Education Futures

Commercial Reality, Law, Innovation and Opportunity

John Boon, J.D.

ISBN: 978-0-9880161-0-1

First Edition, Published by HKMK Management and
Media Corporation, 2012

Contents

Introduction

"John Boon has written a thoroughly researched, carefully crafted, and well organized account of the legal challenges faced by colleges and universities. The scope of the book is broad, and it explores numerous important legal issues in detail, from postsecondary operational concerns through student issues that are regularly litigated. Practicing attorneys, administrators, scholars of higher education law, regulators and students will find this excellent book, with its easily readable format and attention to detail, to be a valuable tool and resource."

—Kerry Brian Melear, Associate Professor, University of Mississippi

John Boon, J.D.

John Boon is a lawyer working globally from Vancouver, Canada. He has represented scores of education providers and institutions. He views education as the most important industry in the world because all persons, business sectors and societies depend on it and because it is a huge economic generator in its own right.

1

Introduction and Executive Summary

1.1 The Future Meets the Past, Current Challenges and Legal Traditions

The practical pursuit of high education ideals requires that those in pursuit have their feet on the ground. The legal foundation for many emerging public and private post-secondary education systems in this time of disruptive innovation can be found with legal traditions that have governed commercial enterprises and transactions for centuries. Strong relationships and effective regulation will be built on that foundation. These laws have greater application to education now as institutions aggressively engage competitive domestic and global markets, more students and more diverse students.

Education is big business today. It is also big news because what happens or does not happen with education impacts everyone. There was a time when education was not in the news very much. Now mainstream and specialized media outlets focus on education issues like never before. Stories often reflect reality and just as often they distort reality. They attack the dysfunction of current systems and describe exciting new events that indicate that major and positive changes are here now and on their way.

Like all business sectors and environments that undergo disruptive innovation—that is now happening in education - there are parties that want to protect the status quo and those that want it broken down. The latter almost always win eventually, but not without a fight. In many countries, the status quo is problematic for those that want to protect it. They either depend on government money to fund it—money that is increasingly scarce - or they operate without government money and in the face of rising costs are forced to set prices that are hard for consumers to pay and finance.

Change is being driven by these factors, by technology and growing and diverse capacity to produce good education, assessment and related products and by social, lifestyle and economic factors that result in new market demands. As always, demand and supply factors ultimately rule the day.

The following quick clips from news headlines illustrate just a few of the news trends.

- Students in Quebec protest (slightly) higher tuition costs and demand free education (Spring 2012).
- Occupy movements worldwide demand major economic change and some demand free education (2011).
- A university chancellor says students do not want to pay more for degrees that do not help them find work—leaving unanswered the question of why taxpayers should then pay more for the same product (2012).
- Increasing numbers of university grads head to technical school so they can get jobs.
- Two thirds of new teachers in one Canadian province cannot find jobs as teachers (2011).
- A university vice-chancellor says no one has figured out what education quality is (May 2012).
- Aspiring Canadian doctors go overseas to study medicine because of limited seats in medical schools.
- Increased recognition of foreign medical degrees is needed so immigrants can fill the need for more doctors.
- Alberta is short 70,000 workers and cannot find people with the skills needed.
- Only half of recent (2012) U.S. college graduates have full-time jobs and student loans are now at $1 trillion.
- Program and operations cutbacks at most government funded institutions are occurring daily.
- Education unions demand removal of education from trade talks because education is a public service and not a salable commodity.
- Students of a private institution use a blog to criticize the institution and regulators and the media jump on it to claim that students are not receiving what was promised (without mentioning the contract or its content).

- Major US universities announce Massively Open Online Learning Courses and their investment of tens of millions of dollars.
- The Mozilla Foundation supports diverse and dispersed, institution based and non-institution based, projects aimed at new assessment and credential systems.
- The amount of private investment money in new education technology ventures increases exponentially.
- A Canadian chancellor says the system is unsustainable given rising research costs and high student demand.
- A US billionaire pays students to drop out of college and develop product. He says university costs outweigh benefits.
- Statistics still show that those with degrees on balance still do better than those without.
- Ontario Courts of Appeal (2011) affirm their inherent powers to hear and rule on student claims validly asserted under contract law or other laws whether or not the issue relates to academic matters.

This is just a sampling. To be clear—this book is pro-learning and personal development. It is pro-formal and traditional education only if it is empirically (as opposed to rhetoric, branding and marketing talk) the most effective and cost efficient way to facilitate learning and the authoritative validation of learning and states of knowledge and only if it allows the student to follow their chosen path and to do what they aspire to do. The issue is never education versus non-education. If there are other ways to better and more affordably accomplish what traditional "college" helps students accomplish then that should be encouraged. As Don Tapscott said in Macowikinomics, the key is effective learning and not just branding and credentials.

The fundamental message of this book is that education issues and problems cannot be addressed and solved if people don't understand or even try to understand what education really is and aspires to do in technical, legal and commercial terms. That may seem cold and unsuited to the world of high education ideals, but it is not. You cannot manage change if you do not grasp the reality of Now. Stephen Covey (Seven Habits of Highly Successful People) said several years ago: How you see the problem is the problem. In other words, if you do not properly identify and articulate the problem you cannot solve it. To carry on the idea, if you do not properly identify and articulate the proposed solution you won't be able to take effective action to implement it.

This is about the search for and a description of education reality. The focus is on post-secondary education, but the observations, principles and conclusions arrived at can have relevance beyond post-secondary education. Even non-commercial sectors can benefit from commercial and legal analysis.

Private and public (government funded or as otherwise defined) education enterprises and institutions - when tuitions are paid and often when they are not—operate in commercial, legal and contract environments and not in a separate and imaginary academic universe cut off from those realities. It is not just a government service or a delegation and extension of a government service.

This work is about the importance of managing and regulating in accordance with this reality. It is about how students, managers, teachers, mentors, regulators and other stakeholders can build on and work with that reality to act more intelligently, effectively, efficiently, fairly and in a legally ordered way in the real world to keep sight of, pursue and live up to high education ideals including that of education freedom for students and education providers.

Education freedom is not about free education. It is about a person being free to choose their path in life which encompasses the freedom to pursue and prepare—with studies of choice - for the opportunities of life, work and business that they aspire to as opposed to those that others choose for them or restrict them to. It is about education providers being free to develop, offer and provide products that students and learners demand and choose without needless (not risk mitigating) regulation.

1.2 How To Read This Book

This book is designed for: students and parents; teachers and faculty; managers from all education institutions; academics that have expertise in education; government regulators working with education sectors or related fields such as student loans, immigration, professions or business development; business leaders; lawyers working in the fields of education and the workplace; and anyone else interested in the current state and future of education.

Although this book is an attempt to address a gap with the legal and business analysis of education it is not an academic work. There is more citation of news items than legal cases. The latter is where the trends are seen.

For many readers, this book can be used as a kind of issues management manual. If there are specific issues that are of interest and current concern they can go to the table of contents and focus on that issue. In many cases though, the broad context and core points are essential to understanding each isolated issue.

This is not a text book that is designed for any specific program of study. It makes very little use of statistics because they can too often be used to hang you later either because they were inaccurate or just became outdated. Most of the trends cited are obvious and statistics do not have to be used as illustrations.

Most of our work has been done in British Columbia, Canada although we have also worked in other parts of Canada and other countries, including the United States. There is no attempt to pick on BC regulators. They just happen to have been major factors in this work over the years.

It is possible to scan the table of contents and this introduction—with main points from each part - to focus on areas of greatest interest, but again, in many cases, it will be necessary to grasp the core ideas presented before isolated issues can be fully understood.

The book is organized around what we call sections as opposed to chapters. There are almost thirty sections because we have tried to keep each one relatively short and more easily reviewed and grasped. The work does not have to be read in a linear way, but later sections may not be clear if earlier arguments and points are not reviewed.

The main points that follow in this introduction are inevitably an inadequate attempt in a few pages to summarize hundreds of pages. Many important points are obviously deleted, but the main points still serve as a useful guide. The diagrams and diagram explanatory notes in the Appendices are also a useful means of grasping key points.

1.3 Part 1 Main Points: Commercial, Contract and Legal Realities

1. Commerce, contracts and law are the simple reality of life for education when tuitions are charged and often when they are

not and the high ideals of education cannot be effectively pursued without acknowledging and working with reality through practical commercial and business initiatives.

2. People learn in many ways and from many persons and formal institutional education is one method or forum.
3. Education always has been in part a media content industry, but it differs from other content sectors because of its systematic use of pre-defined content, pre-defined learning objectives, assessment methods to validate learning achievements and authoritative declarations of that achievement (credentials) to the world.
4. Education serves all industries and society and is a huge economic generator in its own right.
5. In the knowledge economy, every person depends for their social and economic security on being able to access quality and affordable learning systems which must, for practical reasons, often involve formal education.
6. Personal control over that learning and education is vital and not optional. Current systems often do not provide that control. Gateways (obstacles) in the way of personal learning and economic aspirations—program existence, available positions in programs, unjustified admission standards, professions memberships, financing, program quality, credible assessment systems and credit transfers—must be opened.
7. Informed sellers and buyers should make supply and demand decisions and not central planners in government that use funding powers to influence supply decisions.
8. Development depends on freedom and freedom depends on development
9. Because of social and technological change, education is, like other media content sectors have before it, undergoing major disruptive innovation that will be positive over the short, medium and longer term for many persons and negatively disruptive in the short term for parties with vested interests in the status quo.
10. Disruptive innovations rarely come from major current players because they are too invested in current systems and structurally locked in.

11. Despite comforting political rhetoric and hopes, the idea of having a right to an education is, aside from K to 12 sectors in some countries, elusive if one means by a "right" the legal right to claim a remedy at court under law if they are denied the ability to take specific education programs.
12. Learners and education providers do have, however, in our legal and economic traditions, the right to freely contract and to respectively provide and consume goods and services—including education services - in commercial markets.
13. Public and private institutions often operate under contracts with students when tuitions are paid and often even when they are not because other consideration may exist.
14. Governments have no exclusive power to provide education and private education is not based on delegated or extensions of government and public power. It is based on the right to freely contract and provide and consume services subject to consumer risk based regulation.
15. Legal differences between public and private institutions are slight because in most cases both are independent corporate entities that operate and legally exist separately from constitutional government entities. Both are unified in common markets via contracts and contract law. Public institutions are contract parties and not regulators.
16. A contract focus is not about law suits, but about building constructive and productive service relationships.
17. Commercial and contract-based education is legal reality and not a right conspiracy or attempt to create markets for legal services. Education freedom is essential to personal freedom and central to left and right political thought.
18. Traditional institutions are undergoing fundamental change as they move away from the mythical idea of a separate academy into global markets as global corporations to serve increasingly demanding student consumers in competitive markets with other institutions—students that believe in consumer driven capitalism.
19. Courts are now less likely to defer away from considering student disputes and will—while still deferring on minor academic matters like grades—apply their inherent jurisdiction to hear and rule on student claims properly pleaded in contract, tort

or other areas of law. Students are now much less likely to be denied the same commercial rights that other consumers have.

20. Traditional ideas of students being in In Loco Parentis (under the care and parental control of institutions) or Forum Domesticum relationships (parties are seen as a club where parties agree to operate outside commercial forums) have long given way to commercial reality.

1.4 Part 2 Main Points: Systems Thinking, Contracts, Contract Outcomes and Products, Regulation

1. Systems based thinking in the education sector is not esoteric. Systems involve parties and parts that impact each other. Cause and effect relationships exist. Systems based thinking is important for proper business planning and for effective law reform and enforcement. Realistic objectives can be set and achieved within the system because relationships are not too remote and specified and desired results (effects) can be caused by targeted actions.
2. Contracts involve two parties to a current or possible system that need a legal instrument and the application of contract law to bring order to their relationship and to allow each party to achieve goals and protect interests.
3. Regulations are also risk and support based instruments that target the protection and support of specific interests and without systems planning that regulation can become un-focused and ineffective.
4. Public policy and law must distinguish education systems from systems that lie outside them.
5. Institutions and students and their contracts lie at the centre of education systems.
6. Students are consumers and not system inputs, outputs or outcomes.
7. Education managers and regulators must consider pre-contract (student contract), contract and post-contract periods because each period is central to understanding relationships, impacts and interests and how contracts and laws operate separately in those periods to support private actions and protect private interests.

8. Contract law, tort law and other laws are central to understanding education systems, parties, relationships, products and outcomes. Contracts are separate from and do not exist without contract law which is primarily common law.
9. Contract law governs contract formation (or vitiation), terms, what constitutes breach of terms and whether remedies are owed for breach. Contracts are not pieces of paper, but legally enforceable promises. Aside from promises, terms can include representations of fact that induce parties to enter or stay in a contract. Existence of a term called a condition can mean certain events may have to occur before promises exist and are enforceable.
10. Education contracts, like employment or many other service contracts, are often evolving and executory in nature because they are performed and can change over time as the parties modify original terms or introduce new terms expressly or impliedly. Terms can be incorporated by operation of law if the proper statutory authority is in place. That authority must be clear because courts see and tend to enforce contracts as they are - as instruments created and enforced by private parties.
11. Parties to contracts must understand their contracts if they want to ensure performance on the other side, compliance on their side and the resulting avoidance of disputes. Core expectations, promises and inducements relied on must be understood. Real loss, the substantial non-performance of core promises that induced the contract or false representation that induced the contract are normally key to claims for a legal remedy
12. Parties must understand the distinction between business policies, laws and contract terms that are legally enforced. All three may target or help govern common relationships or events, but they operate separately with separate parties, authorities (creators), subjects, objects, rights and duties.
13. Everyone in education talks a lot about outcomes, but there is often an absence of definition and legal certainty. Use of the term "education outcomes" should be confined to contractually promised education products. Consideration of other non-student contract outcomes (jobs, business success) that relate to, but exist separately from education systems can be considered by way of contrast and to link education systems to

other socio-economic systems that are influenced by and that influence education systems.

14. The core outcome is Outcome 1 which is a promised collection of product factor inputs that institutions intermediate and that allow an institution to help a student achieve the set learning objective which is Outcome 2—un-promised by the institution because the student controls it and un-promised by the student for reasons stated. Contracts for specific products group factor inputs in ways necessary for the specified product. Factors used in law school differ from those in medical school.
15. Student contracts define education products which are the objects of quality.
16. It is product factors collectively that form the contract product and not specific individual factors that are not individually sold, promised or purchased. Factor inputs can include: curricula (not content, but a means to organize content and other factors); information and content resources; faculty and other human resources; real, personal or intellectual property; business systems; teaching systems; and assessment systems.
17. Understanding services is a key to understanding education and student contract obligations because services change the conditions of consuming units and changing student knowledge conditions is the essence of education and therefore of student enrollment contracts (See Merchantability). Institutions help with that change, but the student controls it.
18. Quality assurance must focus on the product in the same way other commercial sectors do and on whether the product is merchantable, that is, able to do what the product was designed, produced and sold for and promised to be and do—in this case to help a student learn and achieve a learning outcome objective.
19. The term "merchantable" is used here in the way it is normally used in commercial environments. A merchantable (quality) product is one that is reasonably fit for the ordinary purposes for which it was produced and sold. Education firms (institution) should be and are, like other sellers or producers, required by law to make and sell products of merchantable quality. The ordinary purpose for an education product is to help a student learn (change knowledge conditions—See Services) and to achieve a set learning objective (Outcome 1). That is what the

parties intend contractually and that is all that they as parties can control. The institution also promises an assessment system that validly and credibly validates achievement of learning objectives.

20. Learning objectives relate to subject matter content and levels of difficulty and targeted expertise and contractually promised assessment systems (Outcome 3) must relate to both.
21. A credential is not a promised product that is bought and sold, but a declaration that product specific learning objectives were achieved and that in part validates—if assessment systems and products were sufficient - that Outcome 1 was successful and that contract performance existed.
22. New forms of credentials are evolving to serve changing markets where lifelong learning is a reality and where education providers and products are more diverse. Degrees are not the only option and they too are only declarations that specific packaged courses were taken and that certain learning objectives were met.
23. Uniformity of content, learning objectives and competencies may be desirable in some cases, but it is not a key to quality. Quality is not sameness. Quality is about achieving contract objectives and perhaps minimum standards that also target consumer risk. Uniformity of this nature should be left to private parties to negotiate. It can be a quality factor if it is promised in contracts. Poorly planned uniformity can stifle innovation.
24. The problems of jobs without people and people without jobs can't be solved unless reality is clear. Too many people of policy influence avoid reality—a commercial market between student consumers and institutions—and see education as a government mechanism to supply trained persons to satisfy workplace demand. They talk as if there is a market between institutions and workplace proprietors. This is not reality. Students are not products, outcomes or outputs sold in markets. They are consumers.
25. Producers must listen to the workplace and to students that also listen to the workplace, but the danger is that governments, public (government funded) institutions and workplace proprietors will micro-manage supply based on what they see as the demand from workplace proprietors. Student demand is com-

plex. They want jobs or business prospects and transferrable skills. They do not just want to be cogs in someone's machine.

26. Central planning puts too much power in the hands of those that determine which programs are needed, how many positions will be offered and, with admissions, who gets the prize. Those not making the cut need diverse producers and products that allow them to compete for available positions and they may want other programs.
27. Credible credentials depend on learning results credibly assessed and not specific brands or reputations. Existing and traditional institutions may have some of their market and brand diminished as other credible and authoritative systems evolve to declare learning achievements.
28. The product is the object of quality and not the learning objective. The learning objective is what is achieved if the product is of quality and works to help the student achieve learning objectives.
29. Articulation and credit transfer systems must expand to all providers and programs that meet set standards.
30. Aside from the education and assessment products (Outcomes 1 and 3), institutions may contractually promise (Outcome 4) career and business development or other services. Promised and un-promised services should be clear and contract law rules of reliance and contract inducement are important. Jobs, business success, incomes, immigration permits, professional memberships and similar post contract or contract period outcomes are not promised (Outcome 5).
31. Regulatory jurisdiction over an institution with regard to a student is limited by the contract period of consumption. Regulations and regulator jurisdiction are triggered by specific contract terms. Actions are prohibited because of risks. Legal standards encourage actions that mitigate the risk. Standards are complied with and permissions are granted to engage in the otherwise prohibited behavior. Often the permission must be granted if the standard is met because the risk justification for the prohibition no longer exists. Impossible to achieve standards are not standards, but new absolute prohibitions that cannot be set in most cases.

32. Administrative law rules apply to regulatory agencies so they must only exercise powers granted by statute, act fairly, exercise discretion reasonably without abuse and in accordance with statutory purposes, be unbiased and not make errors of law if they are required to apply—in the course of exercising granted powers - laws other than those in their governing statute.
33. The future of education, if it follows the trend of other content industries impacted by technology, will be of more diverse production and providers, less scarcity, de-massified markets (where more providers reach smaller specialized audiences) and disintermediated systems where product factor providers and consumers may connect in ways outside the traditional intermediating institution. This is already happening (See Case Studies).
34. Education is no longer constrained within geographical boundaries with credible and quality programs being offered online or with institution and student movement across borders.

1.5 Part 3 Main Points: Contracts, Recruitment, Admissions, Dispute Resolution

1. There is no escaping the fact that education marketing—now aggressively engaged in by most public and private institutions—is about inducing persons to enter binding contracts and that means marketers must know the product and realize that pre-contract representations of fact made to induce contracts could have contractual implications.
2. Contracts can try to limit the impacts of pre-contract representations with various limitation provisions, but these methods will not always work—especially in contracts where one more dominant party tends to control contract processes and instruments.
3. Institutions and students must be cautious when working with third party recruiters (agency relationships are problematic) or student service firms respectively and student contracts and third party contracts should have terms that limit liability and carefully govern the relationship.
4. Admissions are about contract entry decisions. Letters of acceptance are generally interim and conditional contracts.

5. Meeting admission standards is usually no guarantee of acceptance because the institution still has the freedom to enter a contract or not, but standards can be a form of representation from the institution that admission will be or was made on grounds based on the students likely ability to succeed in the program. This means representations about program difficulty and complexity could be of contract significance. If a student reasonably believed the program was less difficult and complex than what it turned out to be and failed they could have a cause of action in contract.
6. Application materials, student representations and letters of acceptance can be incorporated into the contract.
7. Institutions contract with individual students and not groups, classes or cohorts and despite being in common classes each student in the class could still have variable provisions in their contract.
8. Public and private institutions now operate in common markets and serve common groups of students and that means the students and institutions should be protected and governed in similar ways.
9. Administrative law based judicial review of institution actions are an historical anomaly. Disputes between students and institutions should be handled: by the parties internally to the contract with mutually agreed to processes; in court under the common law and applicable statutes; through agreed to systems of alternate dispute resolution; or by emerging education sector dispute resolution tribunals. Dispute resolutions by quality assurance regulators should be avoided.

1.6 Part 4 Main Points: Education Regulation In An Era of Disruptive Innovation, Quality Assurance Delimited

1. Consistent legal theories of quality are required and are now absent. Quality assurance should operate as it does with other commercial sectors with the focus on merchantable and quality products—products that are reasonably fit for the ordinary purposes for which they were produced and sold. Education firms (institution) should be and are, like other sellers or producers, required by law to make and sell products of merchant-

able quality. The ordinary purpose for an education product is to help a student learn (change consumer knowledge conditions—See Services) and to achieve a set learning objective. That is what the parties intend contractually and that is all they control. Management and regulation should have purposes and goals that are achievable.

2. The institution's promised assessment system credibly validates achievement of learning objectives.
3. It is common for the terms quality or outcomes to be used in legally uncertain and multiple ways that result in ineffective and unfair regulation.
4. Quality cannot be seen to go up and down as economic conditions and cycles change and workplace and business markets result in different results for graduates.
5. Quality is also not about uniformity unless that is contractually promised.
6. Quality assurance has nothing to do with what might or might not happen in post contract periods with jobs and business. Such factors can at the most be measures of quality and they are not effective measures of quality.
7. Government requirements that institutions publish stated outcomes are ineffective and can have contract impacts. No such statements should be made unless the parties in fact intend that they be included in contracts. In most cases promises or representations regarding post-contract results could be unenforceable because arguably no reasonable person would be induced into a contract on that basis given that the institution is in no position to actually deliver.
8. Quality standards are distorted if cause and effect links between quality and workplace and business results or loan defaults are drawn without any empirical evidence of poor quality and the failure of a product to help the student learn and achieve the set learning objective.
9. Education quality statutes are not about workplace and business results and they cannot be used to control provider and program supply for the purposes of economic policy. Education should be managed and regulated like any other commercial sector with a focus on contract products as objects of quality and contract product performance, merchantability and risk.

Jobs or business success are not promised so unemployment and business failures are not contract related risks.

10. Terms like "Training Required for Employment" or "Employability" do not relate to actual employment and business results. These terms can relate to quality assurance if a product is designed to help a person to achieve a learning objective that is related closely to being prepared for specific types of work. To have contractual impact the learning objective and the work involved would have to be certain enough to satisfy the certainty requirements of contract law.
11. Risks regarding loan defaults are distinct from quality assurance risks.
12. Current challenges to US and Canadian student loan institution designation programs are symptoms of outdated, unjust, uncertain (in terms of policy rationale and purpose) and poorly drafted laws.
13. No immigration permit is under institution control and no contract promise or representation about them should be made even though it would likely not be reasonable for a student to rely on such a term.
14. Professional organizations, credential evaluations and access to professions laws have nothing to do with quality assurance.
15. Student contracts should state that graduation does not guarantee membership in any professional organization unless that membership is arranged, legally structured and intended.
16. There should be improved regulations to protect student funds paid under conditions where paid for services are yet to be performed. This should go beyond assurance funds and bonds to include systems similar to those used with international goods payments to protect funds paid and product delivery.
17. Regulators generally cannot and must not regulate market bargains.
18. Where workplace experience programs are included as part of a program, special student contract provisions must be included. Contracts between the institution and clients or workplace proprietors must also exist and be carefully drafted to address specific agreements. If contracts between the student and those third parties are intended they too must be carefully drafted to address specific facts. Joint student assessments are possible,

but only the institution is ultimately responsible given that assessment is part of the student contract.

19. Attendance is not a quality assurance factor and only represents a consumer decision to not consume part of a purchased product. Institutions must be cautious about basing dismissals on attendance—especially if the student is performing well academically.
20. Reporting attendance to loan or immigration authorities may be required to establish student engagement with the program, but education quality assurance is about protecting the student from the education product and not about enforcing other related laws. Institutions cannot be made liable under quality assurance laws for failures to report unless they have direct legal relationships with and duties owed to those other agencies.
21. Quality is not about price, affordability and debt, but the debate points are similar and insights into product cost and affordability can emerge from discussions about commerce, contracts, products and disruptive innovation.
22. Students should not pay for what they can do for themselves or with other parties where costs would be less.
23. Profit in education is not bad and can serve student and public interests. Public institutions often make profits on individual programs (or occasionally all programs) and often borrow in debt security markets where they must pay a price for the use of that money and that is marginally distinct from private equity investment.
24. The cost per training outcome (to all payors) should be minimized and the best product should be delivered at the best price for students. That classically sought after economic achievement cannot be achieved simply through models that depend on ever increasing government contributions - that are also increasingly being cut back and not increased. New products, new approaches to packaging product factor inputs and new ways to achieve learning objectives must be found and are being found. New forms of assessment and credentials—authoritative declarations of learning achievement—are being developed.
25. Regulators must guard against the natural tendency to think that they can regulate new technologies and new systems in the same way they regulated old systems. New education provid-

ers and products will require new forms of regulation and new forms of decentralized regulation.

26. New forms of accreditation should be developed for parties engaged in specific and isolated functions now performed by institutions as part of their bundled package of products. If an institution can be accredited in relation to their bundled products and operations functions then other independent parties that offer the same services unbundled could also be accredited (where risks require it). For example, an instruction firm, assessment firm, mentor, curriculum developer, information engineer, publisher, recruiter or credential evaluation firm could be accredited for their service area. This would enhance and give needed authority to distance learning or other innovative education and assessment products. They could operate as third parties in relation to students and institutions or totally outside institutions. Students, student groups and service providers could meet in markets and do what now occurs in the intermediated institution environment.
27. Regulators must be impartial and not tied to vested interests. New Higher Education Acts must be created and create new Higher Education Commissions with broad social, government and business community representation. Commissions should have significant power to ensure that law reforms, quality assurance and all elements of higher education are community driven and not controlled by current vested interests that are slow to innovate and that have vested status quo interests to protect.

Part 1

COMMERCIAL, CONTRACT AND LEGAL REALITIES

2

Education Ideals and Freedom, Education Distinguished from Other Media Content

2.1 Education Ideals, Education Freedom Is Not About Free Education, Education Law and Commerce

Private and public (government funded or as otherwise defined) education enterprises - when tuitions are paid and often when they are not—operate in commercial, legal and contract environments and not in a separate universe called Academia that is cut off from those realities. This work is about the importance of managing and regulating in accordance with this reality. This work emphasizes post-secondary education, but its relevance goes beyond that.

Despite the importance of education, it receives scant attention from business and legal analysts. It is often viewed as a government and non-commercial service. That is the view and desired reality of many in academic circles and education unions [1] and that view naturally gets reflected in regulatory bodies that are often dominated by persons with these views. These parties often seem to view private education as somehow a reflection, extension or delegation of that public service or function. This may be a desired reality for some, but it is not reality.

Education should be managed and regulated like any other commercial sector with a focus on contract products as objects of quality and contract product performance, merchantability and risk. The term merchantability is common in commercial regulation and it is explored in detail later. Regulation must focus on: product purpose; contract promises and representations; product consumption risk; prohibitions targeted at extreme risk; legal standards that mitigate risk if they are complied with; and lifting prohibitions and granting permissions when standards are met and risks are mitigated. Jobs or business success are not promised so unemployment and business failures are not contract risks.

Some argue that a contract and commercial focus is cold and calculating and unsuited to the world of education that has such great ideals. Nothing could be further from the truth. This work is about how students, managers, teachers, mentors, regulators and other stakeholders can build on and work with this commercial reality to act more effectively, efficiently, fairly and in a legally ordered way in the real world to keep sight of, pursue and live up to high education ideals including the ideal of education freedom for students and education providers.

Education freedom is not about free education. It is about a person (a student or learner) being free to choose their path in life which encompasses the freedom to pursue and prepare—with studies of choice - for the opportunities of life, work and business that they aspire to as opposed to those that others choose for them or restrict them to because of limits as to who can offer and consume specific products in education markets. It is about education providers being free to develop, offer and provide products that students and learners demand and choose without needless (not risk mitigating) regulation. It involves a provider's freedom to develop, offer and provide innovative products that can prepare a person for new possibilities in life that they were not even yet aware of because sometimes supply precedes demand.

As noted, and to repeat, the most important ideal and objective is to help the individual learner access the providers and products that will help the learner achieve the learning objectives and state of knowledge they aspire to and that will in turn allow them to pursue the opportunities of life, work and business they are inspired by. The terms "they aspire to" and "they are inspired by" are used to distinguish the options and opportunities the person choses and pursues from those that others may restrict them to or impose on and choose for them directly or indirectly.

There are two fundamental reasons why the education system must be built around individual needs and wants. The first reason is based on the reality that education inevitably relates to and reflects the most primal and intimate elements of human experience. Education ideals and education freedom are not just about economic choices and development, but about what it means to be an inquiring and evolving human being that always seeks not only social and economic security, but to grow to their full potential and to be with and serve others. Uses of a term can vary, but the term education comes from the root "educere" which refers to leading out inherent potential. [2]

The freedom of the individual learner depends on the freedom of those that provide education or its elemental services either in traditional institution environments or in new and emerging environments and markets.

Consider these quotations from notable eastern and western thinkers.

"We in our home sought freedom of power in our language, freedom of imagination in our literature, freedom of soul in our religious creeds and that of mind in our social environment. Such an opportunity has given me confidence in the power of education which is one with life and only which can give us real freedom, the highest that is claimed for man, his freedom of moral communion in the human world. I try to assert in my words and works that education has its only meaning and object in freedom—freedom from ignorance about the laws of the universe, and freedom from passion and prejudice in our communication with the human world." (Rabindranath Tagore, 1861-1941, India's and Asia's first Nobel Laureate. [3]

"The purpose of education is to culture the mind of man so that he can accomplish all his aims in life. Education, to justify itself, should enable a man to use the full potential of his body, mind and spirit. It should develop in him the ability to make the best use of his personality, surroundings and circumstances so that he may accomplish the maximum in life for himself and for others." (Maharishi Mahesh Yogi 1966) [4]

"Education is too focused on facts and not focused enough on developing the full potential and creativity of individuals so that the person and society benefit…people are too often no longer inspired to learn and be curious…a revolution is needed and not just the improvement of broken models… people must reject and disenthrall themselves of the ideas and dogmas of the past that arose to face past challenges and rise to face current challenges by thinking anew (quoting Abraham Lincoln, from December 1862)… education must become more organic with an emphasis on setting the conditions or the environment for growth to occur…. that means customization of learning. (Sir Ken Robinson) [5]

The second reason for the focus on learners is expressed in the section below on "Every Person and the Knowledge Economy". As other sections explore in detail, higher education is no longer merely about the pursuit of truth or professional qualifications by a few. It is about economic and social security for all. Individuals must be free to review information on options and opportunities and to make their own choices as to what is best for them as opposed to having choices made for them directly or indirectly by way of limited options controlled by a few vested interests. Diverse needs and high demand must give rise to diverse and sufficient supply and if it is lacking because of limited products and positions or price then other options must be facilitated to cover the demand.

Government rhetoric about learner demand systems is common, but government actions often go in the opposite direction to enshrine existing systems where narrow interests define who offers what in the education market. Determinations of success or failure of the education system depend on who makes the determinations and on their referenced goals and expectations. Lower goals and expectations make success easier. Ultimately education is about learning and that means learning objectives must focus on what the learner seeks to know and not on what others want them to know or determine is economically or socially valuable and affordable given current funding priorities.

Student and learner demand is variable in terms of product and motivation. Diverse economies and societies and the knowledge explosion have resulted in more areas of study and work specialization and given rise to the need for more transferrable skills. In most cases, when you drill down past the cynicism and doubt, students want and need not only satisfying and meaningful work or businesses, but to pursue passions and to learn about the world as it was, as it is and as it could be. They want to develop their genius and creative, intuitive and intellectual potential. Parents have the same goals for their children.

Expectations, wants and needs give rise to and are reflected in market demand and contract expectations. In legal and commercial terms, forces of demand seek sources of supply and the two together determine and agree to the bargain and learning objective and how it will be pursued and achieved. In philosophical terms, seekers of knowledge seek out those that have knowledge and that can help the seeker define, pursue and achieve the desired state of knowledge or learning objective.

This work is not targeted at philosophical or scientific debates about human development, but it is inspired by them. It highlights them in an effort to focus on the legal and commercial infrastructure that must be in place to ensure that needs are met and that learner and education provider freedoms exist. It is about ensuring that the system is innovative and not controlled by narrow, cloistered and vested interests.

The key is to focus on reality and the real nature of relationships. That reality is that education, public or private, for-profit or non-for-profit is—when tuitions are paid and often when they are not - contractual and commercial in nature. A product is promised for a price and consumed by a consumer. There must be clarity about that product and promise if legal expectations are to be met and if consumption related risks are to be addressed by private contract parties and regulators that address common transactions in separate and distinct ways. Managers and regulators must know what it is they manage and regulate. As management guru Stephen Covey (Seven Habits of Highly Successful People) said one time: How you see (Or Do Not See) the problem is the problem. Even when education is perhaps not commercial (e.g. K to 12 public), legal and business analysis is a useful public policy, law reform and management tool.

2.2 Every Person and the Knowledge Economy

Canada's Governor General and Head of State, David Johnston, recently observed [6] that solving problems depends on the diplomacy of knowledge which he defined as the ability and willingness to work together and share learning across disciplines and borders. He said the well-being of nations is now defined by the ability to develop and advance knowledge and not just by military might or Gross National Product (GDP).

One cannot disagree with that, but one can add that the development and advancement of knowledge he refers to must be driven by and emerge from the intelligence and genius of every citizen and not just a select few. That requires the free interaction of knowledge seekers and education providers of all kinds. That requires that we not allow central planners and traditional, cloistered and vested interests to control information and education systems.

Most new jobs require not just some, but high levels of post-secondary education [7] and a large percentage of working age persons in most countries lack the skills needed to pursue the employment or business goals they strive for and the positions available. Predictions are that hundreds of thousands of jobs will continue to go unfilled because there are no persons with the precise skills needed. Immigration is not enough to solve the problem.

The knowledge economy involves, but goes beyond the "Why" issue and the general importance of learning to personal and socio-economic well-being. It relates to "How" we live, work, produce goods and services and transact business. All economic systems are being transformed from mass production systems where the principal source of value was human labour to systems that are focused on constant and never ending innovation where the key component of value creation, production, productivity and economic growth is knowledge. In the past, land (the agricultural age), natural resources and labor (the industrial economy) were more relatively important.

Our understanding of the knowledge economy must encompass not only how knowledge contributes to economic production and growth, but how each individual is empowered to pursue the knowledge they believe they need to compete for the work, business and personal opportunities available. This is not about satisfying frivolous wants, but about satisfying basic personal, familial and community survival needs and then beyond that the desire for greater prosperity and security. They should not have to rely on what others impose on or make available to them because they think they know what is suitable for or of value to the person, society or economy.

With the knowledge economy those in public life charged with achieving economic development objectives must help individuals that need knowledge and the public and private firms that can help them get it. Effective regulation of education providers is important, but the student being protected against must be clear and regulation must not needlessly restrict the creative and dynamic market interactions between learners and providers. Student risks encompass bad business actors and education quality and the risks of limited access to educational opportunity.

Despite the obvious importance of workplace skills, it is also essential that we develop human creativity and genius and build "know how" and a person's capacities for knowledge. It is equally essential that we allow people to pursue their passions because that motivation is often what drives the learner. The path to greater knowledge and opportunity is never a linear process. Employers and society need people that can think and that are creative, fulfilled and integrated and not just people that exercise a narrow skill and do what they are told.

2.3 Learning and Knowledge Are The Key, Formal Education Is One Means of Achieving It, Learners Learn

Political, business and community leaders say over and over again that education is the key to personal, social, economic, business, professional, legal and economic development. This is only partially true and somewhat misleading. The more fundamental truth is that personal learning that results in skill and knowledge is the key to development. Education, in its formal sense, is just one method of learning and knowledge management. It is a crucial, central and dominant method, but it can only be well managed and regulated if it is understood in its essence and entirety and that includes what it really is and involves in a legal and business context.

Governments, institutions, corporations, families, courts and communities do not think and learn. Learning methods may involve others, but learning is done in solitude by a conscious and sentient person that needs and wants to learn. The knowledge gained is central to good decisions, effective actions and innovation. It is central to survival, living life to its fullest, success and prosperity. The person seeks a state of knowledge that can help them pursue their objectives.

2.4 Defining Education and Distinguishing It From Other Media and Content Industries

Education, in its formal or institutional sense, is only one means used by persons seeking to learn and to have the knowledge that they consider to be important to them. Learning is a personal and lifelong process that unfolds from birth to death. Formal education encompasses pre-school, elementary, secondary, post-secondary, post graduate and corporate, community or professional training.

Many great men and women were self-taught. Many persons with high levels of formal education acknowledge that most of what they know they learned outside formal education in ways that complemented their formal education. Formal education is often still essential for many reasons. It helps people learn how to learn and lays down foundations for future learning.

Knowledge seekers learn from parents, family, friends, mentors, spiritual and religious organizations, newspapers, books, TV, films, newspapers, journals, the Internet, seminars, corporate training, designation or professional organizations through professional development and also from formal education institutions. Learning can evolve from personal reflection, observation, reason and pure thought or new ideas, but even that is still often based on previous experiences and learning—formal or informal. Again, knowledge is what is important and not how and over what period of time it was gained and credentialed. The term knowledge can for this purpose encompass the terms knowledge and skill because knowledge lies behind the skill.

Education in the formal sense can be distinguished from other means of learning and the points of distinction are fundamental to understanding what education is, what institutions really are, what education products really are and how they can all best be managed, regulated, produced at less cost, financed and the subject of innovation.

Learning will, in many or most cases, involve accessing content or expressions of another's knowledge contained in a book, lecture, conversation or other media. Institutional or commercial education can be viewed as a process or relationship involving a student or learner and an institution, teacher or trainer engaged in a specific, formal and systematic teaching and learning process.

Dictionary definitions of education focus on institutional learning and this concept of "systematic" training that is focused on a specified learning objective and on some form of credential that is evidence of or a validation that a degree of learning occurred. For example, the Oxford English Dictionary defines education as: The giving or receiving of systematic instruction, schooling or training given to the young in preparation for the work of life or ....similar instruction or training obtained by adults.

This reality and these factors distinguish education from other means or mediums of communication and learning and other forms of content and its delivery. All communication involves two or more persons communicating their thoughts to others. Each party is a source and destination of information or content. This can involve two people on a street, a mass-media TV program broadcast to large groups or networks of people on the Internet.

Education enterprises use the same content and carriage systems used by others, from one-on-one communication onsite to modern TV or the Internet, but the purpose for the communication is different. Content passes from one to another, but education program products are more structured. A learning objective is set and pursued. If the program is developed properly and the student does their part and applies themselves to "their" essential learning task that objective will be achieved in a set period. Assessment systems determine if that happened. If it did then some form of credential is often given as evidence of the achievement. The credential is not a product or property that is purchased and sold.

Education therefore involves the systematic delivery of a pre-defined body of content for the purpose of achieving a pre-defined learning objective where achievement of that objective is measured by assessment procedures before any institution or third party credential is awarded to acknowledge and serve as evidence of achievement of that objective.

Institutions achieve this and promise students in contracts to achieve this systematic delivery and achievement by aggregating (intermediating) a range of factor inputs to create a learning environment that helps a student to learn (See Outcomes One and Two). They promise an assessment system to measure the achievement so the credential means something. They don't promise achievement of the learning outcome objective because the student controls that. They don't promise the student anything out of the institution's control, but which one hopes will result from a good education such as a job, a successful business or a wife and a house with a picket fence. Such promises could never reasonably be relied on or induce a reasonable person into a contract.

In order to define, describe and delimit the education product the first focus is on the nature of the contractually promised and provided product or contractual consideration. The second focus is on the concept of service which is not to commercially transfer property rights to goods but to provide outputs that can change the physical, mental/emotional, legal, economic, "knowledge" or other conditions of the consuming unit. [8] The hope may well be for future employment and business and life success, but the education service is more narrowly targeted because the service provider must, to be sound in legal and business terms, focus on what is achievable by them and on what can be contractually promised and achieved.

They cannot guarantee or promise that knowledge conditions will change because students do the learning, but they can promise to provide a service that provides the learning environment that will allow the student to change their knowledge conditions. An assessment result can be evidence of that success. The focus cannot be on what may happen far into the future because these conditions were changed.

2.5 All Elements of Education Are Open to Disruptive Innovation

The sections below on education products and outcomes explore how all of the above defined elements of education are open to the "positive" and inevitable impacts of disruptive innovation. Tradition and innovation will combine and change how learning occurs, how it is assessed and how it is recorded and declared to the world.

The systematic ways in which products are assembled and dis-assembled are changing. The institutions that intermediate and aggregate inputs to serve student consumers are therefore fundamentally changing. As in many sectors, new forms of providers challenge traditional players. Established forces must not be able to control or limit that change by controlling the reins of government and markets. On the demand side, as stated above, learner need and demand must drive the system. Suppliers must respond to that demand and in many cases provide innovative products that precede and lead to market demand. Internal and third party assessment systems, credential evaluation systems and credit transfer systems are arising to meet new realities. Much of this work focuses on current and likely disruptive innovations and how they trigger the need for responsive innovation in management and regulation.

2.6 Education Supports All Industries and Society and Is An Economic Generator Itself

Learning is centred on the learner and seeker of knowledge, but that person exists in a domestic and international context that is commercial, social, legal and political in nature. The person needs to survive, succeed and prosper in that field of action where they apply and continue to add to their state of knowledge. The familial, community, domestic and international societies they are part of depend on them and their knowledge and skill. They must have their workplace and business needs met and the desire of student consumers for work and income will ensure that they are met. That does not mean that they should dictate and limit what students can learn.

Education enterprises, individually and collectively as an industry, are an essential support to all industries. Education enhances the knowledge base essential to all enterprises, social organizations and domestic and international commerce and politics.

Domestic and international education is also a major economic generator in its own right because it produces jobs, supply transactions, taxable incomes and export revenue. Most countries and states and provinces within most federal nation states have recognized - often in the face of slumping traditional manufacturing, resource or other sectors—that international education can itself be a source of economic development for domestic institutions and national and sub-national economies. Investments in human capital can be as powerful and some say more powerful than investment in physical capital (roads, buildings and equipment).

There was a time when international education referred to having students going to institutions that are not in their home country. [9] Today it is more complex. The marketing to those foreign students is much more aggressive and competitive and immigration issues continue to be major considerations. It still features foreign students attending domestic institutions and now also involves: distance learning; greater transfers of credit and credential evaluation; the movement of institutions to other jurisdictions to enroll students in those foreign jurisdictions; greater movement of persons combining work and education; and other related matters. Factors relating to domestic education apply to international transactions. Students must meet admission and academic standards. Institutions and programs must satisfy accreditation or similar standards. Credential evaluation, transfer and other issues apply.

A recent US report went so far as to say that a weak education system threatens prosperity, global position, physical safety and national security. It cites insufficient preparation of children for science based and technical jobs that both the private and public sectors need to fill, scant and declining foreign-language education and a weakened "national cohesiveness" as a result of an under-educated and unemployable poor population. The report, the result of an independent task force co-chaired by former secretary of State Condoleezza Rice and former New York City schools chancellor Joel Klein says the dominant power of the 21st century will depend on human capital and concludes that the failure to produce that capital will undermine American security.

Ms. Rice said education is the glue that keeps a country together. A factor weakening that glue, she said, is the perception of a smaller and smaller group that is advancing in America. That again plays to the key point made above—that all learners must be able to follow their chosen path, participate and contribute.

3

Education Rights Limited, Freedom of Contract and Commercial Rights

3.1 No Substantive and Legally Enforceable Rights to an Education

It is politically fashionable to talk about students having or needing a "right" to an education. [10] There is usually no use talking about "rights" unless you are talking legally and judicially enforceable rights or, in other words, rights that can lead to legal remedies.

A right can be defined as that which a person has a just and legally enforceable claim to with regard to others.[11] The others could be all persons or specific persons that must do or not do something because the person has the right. Specific legal instruments can vest rights at a specified time. General bodies of law—property law, contract law, tort law or other bodies of laws—will apply to determine if a specific contract instrument, relationship or transaction in fact satisfy legal requirements and result in a vesting of rights.

This brief examination of rights leads to key questions. If the student had the right to an education then who is the "other" that they would have the legally enforceable claim against? Who has the offsetting duty? The State? The institution? How can a legal entity be required to enter a contract? What specific constitutional, statutory or common law provision creates the right and duty? Would that be a right to a free education? Would it be for an under-graduate or a post-grad degree? Does it encompass lifelong learning and all future corporate and professional development training? Would it be in an area of study of the student's choice or something imposed on them?

In most jurisdictions and in technical legal terms, subject to distinctions in some cases between post-secondary and pre-post-secondary education, citizens do not have legally enforceable rights to an education. If programs do not exist, if positions are limited, if persons are not admitted or if they have no money to attend they generally cannot go to court, claim that a constitutional, common law or statutory right has been denied to them and then demand a legal remedy from the courts.

The Canadian Charter of Rights and Freedoms and the US Bill of Rights provide respectively for persons to have the rights to "life, liberty and security of the person" or "life, liberty and the pursuit of happiness", but to date these have not resulted in firm constitutional, common law or statutory rights to an education. There are laws in many Canadian provinces or US states and federally in some cases that make it illegal for persons to be denied access to any service if that denial is based on some form of recognized or listed type of discrimination. That is different from a right to an education. That is a right to not be discriminated against.

Since 1952, Article 2 of the first Protocol to the European Convention on Human Rights obliges all signatory parties to guarantee the right to education. The United Nations' International Covenant on Economic, Social and Cultural Rights of 1966 guarantees this right under its Articles. Generally, however, this has not resulted in specific legal rights to an education. UNESCO and other UN agencies and declarations refer to education "rights", but it is up to individual member states to do what they can and this normally does not result in legally enforceable rights.

Where legal rights to an education do not exist by virtue of a constitution, statute or the common law they can be pursued with contract instruments that are enforced pursuant to the broad body of contract law.

3.2 Learners and Providers Have Freedom of Contract Rights Subject to Risk Based Regulation

As argued in other sections, free citizens have the right to work alone or together with others in an enterprise and the right to offer products to a consumer. They and the consumer, in this case a prospective student consumer, have the right to freely enter a contract under which a product is bought and sold for a price. Regulation and legal standards can kick in to protect consumers when certain contract conditions exist (See Separate Sections).

In most jurisdictions, buyers and sellers of goods and services, including education services, have the right to engage in private contract transactions without interference and regulation that goes beyond the need to address substantial risk. Government regulation is usually triggered by specific types of transactions—for example, education products of a set length and cost that create specific risks for students. President Obama said: "We should have no more regulation than the health, safety and security of the American people requires". [12] That logic applies everywhere.

The only action that can modify this reality would be an outright ban on any kind of education or specified types of education except that offered or authorized by government and state run authorities even if no risks existed or existing risks could be easily managed with reasonable regulation. Such an action in the "knowledge economy" and the "information age" would justifiably be the subject of ridicule. Charter of Rights actions in Canada or Bill of Rights actions in the USA would certainly be contemplated in the face of such a law.

3.3 Public and Private Institutions Often Operate Under Contracts With Students, Tuition Paid and Not Paid, Consideration Issues

When tuitions are paid (and often even when they are not as noted below) to a public or private institution in return for an education product the relationship is contractual and commercial. A contract exists when a legally enforceable promise is made and it can be verbal or written. Contract instruments and contract law are distinguished and discussed later. The education product that is contractually promised is also explored in depth.

Most importantly, the sections that follow will explore in depth what the courts have had to say in the past and what they say today. By way of summary, judicial authorities in Canada, the US and the UK generally state that this relationship is contractual and that courts will assert their inherent jurisdiction to rule on the matter when proper causes of action in contract or tort or in other areas of law are claimed and articulated and presented to the court.

If tuitions are not paid and a student is induced to attend by scholarships or grants and is promised that certain conditions will exist (e.g. equipment or available research funds) then a binding contract could still exist. If the program was not as it was represented and promised to be it is likely that an action in contract or tort would exist. Universities are recruiting the top students and often offering perks. Some universities are promising an exclusive inner circle where membership has privileges—mentoring, advising and invitations to networking events with the president. Promises given must be kept. [13]

As noted in other sections, this issue of education being commercial and contractual or not can come up in many contexts. In relation to international trade it is noted that the GATS includes phrases that refer to a service (education included) being excluded where it is "supplied in the exercise of government authority", that is, not in competition with other suppliers. The reality is that public institutions are generally not government and do compete with other suppliers.

In addition to the examples cited, contract consideration (roughly defined as something of value flowing between the parties to elicit the other's promise of consideration) and therefore a contract can exist in the absence of tuition paid by a student because the student did actually rely on promises and representations made to their real or potential detriment or because the institution did, in some reasonably direct way, benefit financially (with the knowledge and intention of both parties) from that student's enrollment (e.g. payment to an institution based on enrollments). It is of limited use to predict what a judge might say, but the point again, contract or not, is how the commercial model can inform and guide decisions and actions in public and private contexts. It can do so because of how it addresses products, risks, standards, intentions, expectations, promises and representations. Again, if a student pays little or pays more than they think they should have there is still often a legally enforceable bargain. Courts will enforce bargains and not change them unless the facts clearly show abuse of power or duress of some kind.

Institutions and regulators in the U.K. and the USA have a more reality-based approach, but the following examples illustrate that many in Canada have not grasped reality. That is gradually changing.

"The way the [Private Training Institutions Act] is written, it's seen as a contract between the student and those institutions…The protections are different with public institutions because they are not overseeing the relationship the same way as the non-profits or the [private] institutions." SFU Professor, BC Business Magazine Dec. 2, 2011.

"…universities are increasingly seen as instruments of economic and social development. But he noted other issues of concern as well, including huge first-year classes, a consumerist sense of entitlement among students. Headline: Universities becoming too business-like. [14]

"We are not commercial entities. We are public bodies that are accountable to government and taxpayers." [15]

"As the courts move towards a more commercial view of the relationship between universities and their students, universities should make sure they have clear documentation. We have always relied on the calendar and university policies as the closest thing to a contract that we have. It has not been seen as a business arrangement. But students, parents and courts are more consumer-oriented today. If people are struggling to get the money for tuition, they expect to get something for it—their degrees." General Counsel for York University, Toronto Canada [16]

These are a few examples to illustrate the denial at many institutions about the commercial and contract nature of their enterprise. These attitudes and positions no doubt arise from traditional thinking that surrounds the academy. Other sections address how institutions have evolved from the academy to global corporations focused on consumers, but attitudes are slow to change. Many of the old non-commercial Club or In Loco Parentis ideas are still found in institutions and with regulators that often come from the traditional academy.

Where the contract and commercial reality is accepted with many institutions it is often for the stated and limited purpose of tying the student to their payment obligations and obligation to comply with institution regulations with nominal or no attention paid to the product and other promises made to students.

In response to the quote from the General Counsel at York University, it is made clear in later sections that students do not buy or demand degrees. The degree is a declaration that they learned something and the contract product just helps them do the learning. The benefit of the doubt is given to counsel because no doubt they made a quick comment for a media interview.

3.4 No Exclusive Government Power to Provide Education, Private Education Is Not Based On Delegated Public Power

Constitutionally designated governments generally have the power to make laws in relation to education, but not the sole power to provide education. That leaves regulation for the purpose of protecting consumers from specified market risk that arises from the consumption of contract products. The reality begins with freedom of contract. Education is not exclusively a government service that is somehow delegated to private parties. It is a commercial sector, public and private, that offers products to consumers under contracts.

The right to provide education program services under contract is not a right that belongs only to government and that only government can either do directly or delegate to others. Education programs are not a scarce public resource that governments can or must apportion or grant to applicants in the same way they grant a right to "own" a limited land base or a right to harvest or use a limited public resource.

Governments can deliver education via constitutional powers where given or they can exercise inherent powers as legal entities to enter into service contracts. Neither alternative blocks private entities from competing. Private commercial education is not a public service delegated to the private sector and supervised by government. It is a commercial industry based on freedom of contract that should be regulated like other commercial industries with a focus on product, consumption and product and consumption risk.

Private education is not about the privatization of education as a public service. Government is not hiring private firms to do a government job. It is a decision to regulate a commercial activity in the public interest.

3.5 Legal Differences Between Public and Private Institutions Are Slight, They Are Unified In Markets With Contracts and Contract Law, Public Institutions Are Contract Parties and Not Regulators

There are only slight differences in legal terms between so-called public institutions and private institutions and the two are unified at the market level through the mechanism of contract law. Both enter contracts with students (often even if tuitions are not paid). Contract law applies to those contract instruments.

Education regulation should target contract products and consumption risk. It should operate separately from, but alongside contract law to ensure students receive what was promised to them and that products satisfy legal standards also focused on mitigating consumer risk. Students in all sectors should have the same protections and different regulations can only be justified where risks differ. Regulations and contracts operate separately because parties to the regulatory relationship are the institution and public agency while the parties to the student and institution contract relationship are only those two parties. The rights and duties of the parties are distinct.

Few involve governments actually acting on their own as legal entities without the creation of separate corporate entities. Public institutions are usually autonomous to varying degrees and most fight hard to be free of government and political influence. Most are corporate entities created by statute that are legally separate from government. The nature of public institutions often relates to the contractual and funding relationships they have with government.

Governments can deliver education via constitutional powers where given (USA states) or they can exercise inherent powers as legal entities to also enter into contracts to provide services. They can also create statutes that allow for the creation of new legal entities that they may or may not control through various means.

One can view these "public" institutions and private institutions as being on a continuum. At the far left would be the pure government institution with government itself as the Crown, Republic or Commonwealth being the actor and contracting party. Then would come the entities created by statutes dedicated to education entities that are then funded by government. At the far right would be the pure private option with institutions being created as for profit or not for profit firms under general corporation statutes.

The regulation of education can fall under a property and civil rights clause of a constitution (In Canada) or a dedicated education clause. The reality begins with freedom of contract and risks arising for consumers under that contract. In the US, the federal government has asserted some jurisdiction over education with the use of some general provisions in the US Constitution that relate to providing or promoting the general welfare of the union, but that jurisdiction is limited. In general, the Tenth Amendment says powers not delegated to the federal government by the Constitution or prohibited to the states are reserved for the States. Since education is not mentioned in the federal constitution it is a power reserved to the states. Most state constitutions then state that the government can provide for systems of public education. [17] Private education is untouched and private businesses are regulated.

Having the capacity to grant a degree or use the term "university" does not make an institution "public" or part of government. If government initiates the creation of a new corporate entity, funds it and controls the board that does not make the firm part of government. Often it is a community group that initiates the creation of a new institution and these statutes dedicated to educational institutions are just the vehicle.

In the absence of specific law, public institutions are not regulators with power over student consumers as regulated parties. They are corporate bodies created to provide services under contract. Students become students because of contracts they have with institutions. Institution regulations are, in most cases, where the parties so agree, terms of contract, but we recommend minimizing broad contract incorporation of every "rule" put forward by the institution. Some can remain as non-legal policies or guidelines. If they were to be given the power to regulate students they would have to be both regulator and contract party. Since regulators normally regulate commercial relationships the public institution would be regulating itself since usually it is the provider and not the consumer that is regulated.

3.6 A Contract Focus is Not About Law Suits But About Constructive and Productive Relationships

This emphasis on contracts is not about encouraging or managing contract litigation. It is about pursuing education, social and personal development ideals and objectives in the real world. It is about dealing with reality and about building a strong business relationship that results in all parties to a contract leaving that relationship with a sense that well understood promises were substantially kept. That results from having a clear contract that can be reasonably complied with. It is about understanding what regulation is needed to address risks arising from the mutually understood contract. These objectives are crucially important as all parties continue to grapple with the disruptive innovation now underway in the education sector.

This focus arose from the observation that the parties were often not that clear about the reality of their legal relationship and that was often reflected in needless disputes, irrational claims, weak management and un-focused, unrealistic, ineffective and inefficient regulation.

If institutions, students and education regulators, funders and other stakeholders have a clear understanding of the commercial products involved, the true "outcomes" sought, the risks targeted and the contract and regulatory standards needed to mitigate risk then they can all set and achieve realistic and achievable contract and regulatory objectives. Contract (students and institutions) and regulatory (institutions and government) relationships are distinct and deal with separate parties, rights, duties, subjects and objects, but they often target the same risks and work to ensure that the student receives what they were promised under the contract.

3.7 Commercial and Contract-Based Education is Legal Reality and Not a Right Wing Conspiracy

This idea of education contracts and commerce is not some right wing political idea, objective or ideology. It is not an idea concocted to market legal services. It is the legal reality for most public and private post-secondary institutions and for some pre-post-secondary institutions. There is market demand and supply. Demand starts with individual learners and aggregate demand arises from that. Buyers and sellers meet in markets and enter legally enforceable contracts under which student buyers promise to pay a price in return for the institution seller's promise to provide an education product that is more complex than many acknowledge (See Below).

3.8 Student Gateways, Product Quality Risk, Product Access and Choice Risk

Gateways are obstacles, some justified by solid policy rationales and some not, that stand in the way of a person achieving: the state of knowledge desired; the credentials that validate that academic achievement; a desired professional status; or any other status they want or must have to achieve work, business, professional or personal aspirations. These gateways generally parallel education and workplace processes.

Students and learners are hurt by poor quality education and by the lack of access and choice. Institution and product quality can be measured in terms of products that create learning environments for students that help them to achieve the state of knowledge desired. The institution can promise that, but not achievement of the learning objective because the student controls that outcome (See Outcomes). Access and gateway issues such as program and enrollment position availability, program cost, financing, admission standards and other issues do not generally relate to product quality but to education system quality.

3.9 Informed Sellers and Buyers Should Make Supply and Demand Decisions and Not Central Planners

Markets work when supply is not limited to specific persons. Competitive and dynamic buyer-seller markets are imperfect, but relatively speaking they are more intelligent, effective and efficient than centrally planned forums. Controlling supply won't change demand in most cases. Government funded institutions generally make their own program decisions, but constraints on public funds are real and they influence what these institutions can do. If programs are dropped or if positions are limited that impacts on a person's ability to pursue the education they want. It is important that other sellers be free to meet this demand.

Stalinist era central planning - where apparatchiks decided the soviet economy needed three blue cars and five red cars - did not work. Education products are no different. They should be treated like any other commodity where markets are the primary forum for demand and supply decisions. It is impossible to track hundreds of institutions and thousands of programs worldwide in terms of their ability to result in specific employment or business results. It is equally impossible to grasp all available fields of action in order to determine how many persons in each field of study are needed to fill projected jobs and serve projected market needs. The causes that influence specific effects are unfathomable and conclusions will always be based on partial and questionable evidence.

This does not mean that this type of projection and analysis is useless. It just cannot be relied for two reasons. First, it is often not effective and surpluses and shortages inevitably result (See later citations). Secondly, if available positions are limited and based on projected needs that can restrict the ability of others to seek opportunities in that field. The power to decide futures should not be left in the hands of a few admission officers. Each institution must make choices, but others should be allowed to compete.

Governments should not dictate where students will study, how they will study and what they will study and work at based on what they judge to be economic needs based on questionable information. The

BC Government (Campus 2020) says education systems should focus on learner demand, but officials also say they may not provide loans for programs "they" think do not deliver (undefined) employment results. They say a program's risk profile in the future is not likely to be just based on past student defaults.

Government and professions-based public servants and education regulators or public institution executives should not be, as they often are now, setting quotas that amount to them dictating that they know best and that the economy needs or can absorb a set number of lawyers and doctors or other professionals and tradespersons. Based on that they allocate funding and a set number of programs and positions. Limited public may make restrictions essential, but they should not then encourage policies that restrict the ability of others to meet existing demand.

Trying to predict future labor needs is unwise and difficult and usually ineffective in terms of coming up with data that can lead to wise policy and legal decisions. The BC government, [18] despite having studies that said they cannot accurately predict the future, have proceeded to set policy as if they had that data—for example by pursuing policies that consider industry average rates of employment as factors of quality assurance used to accredit institutions or by equating student loan defaults with poor job results and quality education. In most cases there is no correlation.

The last thing governments should do now is try to micro-manage and engineer knowledge economy relationships because they think that they know what the forces of demand and supply are. They can act positively to support institutions and programs where students make choices, but government must not needlessly restrict the actions and decisions of informed providers and consumers. Where government funds are limited and these supply decisions are necessarily restricted then the system must allow other providers to serve that demand where they can.

Individual learners should make their program, institution, life, professional and business choices. Then the market will decide who is the best doctor, lawyer, engineer or carpenter. New people coming up may be better than those already there or better than those that admission control officers with limited positions to dole out may choose.

The steady stream of stories [19] about too many graduates in one area and not enough in others areas and of unfilled jobs or long waiting lines of under employed persons tells you that central controls do not work. It also tells you that in many cases markets are also not working because people perhaps made decisions that were uninformed or unrealistic. The latter is still the preferred mistake because at least persons that did not make the cut and get the job they wanted at least they had a shot that might not have existed with central market controls. Market systems are imperfect, but at least there the decision making and demand and supply mechanisms are de-centralized and exposed to a multitude of points where informed and intelligent buyers and sellers make decisions.

3.10 Education Freedom is Essential to Personal Freedom and Central to Left and Right Political Thought

Learning is so essential to personal, business, economic, social, legal and political development that persons must have the individual freedom to access and pursue what they need and want. They should not have to rely on what others impose on or make available to them because they think they know what is suitable for or of value to the person, society or economy. It is a waste of human potential and resources to have highly skilled persons driving cabs and equally a waste to not allow a person to develop the knowledge and skill they want to have and use.

America (Canada and the United States), has been a magnet for people seeking adventure, fleeing from tyranny or just trying to make a better life. [20] They had to learn and work. In these and many other countries, economic and political progress was based on free market systems that allowed individuals to freely pursue their own objectives, interests and goals. Even with many of those that favor a robust role for government in the provision of services, including educational services, a high degree of personal choice has still been advocated.

The thought was that if cooperation and deal making is voluntary no exchange will take place unless both parties benefit. The contractual doctrine of consideration—where something of value flows between the parties to essentially buy the other's promise - was the foundation. No external force, no coercion, no violation of freedom was seen to be necessary to produce cooperation between benefitting individuals. By pursuing their own interests they were seen as promoting the interests of society. Economic freedom was seen as essential to political freedom. Allowing and enabling people to cooperate with each other without coercion or central direction was seen as a way to reduce the area over which political power had to be exercised.[21]

Related ideas were embodied in the US Declaration of Independence and more recently the Canadian Charter of Rights and Freedoms. The US Declaration was established in large part on the principle that every person is entitled to pursue their own values: We hold these truths to be self-evident that all men are created equal, that they are endowed by their Creator with certain unalienable Rights: that among these are Life, Liberty and the pursuit of Happiness.

The Canadian Charter similarly states that Canadians have certain fundamental freedoms, including the: freedom of conscience and religion; freedom of thought, belief, opinion and expression, including freedom of the press and other media of communication; freedom of peaceful assembly; and freedom of association.[22] In addition, Canadians have[23] certain legal rights including the right to life, liberty and security of the person.

The split between right and left is not so much on the issue of personal choice, but about how to serve the accepted need for universal access—government service or mixed public private services. If persons believe in choice and government supported providers do not provide that choice then they should reasonably side with choice and not the political dogma surrounding state supported providers.

Keeping education markets free and accessible is not a right or left argument. The Fraser Institute in Canada (what some call a right wing think tank) has said government should stop deciding how many professionals and other workers are trained because it usually results in shortages or surpluses. More liberal minded persons say let people dream and freely try - without unreasonable restrictions - to fulfill their study and professional aspirations while letting markets and not government or professions gatekeepers determine who ultimately works and competes to have a chance at success in a specific area.

Liberal Philosopher Isaiah Berlin[24] said a person or group is or should be left to do or be what he is able to do or be, without interference by other persons. He also questioned who else could be justifiably given the power to restrict those choices. In Canada, Jack Layton, the former leader of the NDP (about as far left as you can go in Canada without really being that far left) said in a 2011 election campaign that he wanted to ensure young people were able to pursue their personal dreams. In the same campaign, Liberal leader Michael Ignatieff said "If you get the grades you get to go" and he did not mean you get to go into a program that the government chooses for you.

3.11 Development Depends on Freedom and Freedom Depends on Development

Nobel Prize Winner Amartya Sen and others rightfully states that development creates freedom and freedom creates development. [25] Development should expand the freedoms people enjoy. Expansion of rights should be the standard. This contrasts with narrower views of development focused on the growth of GNP, a rise in personal incomes or technological advances. As Sen argues, if freedom is what development advances then we should concentrate on that overarching objective rather than particular means, measures or lists of instruments.

Viewing development this way directs attention to the ends that make development important, rather than merely to some of the means or measures. Development requires the removal of major sources of un-freedom: poverty; tyranny; poor economic opportunities; social deprivation; neglect of public facilities; intolerance or over activity of repressive states. What people can positively achieve is influenced by economic opportunities, political liberties, social powers and the enabling conditions of good health and basic education.

As economies mature, the threshold for what basic education means moves higher. The institutional arrangements for these opportunities are influenced by the exercise of freedom through the liberty to participate in social choice and in the making of public decisions that impel the progress of opportunities. As this threshold for basic education moves higher it becomes more difficult for governments alone to centrally plan for and meet all education demands.

Markets are part of development. The ability of markets to contribute to economic growth and progress is widely and rightly acknowledged, but it is a mistake to understand markets only in derivative terms, that is, in terms of what they lead to. [26] The freedom of exchange and transaction is itself one of the liberties people value. Sen says to be generically against markets would be like being against conversation. The freedom to exchange words, or goods or gifts does not need defensive justification. They are part of the way we live and interact with each other unless stopped by regulation or fiat and those restrictions must be justified because they are needed to protect specified interests against specified risks. The contribution of markets to economic growth is important, but this comes after the direct significance of the freedom to exchange words, services, goods and gifts has been acknowledged.

3.12 Freedom of Contract, Academic Freedom, Out of Sync Supply and Demand, Private or Public Investment

The kind of freedom most commonly cited in education circles is academic freedom. There was a time in history when universities were the only place where books or those with knowledge were and both teachers and students needed that institution—one for teaching and one for their studies. Principles of academic freedom evolved to ensure that persons that had this special and to some extent exclusive cultural role in developing and holding knowledge for current and future generations were not subject to political or corporate control.

Academic freedom takes different forms and depends on how individual institutions articulate it. The courts have often held that such policies are not contractual in the sense that faculty cannot always claim contract breach if institutions do not adhere fully to that expression of what academic freedom means. There is no logical rationale to restrict it to state run institutions. It is not a constitutionally protected right except to the extent it fits within existing constitutional rights and freedoms that extend to all persons no matter whom they work for. Constitutions constrain governments and do not provide private law rights.

Academics still pursue and develop new knowledge and society must support them, but knowledge is now dispersed and pursued and developed by government agencies, independent researchers, professionals and corporations. Universities are also now commercial enterprises marketing to global audiences and competing with other institutions. Teaching, education and training are also dispersed and it is hard to argue that only certain persons teaching certain things in certain places have academic freedom.

Academic freedom and the ability of instructors to teach what they decide should not be the sole determinant of what is available in markets to meet demand. The institution and student consumers must dictate what products are provided and consumed in a market. More than one university president has commented that they are constrained in their ability to act because any attempt to influence product and content is met with departmental opposition based on academic freedom arguments. A contract is a two way street and academics cannot and should not dismiss what students want. The "we know best" attitude may often be perfectly valid and at other times be nothing more than an anachronism of the past. Students could assert more market influence if they perceived themselves as active and not passive players.

Another context in which these debates play out relates to private investments in public institutions. The same principles can be involved with public investments. Private investments in education often still flow to the public sector because of their size and prestige and their research and teaching involvement in key sectors of the economy. This is often fine and good and perfect understandable and appropriate. In many cases, these investments are not tracked in terms of returns. Investments in private institutions or the creation of new institutions may be more effective and open to monitoring. Often investments in specific institutions or programs would be better invested in scholarship funds that are available to students from all institutions or sector specific institutions.

Two articles appeared in the Canadian media in March of 2012 [27] to illustrate the point. As the articles point out, whenever universities move toward significant corporate collaborations it raises issues of autonomy and integrity. For one thing, if the academics insist on absolute control over what happens then it is not really collaboration, but a straight donation. They are not really doing anything together subject to the terms of their collaboration contract.

In a desperate search to secure funding, universities are entering more complicated donor relationships that go beyond passive donation. That results in issues around proper governance structures that allow universities to accept funding from outsides while also protecting their autonomy and integrity. Faculty associations take a firm stand that no one other than academics has any business directing what happens in terms of research and teaching. As discussed in other sections, they are still viewing "academia" (academic affairs) as this separate world that is isolated from the world of commerce. In our view donors have every right to set conditions on their funds and if the academics don't like it then the donor should invest the money elsewhere. The assumption again is that the only smart people that can make these decisions and do the work are in academia and that idea is outdated.

3.13 The Evolving Higher Education Social Contract

The old social contract involved a majority funding the education and research activities of a small minority because they benefitted from their activities. Now everyone needs higher education and higher education involves a greater range of disciplines, professions and vocations. No one institution or group of government funded institutions can meet this diverse and almost infinitely deep demand. Students want to learn in different ways and at times and in places that suit their needs and lifestyles. Government funded institutions should not control markets or dominate and influence regulatory regimes for their benefit even if they could meet demand on their own.

As noted, there are only minimal and illusory differences between public and private institutions. There is the growing capacity, impact and influence of private institutions in some education sectors and the changing nature of traditional institutions as they shift away from older In Loco Parentis and "club" models to become commercial and market oriented institutions that compete with other public and private institutions in domestic and global markets. All of these factors contribute to the need for a new social contract written around diversity and learner choice.

Institutions of higher learning were given special powers and privileges because they were seen as having special cultural influences. They were seen as holding and developing knowledge for current and future generations. Few people went to them, but those (the vast majority) that did not still saw the value. Today, knowledge not only resides and is not only developed in these institutions. These institutions still have great influence and benefit and should be supported, but they cannot be only focus or centre of attention.

With special privileges come special duties. Some people may not buy into the old social contract because their needs are not met. They want to make sure that institutions with special powers are not working behind the scenes to protect their special powers and to restrict those that can also meet needs. Even if needs are met by older institutions those institutions should not support policies that restrict student choice. Special privileges were granted because others could not do what they did. That is not always the case now. If needs can be met by new providers they should be enabled. Risks should be addressed by proper and uniform standards applying to all.

The social contract frays at the edges when you have one student's family paying taxes for government funded institutions and programs that the student is capable of being successful in, but is blocked from taking because of limited enrollments. The denied student is forced to pay the full cost of a private program or perhaps denied the freedom to pursue their dreams at all. Well managed and regulated private sector training firms can and do save governments and taxpayers money and in many cases without sacrificing quality one iota. Denied students get hit again in terms of credit transfer and market recognition if the credential they gain is less valued unjustifiably in real state of knowledge terms because again their tax money is used to establish the government funded program and brand as the best program and brand.

The social or economic value of an institution, class of institution or specific program depends on many factors and that value does not vary with public or private institutions. The value focus should be on helping achieve learning outcomes because that is the essence of what education is about. It does not matter where the learning occurs.

Traditional media and content producers are losing their de facto monopolies on the delivery of content. There is no reason to believe that traditional education providers will escape that reality except for the fact that existing large providers tend to control or greatly impact the regulators that impact competition. Traditional authority is being challenged politically, socially and in academia. Current institutions will survive, but not as exclusive addresses for learning. The taxpayer funnel (taxpayer money in at the top) option is not going to be the only or major option.

The social contract on higher education—as it manifests in properly balanced law reform - should reflect these points and the points expressed in other sections.

4

New Institutions, From Academy to Global Corporation and Customer Driven Capitalism

4.1 The New Institution— From the Academy to Global Corporation

Public and private institutions have evolved beyond (arguably they could never be described that way) the traditional and isolated "academy" to become more market, commercial and contract focused enterprises. [28]

Elementary and secondary institutions also, but especially post-secondary institutions are very different than they were fifty years ago. They have adjusted to different lifestyles and needs. In the 1960s most Canadian and US university students were young, part of social elites and studying and participating full-time on campus without working on the side. Employment or career opportunities were more assured. Careers lasted longer. University executives presided over the academy and acted like headmasters providing moral leadership. [29]

Today, more people, from all income and racial or social groups, attend post-secondary education. Students are often older, more diverse and often working or raising children at the same time. Students often commute over distance and are more job-oriented. People change jobs and careers often and must constantly learn new things and enhance their state of knowledge. Students have a greater sense of entitlement as customers. Recruitment agents help with marketing and administrators are market driven and often in conflict with self-focused academics. [30] Competition between public and private institutions world-wide is greater.

Costs are rising and government and philanthropic funds are limited so tuition fees are rising in most jurisdictions. The dollars spent per student are often decreasing and there is increased competition for scarce resources. Institutions [31] are less removed from mainstream society, more tied to events and interests outside the academic world and more focused on solving immediate problems.

Institution executives lead organizations that are part mid-nineteenth century ecclesiastical entities and part late-twentieth century corporations. Being a university president today is like being a CEO of a major corporation, but they manage departments that often view themselves as separate and beyond the reach of central institution or government planners. Many institutions are larger and need to grow to be viable. Operating budgets alone, without considering capital budgets, involve tens or hundreds of millions of dollars. Leaders must serve students, bargain with unions, keep the organization updated technologically and lobby government and off-campus stakeholders. They try to have distinctive brands that highlight distinct product features and market plans. No single university can address all the needs of modern life. [32]

4.2 Education Institutions, Shareholders, Stakeholders and Customer Driven Capitalism

In the past, higher education institutions were often seen as being separate from society. They were somewhat isolated and given deference by courts often because they were perceived as having a special cultural value to society. They were seen as developing new knowledge in the pursuit of truth and committed to passing it on to future generations. That is still the case, but society is less dependent because knowledge and expertise is more diverse and dispersed. Knowledge is developed and held at many levels by knowledgeable people that work in professions, trades, government, a broader range of public and private institutions and non-profit and for-profit corporations. These institutions are more engaged in education markets as equals with public and private domestic and international institutions.

In that olden time, students were either treated as children (in loco parentis) or as members of a larger group that effectively gave up any commercial legal rights in return for the privilege of being part of the "academy" or special "club". [33] That world is largely gone although remnants of the culture remain to impact remaining managers and regulators that emerged from that world.

In that other world the emphasis was often on everything that the university or institution did "for" the broader society (a kind of shareholder group) because they had something no one else had—knowledge and knowledgeable people and the capacity to generate new knowledge. The individuals attending benefitted, but at one time there were very few of them and still most people do not attend university.

The student consumer and commercial focus in education arises so that students are the centre of attention and not the broader society or "shareholder" group. In the commercial world also the focus was often on shareholder value. That was seen as the ultimate goal and that element remains and always will. Again the balance is shifting. Selling to consumers was seen as the way you achieved that shareholder goal. The economic crisis late in the first decade of the new millennium revived the old debate about whether firms should focus on their shareholders, customers or workers.

In the Economist magazine in 2010 [34] it was observed that the era of "Jack Welch capitalism" may be drawing to a close as more people question whether a firm's sole and primary aim should be maximising shareholder returns. Even Welch was quoted as recently having said: "On the face of it, shareholder value is the dumbest idea in the world".

In the Harvard Business Review, Roger Martin, Dean of the University of Toronto's Rotman School of Management, said all stakeholders—consumers, employees, suppliers and society at large—should get more attention and that specifically shareholder value should give way to "customer-driven capitalism" where firms aim to maximise customer satisfaction. Education providers, public and private, and those that regulate and govern them cannot escape this idea. Governments rhetorically embrace "learner demand systems", but their policies and actions often tell a different story.

This fits with our analysis and assertion that educational institutions and those that regulate them should also focus on the provider, the product, the product consumer and the risks associated with product consumption.

In reality, private and public institutions serve many masters. Corporations are legally responsible to shareholders (or non-profit members) under one line of legal accountability and responsible to student consumers under another line of legal and contractual accountability. They are liable to regulators under yet another line of legal accountability that is separate from, but related to and arising from the student contract (See Sections on Public and Private Duties).

In the public sector (subject to sections questioning public-private distinctions), the institution has no direct legal line of accountability to the broader society. Their legal responsibilities are as set out in their constating documents and governing statutes. The broader society had and has expectations and we talk about that more as that "social contract" may be about to be challenged given that institutions and society are undergoing major change.

5

The Courts Have Spoken—Education is Commercial and Contractual

5.1 The Decline of Student and Institution In Loco Parentis and Forum Domesticum Relationships

For a long time and even until relatively recently, in Canada and the USA, courts tended to treat the relationship between an institution and student as one of in loco parentis. The institution was seen as and often expressly contracted to be a form of parent wielding strict control of a child and as being responsible for their social, physical, mental and moral well-being, care and development.[35] The theoretical construct of in loco parentis was not related to duties owed to the student by the university.

For centuries prior to WWII the university was seen as a private institution that best regulated itself through the consensual agreement of its members much like a Victorian gentlemen's club. The University environment was thought to foster heightened virtues among scholars who through their distance from society and personal financial sacrifice for the purposes of education were responsible for developing knowledge for future generations. [36] Courts would often defer determining the rights between the parties on the grounds the parties had implicitly agreed to rely on their own means to settle disputes. [37] This changed when institutions changed.[38]

The 1960s period, with its surging student activism, was when the shift began to occur to a more student and institution contract focus. [39] In the USA, in the anti-Vietnam War era universities began dismissing students for protesting. The courts intervened in disputes over the dismissals by applying the lens of the due process clause of the 14th Amendment, which guarantees procedural fairness when the state government would deprive an individual of their property or liberty. This understanding of higher education as a property right or entitlement helped usher in the concept of the student-university contract under which the institution provides a service product in return for fees paid by the student. The notion of higher education as an entitlement and the student as consumer was introduced and the in loco parentis idea began to die. [40]

In Canada the same kind of traditional reasoning [41] was used by courts for deferring and not ruling on academic matters. Following a forum domesticum line of reasoning it was assumed there was a preselected jurisdiction where the parties had agreed amongst themselves as to how disputes would be handled within the forum. This was considered practical, faster, cheaper and less formal. As in the USA, the nature of the student-university relationship also shifted from in loco parentis to a consumer-provider relationship. Universities were acting more like corporations competing in a marketplace for students and less removed from mainstream society. Romantic notions of institutions gave way to modern realities and it became harder to justify traditional judicial deference in student grievance matters. Judicial intervention was not political obstruction and institutions could still live up to their social obligations. Students expect access to judicial forums and remedies after they exhaust internal recourses. [42] Courts may defer on academic matters like grades as they may defer on some family matters, but at a point any family or academic matter can attract judicial attention if a claim alleges that legally protected rights are being seriously infringed.

These issues are examined again in relation to systems thinking. When looking at the nature of the institution and student relationship you must deal with reality. You cannot pretend it is an in-loco parentis relationship or a relationship involving membership in some kind of ancient club when the reality is a commercial and contractual relationship. The models and ways of thinking that dominated higher education in the past continue to influence attitudes and management styles or decisions. You cannot effectively manage or regulate that relationship unless you understand what the contractual promises, representations, intentions and expectations are.

5.2 Contract Law Always Applied, But the When and How Became More Clear

Courts in most jurisdictions have always held that contract law applied to the institution and student relationship to some extent. [43] Judicial deference was more about when and how. Contract law applied to public and private sectors, but most cases concerning representations came from the private sector where institutions were not often subject to other forms of judicial review. It is argued in other sections that these traditional uses of judicial review, more commonly applied to public decision makers, are no longer (if they ever were) the proper method for handling student complaints and disputes.

In circumstances where claims and pleadings set out a proper legal cause of action and where students placed new demands on institutions for less paternalism and more accountability for services promised and rendered, the courts began to see higher education as being contractual in nature and the student as a consumer with every right to legal protection—and specifically the protection of the common law of contract and tort. This occurred in both Canada and the USA.

Courts often adhere closely to contract theory in some areas and apply it more liberally in others. In the USA, for example, the courts for a time would often defer and not consider cases involving academic and disciplinary matters [44] and decisions while still regarding the relationship between the student and institution as contractual. The lack of a unified legal doctrine has led to confusing and unpredictable legal decisions. Grading policies, admissions and discipline were examples of where deference continued with the same justifications [45] noted above to avoid students running off to court every time they have a beef about a grade. [46] Deference may be justified in some cases, but later sections show how so-called "academic" areas still have contract elements.

In other areas like tuition, fees, scholarships or loans, courts, especially US courts but Canadian courts also, interpret the contract with exacting scrutiny, tolerating little deviance from agreed-upon terms of contract. Student consumers contend they can rely upon contractual relations with institutions from application to graduation. [47] The real nature and content of the contract and its contained promises, representations, conditions and statements that give rise to rights and obligations are explored more in later sections.

5.3 Judicial Deference and Academic Freedom

One of the troubling aspects of deference arguments is the tendency for institutions to seek immunity for themselves from judicial oversight because it would impact their academic freedom. Academic freedom has its place although that place is changing as the social contract with institutions of higher education evolves. Academic advocates seem to forget that the common law also has a slightly important place in our legal culture. They suggest that their academic freedom—a highly uncertain legal concept at the best of times—can override a student's right to present a claim in contract or tort law to the court. They suggest that judicial intervention is government intervention. Judicial oversight is not government oversight, but judicial reference to the common law and principles that have guided our personal and commercial affairs for centuries.

5.4 Canadian Courts Assert Inherent Jurisdiction to Give Students Common Law and Contract Law Protection

Canadian courts have, as in the USA, clearly stated that contract law applies to the institution and student relationship and that the courts will assert their inherent jurisdiction. [48] This was affirmed with important judgments from Ontario in 2011. These cases can impact universities across Canada because they came from the province's Court of Appeal. They impact whether a student's academic grievance will be heard by a court.

In the Gauthier case the court stated several relevant principles. [49] It said the Superior Court is a court of general jurisdiction and its jurisdiction may only be delimited by clear and express legislative or contract provisions. It said if there are no provisions like that then the court is competent to rule on the dispute even in matters of an academic nature. It said that with purely internal academic decisions the appropriate proceeding may still be judicial review, but it said where there is a contractual aspect to the relationship with the university and a breach of contract is properly alleged, the court has jurisdiction to hear the case. Serious arguments can be made against the idea that judicial review is the appropriate approach with public institutions because they are legally, according to Canadian case law, not government and not subject to the Charter. That issue is discussed in another dedicated section.

The university argued in Gauthier that the court did not have jurisdiction over the subject matter identified by the student. It said that even though the matter was framed as a contractual dispute it said the student's claims were academic in nature. [50] This was rejected by the court because of the specific facts that we do not review here.

Another Ontario Court of Appeal judgment (Jaffer) [51] alleged breach of contract, breach of good faith and negligent misrepresentation. York University claimed matters were academic and outside the court's jurisdiction and that Jaffer had initiated a human rights claim that fell within the exclusive jurisdiction of the Human Rights Commission. At the Superior Court of Justice, the University tried to strike the appellant's Statement of Claim on the basis that it failed to plead a known cause of action within the jurisdiction of the court. Pitt J. agreed and held that the issue was academic, within the university's discretion and involving a human rights claim. The motion judge maintained that if the core of a student's grievance involves academic conduct then it cannot be heard by the courts even if issues involve contract or tort. These lines of reasoning did not ultimately carry the day.

Madam Justice Karakatsanis, in a unanimous decision, rejected that position and stated clearly on the basis of Gauthier that where the elements of a breach of contract or negligence are properly pleaded, the Superior Court will have jurisdiction to hear a claim even if the dispute is academic in nature and arises out of the academic activities of the university.

Noah Sarna observes in his book on the Law of Schools and Universities that the courts rejected similar claims by other students not because the court lacked jurisdiction or because judicial review was the appropriate form of claim, but because the claims were untenable. The Jaffer judgment quoted Gauthier: "In my opinion, to determine whether the court has jurisdiction it is more useful to look at the remedy claimed by the plaintiff. When a party is seeking to have the internal academic decision of a university reversed, the proper procedure is judicial review (Again, arguments against using judicial review at all are addressed separately.). If the plaintiff is alleging the basis for a cause of action in tort or breach of contract and claiming damages, the court will have jurisdiction even if the dispute arises out of the scholastic or academic activities of the university in question".

Both universities in the Gauthier and Jaffer cases applied to the Supreme Court of Canada for leave to appeal the Court of Appeal rulings. In March 2011, both applications were dismissed.

Again, both cases referred to an implied contract where students may have a claim for damages if the university did not deliver on promises and actions exceeded their jurisdiction over their academic programs. Students cannot just be trying to appeal decisions of an academic nature. Put another way, Jaffer and Gauthier [52] confirmed that courts will dismiss student claims unless the matter falls outside discretion granted to universities over academic matters. Falling outside that discretion though is a proper cause of action in contract or tort law. These bodies of law are triggered respectively by the existence of volitional contract instruments and non-contract relationships that give rise to legally enforceable duties of care.

It is hard to believe for some that in 2012 many public (government funded or as otherwise defined) institutions are astonished that they are actually subject to Canadian common law as it relates to contracts. Finally they are starting to acknowledge: that universities and their students must have clear documentation; that they have always relied on the calendar and university policies for the contract; that it has not been seen as a business arrangement; and that students, parents and courts are now more consumer-oriented.

Some refer to a mindset that has existed in the U.S. for a long time, but this is not about mindsets. It is about primary powers within the Canadian system consciously avoiding what they must always have known - that these laws apply to them. They seemed to think that students and institutions in other countries had the burden and protection of the law as did private institutions and their students in Canada, but not the public institutions and their students in Canada.

A big question must be—Where were their regulators? The same Ministry regulators require private institutions in Canada to have written (not implied) contracts. They should be aware that the UK (public and private institutions) and BC (private vocational schools) governments have given non-court agencies the ability to consider some contract complaints. [53] Under those complaint systems both sides must have the protection of the common law of contract and tort as administered by competent and impartial persons because a dispute or Lis Inter Parties would exist. The law is a unified whole and cannot mean something different in courts and at tribunals. Any decision to the contrary would be a reviewable error of law. There is a difference between administering the statute and the application of administrative law to that function and the adjudication of a dispute between two parties.

They somehow thought and many still think that they are outside the legal system and that government funding for what are still independent corporate entities put them outside the law. The public sector newsletter cited in this section was published a year after these recent cases cleared the courts, but it is an indication that reality is setting in.

Student complaints are growing world-wide. [54] Many are not reasonable and easily dismissed by courts because no real cause of action is shown. There are also growing numbers of valid complaints that the courts are ruling on. What is clear is that the broad term "academic affairs" must always be questioned and cannot be hidden behind as a reason for judicial deference because virtually everything that happens in the education train of events from recruitment to graduation can have contractual implications.

As discussed in other sections, there are only slight legal differences between public institutions and private institutions and the two are unified in markets through contract law. Both enter contracts with students and contract law applies. Again, as argued in other sections, education regulation should be targeted at contract product risk. Regulation should operate separately from, but alongside contract law to ensure students receive what was promised and that products satisfy legal standards also focused on mitigating consumer risk. Students in all sectors should have the same protections and different regulations can only be justified where risks differ. Regulations and contracts operate separately because parties to the regulatory and contract relationships are different. The rights and duties of the parties are distinct.

It is not just Ontario courts that accept the contract reality of education. In many cases from many provinces, courts have acknowledged contract reality and either decided the case on contract principles or referred to the contract and then still relied on administrative law and judicial review principles—a practice that arguably is an historical anomaly (see that section) or that could often be avoided with proper pleadings when facts allow for it. In the MacDonald v. UBC case, cited below and in other sections, the court relied on a university calendar provision that expressly said a contract existed to establish payment obligations and to give the institution the power to unilaterally increase fees, but it still decided the case largely on administrative law grounds rather than contract law grounds.

One cannot avoid observing that large public institutions will often rely on their catalogues as contracts to protect their interests (fee collection or increased fees) and then argue strongly against the student being able to assert their right to contract law protection by insisting that judicial review (under which private remedies are difficult) is the appropriate procedure rather than a civil contract action. They try to insist that everything associated with the student falls under the "academic" umbrella and thus justifies judicial deference. Those times are clearly ending and when serious legal causes of action in contract or tort exist the courts will hear and rule on the case.

Part 2

Systems Thinking, Contracts, Outcomes, Products, Regulation

6

Systems Thinking and Education Systems

6.1 Systems Thinking, Contracts and Law

An understanding of systems is essential to good contract and regulatory management and it is sometimes absent in the education sector. Systems are relationships of legal entities (persons or corporations), things or parts. A system is an integrated whole whose essential properties emerge from the relationships between its parts. Systems are separate from their parts and form greater and higher level systems or relate to other systems. Emergent properties are revealed at a particular level of organization and are not possessed by constituent sub-systems. The whole is more than the sum of the parts.

System success depends on it having its own "achievable" objectives, interests, motivations and plans, but these evolve from those held by its constituent players and parts that may in fact be complementary or in conflict. Systems are systems because they reflect and encompass cause and effect relationships and the parties and elements that cause the effects and that are affected by the cause.

The link between systems and law is obvious. Laws are risk management tools and seek order in relationships where two or more parties can, through their actions or omissions, impact others, that is, cause an effect for others. As noted in other sections, volitional contract instruments, governed by contract law and public law regulation can target the same parties and relationships and operate separately to establish and maintain order for them. The essence of a contract is an attempt by two or more parties to establish and maintain a relationship that has mutual benefits and that means they must often each commit to be legally bound to do or not do certain things and to only make representations of fact that are true if those representations can induce others to enter a binding contract. The contract can then trigger the application not only of contract law, but other laws. Other sections explore this.

Education institutions and students have complementary and conflicting interests. Contracts are what they are and they do what they do because of such relationships. They need and want each other and want to achieve a shared objective, but to get there they have to sort out conflicts and mitigate risks that arise from their relationship. As we see later, education management and regulation are doomed to fail if they do not grasp this fundamental reality.

6.2 Institution and Student Contract Relationships Lie at the Centre of Education Systems

Education systems are about "education" and learning. As a result, the student and institution contract relationship lies at the centre of the education universe or system. The student is easily defined and delimited. The student is an individual learner. The institution is more complex. As noted in other sections, institutions are just corporate shells at an address (traditionally) that assemble, aggregate and intermediate various product factor inputs in order to create a product that can help the student learn.

The three core players are the student, the institution (as an aggregator of product factors) and the education regulator, but the other parties are numerous and their relationships complex. The legal entities, things or parts that revolve around the institution and student are not necessarily part of the education system. Faculty, information and instruction resource providers, intellectual property licensors, landlords and others that are or provide product factor inputs are part of the system because they contribute to the education product and to learning objectives being met. Many of these relationships are contractual.

Other players and parts are more peripheral. Surrounding the institution and student relationship are stakeholders that have direct and separate legal relationships—many of them contractual in nature - with an institution, student or third party or that have a stake in student and institution relationship outcomes. Most of these parties and relationships would not exist without the student contract.

Some may want to influence the institution and student contract, but more importantly a student may wrongly assume they have rights in relation to other stakeholders that they can enforce under the student contract. Those possibilities (e.g. articulation partners, professional organizations, immigration authorities) are discussed in other sections. There are no broad conclusions that can be drawn about inclusion or exclusion from education systems. It is an individual assessment on the facts. In one case a professional organization may be part of the system because they contribute to curricula development. In other cases they only come into the picture in the post contract period to admit grads and to regulate members in the interests of those that consume member services.

The list of parties that may (Emphasis Added) be part of or revolve around education systems includes, but is not confined to: faculty members; industry groups; trade authorities; employers or service consumers; trade and economic development authorities; immigration and border control authorities; groups of schools; student loan lenders; student loan institution designation authorities; market brand officials; professional groups; quality assurance regulators; information and content engineers and providers; third party recruitment or student service firms; student assessment and credential evaluation firms; or any person or firm that provides services to help institutions assemble a modern learning environment.

Some of the ways these parties are impacted by or relate to the student contract can be listed. Student contracts trigger regulation and specific regulations suited for unique risks. Student contracts create the payment obligations for students. Student contracts establish the legally enforceable rights and duties of students and institutions. Marketing and recruitment are about inducing persons into contracts. Admissions decisions are about a decision to enter the contract. Program operation is about delivering on contract promises. Supply contracts the institution enters into (faculty, equipment) arise because of the student contract. Assessments measure if education products helped learners learn as contractually promised. Student loan eligibility is triggered by enrollment contracts at designated institutions. Study permits are normally given if a student is enrolled under contract at an institution. International trade rules relating to education are about entering into cross border transactions and contracts. Articulation, credit transfer and credential evaluation are about evidence of contract results.

6.3 Education Systems, Success, Students Are Consumers and Not Inputs, Outputs or Outcomes

Education issues cannot be addressed without understanding the nature, boundaries and objectives of the education "system". It is only at the contract level where students and institutions provide and consume products and where cause and effect relationships have real legal significance because of substantial and real impacts, proximity, intervening events and other factors.

Effective regulation and management involve setting realistic and doable goals. Success and achievement must be based on those realistic and doable goals. Success should be measured by evidence and not conjecture or assumptions. Risks addressed by one set of contracts and regulations must be separated from risks associated with other contracts and regulations. If an actor cannot realistically achieve an objective then he is not acting within an environment where real objectives can be set and achieved, that is, not acting within a "system".

Some refer to students as education system inputs and others refer to them as education system outputs or products. They are neither. If they were an output that would mean the purpose of the education system is to create a worker for a benefitting economy. If you consider the broad socio-economy as the examined "system" that may be appropriate. Institutions do not normally have contracts with companies or public sector economic development authorities to produce specified workers. They are not an input to a product because they consume a product composed of factor inputs.

The student is simply a consumer that buys a product for a set price when tuitions are charged. In public subsidized systems that price may be at a lower level that does not reflect real input cost, but that is a separate issue. The nature of the bargain does not change the contract reality. Politicians or the media commonly say we train too many teachers or lawyers. They imply that this is the purpose of education. That may be a broad socio-economic objective, but the education system, which is part of the socio-economic system, must be more narrowly focused. Its purpose is to help students achieve a state of knowledge that can be assessed and validated. If the purpose is expanded too far then fulfillment of that purpose would be jeopardized by factors that lie outside the control of those that participate in the education system. That is the antithesis of what systems thinking tells us.

6.4 Education Systems Relate To and Are Separate From Other Systems, Contracts and Systems

A legal entity can, in its own right: enter contracts; own property; earn income; pay tax; sue or be sued; claim and have vested rights and powers; have obligations (duties) and restrictions imposed on them; and have or assert needs, wants, interests, motivations, principles, values, beliefs, goals and objectives. With education the three key entities are the student, institution and regulator with other stakeholders and relationships revolving around them.

This is one more way to look at the nature of the institution and student relationship. You cannot pretend (See other sections) it is an in-loco parentis relationship or a relationship involving membership in some kind of club when the reality is different and that reality is a commercial and contractual relationship. You cannot manage or regulate that relationship unless you understand what the contract promises, representations, intentions and expectations are because those are the things that create and shape the relationship.

Distinct systems exist at the level of the institution (the aggregated and intermediated elements), the institution and student, the industry, the regulator, the workplace and the socio-economy. They form larger systems together, but for legal and business purposes lines must be drawn between them. Effective management and regulation depend on having realistic and doable objectives. Each system has its own objectives and cause and effect (accountability) relationships that are close enough to have legal significance and practical function.

Education regulators are often not properly distinguishing the workplace and socio-economic systems from education systems. Education, in the formal sense, involves a contract between an institution and student and that has a beginning and end. The system should be analyzed and understood in that context.

A job, work or business is not an education system or outcome, but an outcome that emerges from countless education, social, personal, business and economic factors. Education should be regulated as other commercial sectors are regulated—with a focus on product, product risk and risk mitigation. Reluctance to articulate matters in contract and product terms may be because persons from the traditional academy have not yet acknowledged the reality that education is contractual and commercial and not just a public service delivered with tax money.

6.5 Pre-Contract, Contract and Post Contract Periods, Players, Contract and Non-Contract Outcomes

There are three core periods to consider—pre-student contract, student contract and post student contract periods.

Even before the student contract is finalized there are legal relationships beginning to form. Prospective students are protected by tort law (where duties may exist to conform to standards in the absence of or in addition to contracts) or perhaps by collateral contracts and statutes that protect prospective institutions and students. It is here that recruitment and marketing initiatives occur, where applications are made, where student loans are applied for (not granted until a contract exists) and where other education-related activities play out.

Most everything involved with education revolves around the student and institution contract and the contract consideration, promises and representations each party makes and offers the other. If the contract product involves a specific type of training (of a certain type, length or tuition cost) then that often triggers the regulator's jurisdiction. The nature of the contract will also impact the specific goals and risks that exist and therefore the specific regulations that may be required. Management and regulation should focus on the major goals and risks and not on building institutions that look like institutions of the past unless that is necessary to address goals and risks.

It is that product that is "consumed" by the "consumer" during the contract period that normally has a beginning and an end. It is that product that has a goal in mind and creates a need to protect consumers from risks associated with product consumption. Education (Quality Assurance) regulators are not tasked with protecting all students from all risks associated with all programs and certainly not from risks associated with unemployment or business prospects that may or may not occur beyond the contract, consumption and risk period.

The first two core outcomes outlined below (the Product promised and the un-promised [because the student controls it] learning achievement) are achieved during this student contract period. In the post student contract period the contract and legal relationship between the student and institution has ended and the jurisdiction of regulators over that relationship has also ended. It is here that the opportunities sought are pursued and hopefully seized. This can relate to a job, self-employment and professional work or business and entrepreneurship.

These "Outcomes" are not and cannot legally be promised and fall outside the education system because the objectives are not achievable within the education system. It is also during this period that student loans come payable and are in most cases paid back.

7

The Private Law of Obligations—Contract, Tort and Restitution Law

7.1 Legal and Contract Literacy and Future Management and Regulation

As already noted, the student and institution contract is the centre of the education universe with all contract management, regulatory enforcement and stakeholder relationships revolving around it. It is often alarming to see regulators, the media and students in a frenzy making allegations while ignoring the legal, commercial and contractual realities of the student and institution relationship.

Management and quality assurance regulation should focus on contract products, product consumption risk and standards that mitigate consumption risk. They should focus on ensuring that promised products are systematically delivered to students and do what they are designed to do—help students learn, assess if learning occurs and credibly declare that achievement to the world. Again, jobs and business success are not promised so unemployment and business failures are not contract risks.

Students, institutions and regulators must understand what contracts and contract law are and how they operate separately from, but alongside public law regulation and administrative law. They must understand the contract and its parties, promised products (objects of quality), represented facts (that may induce contract entry or continuance), product consumption risks and provisions that address party risks. This is what gives rise to the legal relationship and the possible risks that may need to be addressed by public law and regulation.

This section is not written for lawyers. It does not quote and summarize countless cases. It relies more on contract law texts. [55] Basic points are presented in summary format. There can be variation from jurisdiction to jurisdiction and there is no attempt to cover all possible variations. In most cases, the fundamental concepts do not vary that much. Canadian law is the primary focus and no attempt has been made to ensure that the review is absolutely up to date with references to the most recent case and statute law. Core ideas are the key.

7.2 Public Law and Private Law

Public law is common law and statute law made and enforced to protect the public interest as opposed to specific private rights. It addresses relationships between private individuals or corporations and government. This can include: Constitutional Law; Administrative Law; Criminal law; Taxation Law; Immigration Law; and Military Law. Education regulation targets a contract relationship, but it does so for a public purpose, that is, an orderly education market where consumers and the integrity of providers and products are protected. That happens in parallel to contract enforcement by the parties in private law.

Private common law or statute law (contracts are volitional instruments enforced by law) addresses relationships between private parties—individuals or corporations. It can involve contract, tort, property or company law. It is often concerned with lawsuits where one party seeks compensation. Events or relationships can involve and trigger both public and private law. Deceptive promotions may give rise to criminal prosecutions or private actions for breach of contract or damages. A misleading prospectus or insider trading action may give rise to criminal or administrative penalties and civil actions for damages.

7.3 The Private Law of Obligations—Contract, Tort and Restitution Law

The private law of obligations—the duties that private persons owe to each other - is usefully divided into the law of contracts, the law of torts and the law of restitution (unjust enrichment). In common law systems those duties are typically the product of judge made law although statutes are relevant.

Contracts are voluntary and based on establishing and enforcing legally binding promises. Tort law enforces duties that exist between parties that have special types of relationships even when no agreement exists. In that sense they are involuntary. With contracts persons must intend to be contractually bound. Intention exists or it does not although it can sometimes be implied. With torts, the mental state, thoughts and intentions of the party are less, but still relevant because torts can vary from intentional torts to gross negligence or simple negligence. The remedies that may follow from contract breach or torts are referred to below.

Restitution is about unjust enrichment occurring at the plaintiff's expense. Elements of the common law involving the law of quasi contract and a body of equitable doctrines were restated as a new legal subject. The measure of restitution relief is the value of the benefit received or obtained by the defendant. Restitution law is not explored in depth here.

7.4 Tort Law

A "Tort" is a breach of law not arising from an agreement. Tort law strives to compensate persons or entities for harm done. It tries to return them to the status quo. There are intentional torts that involve interference with persons and property. These are generally actionable without proof of harm or damage because of the intentional element and judicial inclination to punish the wrongdoer for having the intention. There are also non-intentional torts where negligence is the basis for the liability. Here it is the negligence that is the basis of the liability and not the state of mind (intention) and damage may have to exist before one is liable.

As with contracts, certain key elements must exist before rights and obligations exist under tort law. A person must "owe" a duty to persons harmed to conform to an applicable standard. The existence of this duty depends on the facts and relationships involved. Damage caused by the breach is generally required.[56] The action or non-action should reasonably directly "cause" the harm so one must consider the proximity or intervening forces. Damage should be reasonably foreseeable. If it is too remote or uncertain liability may not exist. Strict liability makes a person liable even if there was no intention and no fault and this is generally not what the common law does. Contributory negligence or the voluntary assumption of risk is always a factor.

In the education context if representations made in the pre-contract phase result in loss even if a contract is not consummated and if the contract is finalized those representations can be integrated into the contract as contractual warranties. One issue may be whether a reasonable person would rely on and be induced into the contract by the representation.

7.5 Contracts Are Not Pieces of Paper or Online Documents, They Are Enforceable Promises

Too many managers and regulators view the student contract or any contract as a paper document that they must get signed and that they can then put out of mind. Nothing could be further from the truth. A contract is any legally enforceable promise. A piece of paper or other written virtual or physical form of contract is just evidence of promises and a contract existing. The contract between a student and institution is rarely fully expressed in one piece of paper or document and may unfold and evolve over time. It can be partly written, verbal and implied.

Contracts are volitional. The authorities behind them are the parties involved and their freedom to transact and enter into contracts on their terms can only be seriously restricted and imposed on if clear and expressed statute or common law allows for it. Only the parties are bound and protected by and enforce the contract. No party to the contract can impose terms on the other parties.

That collection of promises lies at the core of what the parties do together. It lies at the core of what regulators are tasked to do, that is, protect persons from risks associated with the consumption of products promised.

7.6 Contracts and Contract Law, Conflict of Laws, Parties and Privity Doctrines

The body of contract law - largely common law, but also often impacted by statute—is separate from the contract instrument. The volitional contract instrument entered into by the contract parties is given legal life by and enforced under the law of contract. Contract parties claiming breach of contract must use or refer to the full body of contract law to show: that the contract was properly formed and enforceable; the existence of a specific implied or express term in the contract; breach of that term that resulted in harm to the claimant. They must also use contract law to establish that a specific remedy is warranted given the breach.

Contract parties seeking to enforce and comply with the contract must understand whether the contract was properly formed, its terms and what must be done to ensure performance by all parties occurs so breach is avoided and remedies for breach are unnecessary. Regulators that are focused on quality assurance must focus on the object of quality which is normally the contract promised product and on protecting consumers from risks associated with consumption of that product. That involves risks associated with non-performance. Regulators do not enforce the contract, but they help the consumer and the consumer only exists because of that contract product consumption. Effective regulation requires an understanding of the contract and its products and promises and of contract law.

A contract is only properly formed and enforceable if there is offer, acceptance, consideration (something of value flowing between the parties that effective purchases the others' promises), intention to be legally bound and certainty as to terms. These elements of an enforceable contract can be expressed in written form or not. A contract can be verbal or arise because of the parties' actions. If they perform or start to perform a service and take money then intention to be bound can be implied. If they take money then in the absence of evidence of a gift there is an implication that the party giving the money reasonably expected something in return. As noted below, these written and verbal elements can evolve over time and now (despite parol evidence rules regarding written terms overruling claims of additional verbal agreements) often co-exist—especially with evolving and executory contracts (Below).

Briefly put, there are a few basic types of terms to enforce and comply with. Covenants are promises that something will or will not happen (or be done or not done) in the future. Representations are assertions about a statement of fact where no action is promised. These can be contractual or non-contractual because not everything that is said has contractual import. The key is whether what was said induced a party to enter the contract (See Torts). This is where many disputes arise. Poor legal knowledge results in different perceptions of reality. Conditions are statements of fact that must exist or events that must occur before a legal right or obligation arises or vests. A conditional promise is one where the condition must occur before a particular promise arises, but other clauses in a contract operate in any event. Statements are just statements made about the contract itself (e.g. governing law).

When contract law is applied to a contract relationship you are left with questions surrounding which contract law that will be. That is what conflict of laws is all about. It can be an issue with relationships that cross international or federal and domestic boundaries. If the parties do not state in the contract which jurisdiction's laws they want to apply to their relationship then courts will decide for them based on established legal principles. These issues are not explored here.

The only persons that are privy to and bound and protected by the contract are the contract's parties. Other parties may benefit from or be negatively impacted by how the contract is performed or not performed by these parties, but they generally can't take legal action under the contract. Contracts can't impose obligations on non-parties. They would have to act under separate contracts they may have with all or one of the parties or in some kind of tort, trust, assignment or other action that may be available under third party beneficiary laws. Courts do not want to pierce doctrines of privity, but they may or find alternatives to accomplish the same end if a unfair results cannot otherwise be avoided.

7.7 Executory and Evolving Contracts, Controlling the Four Corners of the Contract

If you buy a chocolate bar and eat it the contract is executed. Promises are made and immediately kept. Both parties performed their obligations. With most education relationships, as with most employment or workplace relationships, the contract begins at one point and then runs and evolves over time. Unlike employment contracts, student contracts are rarely indeterminate. They have a clear beginning and an end. This can make it hard to grasp its full contents and consequences and this can create problems and liabilities down the line as schools have found out.

In contrast with the chocolate bar executed contract, there are executory contracts. These involve an exchange of promises to do something in the future although promises are binding when they are made. An executory contract has not yet been performed or executed in full. Although material, an obligation to pay money in the future does not alone make a contract executory. A contract that is fully performed by one party but not by the other party is often not executory.

With education, both parties have duties and obligations that are agreed to earlier and performed later. Terms of contract can also arise throughout the relationship with new expressed and written terms, verbally agreed to terms or terms that are implied and enforceable because of the law of implied terms which tends (not always) to still depend on what the parties intend (or reasonably likely intended) to be bound by. They run to contract termination. Contract terms can therefore evolve, but there must still generally be expressed or reasonably implied agreement as to new terms. The distinction between contract terms, policies and laws is important (See other sections).

The nature of the contract and the governed relationship are separate from regulations and the regulatory relationship, but the contract and its nature and content often triggers the jurisdiction of regulators and the nature of the regulation that is required so that too is made difficult by this evolving nature of the contract.

Well drafted contract provisions and careful business practices are necessary to place some kind of reasonable control over the four corners of the contract. This goes beyond traditional "Entire Agreement" clauses. This is necessary not just because the relationship can go on for relatively long periods, but because there are so many parties that can potentially create expectations or lead students to believe that certain things are promised or represented as fact in ways that can induce student to enter or stay in contracts. Other sections go into more detail.

To deal with uncertainties it is common to use an "entire agreement" clause that tries to draw four corners around the parties' rights and obligations by limiting them to what is expressly stated. This is a good idea, but with this type of evolving contract and a contract where one party is stronger and more in control of contract content and procedures the courts may not always enforce this entire agreement provision. It is still a good idea to include it along with a provision that states what is included in addition to expressed terms and that can be a summary of the law of implied terms. The latter may guide judicial interpretations.

7.8 Unequal Balance of Power and Adhesion Contracts

If one party (e.g. the institution) is the more powerful party in a contract relationship and the one that drafts most contracts and terms that the parties agree to that reality will be considered by the courts when the contract is interpreted and enforced. Theoretically, students, as parties to a student contract, have some control over the content. In reality formal, written or largely implied contracts leave little room for individual student input. Contracts set down the parties' promises, representations, rights and obligations and the standards the parties want each other to adhere to.

An Adhesion Contract is a type of contract between two parties where one side has all the bargaining power and uses it to write the contract primarily to his or her advantage. An example of an adhesion contract is a standardized contract form that offers goods or services to consumers on essentially a "take it or leave it" basis without giving consumers realistic opportunities to negotiate terms that would benefit their interests. When this occurs, the consumer cannot obtain the desired product or service unless he or she acquiesces to the form contract.

There is nothing unenforceable or even wrong about adhesion contracts. In fact, most businesses would never conclude their volume of transactions if it were necessary to negotiate all the terms of every contract. Insurance contracts and residential leases are generally adhesion contracts and educational institutions will generally have one common contract although many don't have formal contracts. This does not mean, however, that all adhesion contracts are valid. Many unconscionable or so unfair to the weaker party that a court will refuse to enforce them. For example, if key provisions were hidden or not highlighted, a court can find that there was no meeting of the minds of the parties to the contract and that the weaker party had not accepted the terms of the contract.

7.9 Dispute Resolution, Expectations, Inducement, Reliance, Real Loss, Materiality, Repudiation, Remedies

Contracts only exist and are only enforceable if the demands of contract law are met. A breach of contract is a pre-requisite to a remedy and breach is only actionable if there is a real and actual loss. The consequences of breach may be considered in the light of the known purposes for which the contract was entered by the party not at fault. Expectations are relevant and where the value of performance expected is destroyed or substantially undermined then serious breach may be found and the contract treated as ended.

Repudiation of a contract is usually only possible if terms contravened are conditions, that is, terms so important that survival of the contract depends on its performance. If they had no expectation of that result when they were induced to enter the contract and the matter only arose later then arguably no remedy is owed unless at that later time there was incorporation of that term and expectation into the contract.

Compliance under contract or regulation can never be 100%. Substantial compliance rules apply in contract law and arguably they apply in regulatory law because of context, relevancy and risk management rules.

The test for misrepresentations inducing a contract requires that the representation be "material" in the sense of it being relevant to the decision to enter the contract and also not trivial or insignificant. Contracts may state that breach of a term setting out representations and warranties occurs only where the contract misstatement is materially false.

Parties can claim that the contract should be vitiated, that is, impaired, void or voidable and of no force or effect even if the contract is otherwise enforceable. Some of the possible grounds are: impossibility and frustration; illegality; misrepresentation; mistakes; frustration; or duress and undue influence.

The principle remedial objective of the law of contracts is to place the victim of a breach of contract in as good a position as they would have been in if the contract had been performed. This expectancy principle looks forward. In some cases courts may try to restore the person's pre-contractual position. Damages in tort are backward looking because they are calculated with the objective of restoring the victim to the position they were in before the tort occurred. Contract and tort both measure losses suffered by the plaintiff. Many breaches of contract may also constitute tortuous wrongdoing.

The principal remedy for victims of contract breach is an award of compensatory damages. The "Expectancy" principle establishes the remedy amount. If a party sustains loss due to breach it calculates damages that give a plaintiff a monetary equivalent of performance. It does not just restore the plaintiff to the position they were in before the contract although on some facts that can be the remedy. With the expectancy principle the defaulting party is liable only for losses caused by the breach. Damages cannot be remote, that is, related to a loss that was not reasonably foreseeable by the parties when they entered the contract.

The most important exception and limitation with respect to the above facts and the expectancy principle is that the breach victim can't recover losses that the victim could have avoided by taking reasonable steps subsequent to the breach to mitigate loss.

7.10 Business Policies, Law and Contracts Distinguished

While contracts are made by its parties and laws are made by those with law-making authority, business policies are set by those in an organization with the authority to set them. The subject persons are those directed to take action. The benefitting objects are any party that so benefits, but as with law and contract those benefitting parties do not have direct legal rights under them and policies do not create legal rights unless they are properly and legally incorporated into contracts or laws.

Policies do not automatically vest contract and legal rights or obligations because the fundamentals of contract formation still apply (offer, acceptance, intention, consideration and certainty). Merely requiring that policies be read by a student prior to a contract being signed would not necessarily incorporate that policy into a contract. It is common for regulators to adopt bylaws that require institutions to have specific policy types. Often these regulations do not mandate specific policy content and generally they should not. The intention of lawmakers is often just that the matter be addressed so that uncertainties are minimized. Business policies are not public instruments even if a statute requires that they exist. The institution would in that case have a public duty to make the policy, but the policy is not a law and the student or other benefiting party or object has no rights generally to enforce that public duty which also does not create a private right.

Similarly, laws and regulations are separate from contract provisions. Violations of laws do not create private rights for contract parties. Violations of contract provisions are not automatically violations of law. These ideas are explored more in relation to how private and public law interact.

Again, there should be no broad inclusion of all business policies unless contractually enforceable rights and binding duties are intended and that intention is made clear in the policy statement or contract document (or verbally which leaves evidentiary problems). The business policy (asserted by authorized persons in the firm and not the contract parties jointly) is no longer then just a policy, but a contract term. The policy alone vests no legal rights or duties. Policies can be changed by authorized persons in the firm. Contract terms are agreed to by both parties unless the parties agree that one party can unilaterally make the change and if that is too open ended the certainty of terms and the enforceability of the contract come into question.

8

Education Products (Outcome 1), Achievement of Learning Objectives (Outcome 2)

8.1 Introduction to the Education Product, Product Elements and Outcomes

This is about assessing what happens in real life with education and what that means in business and legal terms. A student: attends an on-site or online class and listens to a lecture (or not); reads a physical book or goes to the Internet for text or video resources); learns (hopefully); asks questions onsite or online of faculty or other mentors; works with other students onsite or online on projects or to aid their respective academic efforts; writes an exam or project paper or does other project work; has that work assessed in relation to the class cohort or an independent reference standard; receives credit if academic standards for the assessed work are met; assembles various credits for application toward a "credential" that declares to the world that a learning achievement existed; and has the credential and learning achievement recognized by others.

A product or series of products can be found in all of that. Products change and are never complete. [57] Institutions talk about how they must change to deal with budgetary constraints, tuition increases and other challenges, [58] but you cannot change and seek new ways of doing things if you ignore business and legal realities and do not understand the "Now", that is, what it is that is changing.

8.2 Contracts Define Products, Create Objects of Quality and Constitute Legally Enforceable Promises

Again, contracts are central to understanding products and quality because they define and describe the product that is contract consideration flowing from the education provider to the student and the object of quality. The contract is central to understanding quality standards and assurance and "consumer protection" because it defines the consumed product that gives rise to the risks being protected against.

There is no student consumer without a contract. Contract law determines when the contract exists and ends. A consumer is a consumer because they "consume" something under a contract and that consumption gives rise to specific risks. The object of quality must be the contract product promised and provided. If no contract exists then no legally enforceable promise exists to do anything.

8.3 Collective Intermediated Product Factor Inputs Are the Product (Outcome 1) and Not Specific Factors that are Not Individually Purchased, Four Corners of the Contract

The core outcome is Outcome 1 which is a collection of product factor inputs that institutions intermediate and that allow an institution to help a student achieve the set learning objective which is Outcome 2—un-promised by the institution because the student controls it and un-promised by the student for reasons stated. Contracts for specific products group factor inputs in ways necessary for the specified product to be delivered and assessed. Factors used in law school differ from those in medical school.

Institutions are aggregators and intermediaries. They pull together resources - product factor inputs - and create a learning environment for students. It is up to the student to do the learning. It is these product factors acting collectively together that form the contractually promised product and the capacity to help the student achieve the learning outcome objective and not each individual factor. Most individual factors are not indispensable and conditions precedent to contract performance. Many, but not necessarily all factors will contribute to the education product, assessment product and other service products. These factors can include:

- Faculty members (onsite classroom or online instruction services).
- Mentors and tutors (academic assistance).
- Curricula (not content, but organizes how content, instruction, information resources and other factors or their providers) are organized.

- Real estate facilities (for onsite instruction, administration or online infrastructure).
- Equipment, technology and other chattels (personal, corporate property to facilitate onsite or online services).
- Intellectual property (curricula or information resources).
- Business systems.
- Teaching systems and methods.
- Instruction and reference information resources.
- Other human resources and any factor that is used to help the student achieve set learning objectives.

The University of British Columbia (UBC) and other institutions get it right when they state that their Vision is as follows: As one of the world's leading universities, The University of British Columbia creates an exceptional learning environment that fosters global citizenship, advances a civil and sustainable society and supports outstanding research to serve the people of British Columbia, Canada and the world. It is no more complicated than that and those that insist on bringing in concepts like hard employment numbers or future income to define quality are just deceiving themselves and not living in a state of commercial and legal reality.

Contracts generally do not state that institutions promise specific input elements. For example, they may promote that certain faculty members are there, but that is not normally and should not usually be stated as a specific promise. If that faculty person leaves to teach at another institution then that should not be a breach of contract by the institution. The student may see it otherwise if they gave up other opportunities because they wanted to be with that specific faculty person. The issue of reasonable reliance arises. The same could be true of other elements. Contract clarity is required.

The Education Product or what some would call the learning environment must be defined as the product factor inputs collectively and not how they passively exist, but how they actively work together to help the student achieve a set learning outcome objective as measured by the Assessment Product. It is that reality of aggregation and intermediation of factor resources that creates the foundation for current and future disintermediation and disruptive innovation in the education sector. Other sections go into detail on this point.

When most institutions charge fees they do not state that specific fees are for specific parts of the product. They do not pay set dollars for the instructor and another amount for the computers. They are offered collectively to achieve a specified purpose (to help the student achieve the learning outcome objective) and must be viewed and judged collectively as one promised offering in relation to that purpose. For example, if a student had ten teachers and one was not qualified then that factor alone would not be determinative of contract breach if on balance the inputs collectively were sufficient to facilitate the desired learning.

Specific services provided for separate fees (a road trip) are manageable, but the problem comes with general services that are provided with no special fees outside general tuition fees. Litigation has occurred involving disputes over tuition, fees, scholarships, loans, and related pecuniary matters.[59] In these cases, judges tend to examine the express terms and specific language of the contract contained within the "four corners" of the contract document and issue opinions accordingly. These four corners should be clear.

Despite these assertions it is possible for an institution to break out input factors and sell them individually. They can never legitimately give a credential without work because a credential is not the product or transferrable property, but evidence that the institution helped (as promised) the student achieve the learning outcome.

For example, an institution could choose to offer instruction without a promise of assessment or a credential. They may do this in a part-time format—same teacher, same content, no tests and no credential. That is legitimate. This is different from disintermediation where certain product inputs (e.g. faculty, assessment firms) reach around the institution intermediary to deal with the consumer directly or where the consumer reaches around the intermediating institution to access content, instruction, assessment or other elements.

Student contracts should make it clear that without express agreement no promises are made and no attributed fees are set for specific inputs like faculty or equipment. Contracts must state that specific inputs and resources are not contractually promised and that inputs can change provided the institution's contract obligation to provide a learning environment capable of helping the student to achieve the learning objective is satisfied. Again, the student controls that ultimate learning outcome (Outcome 2).

The student contract must state that the institution's contract performance and Program quality will only be measured by whether the Program (combined with student contributions) is sufficient to allow the student to substantially meet contract learning objectives. It cannot be measured by what may or may not happen months or years after graduation because of countless decisions and actions made by unforeseen parties. In other words, the institution can only promise a product that is capable of helping the student achieve that objective and cannot promise the achievement. That is up to the student.

8.4 Understanding of Services Illuminates What Education Is and Does and Education Quality, Focused Management and Regulation

As stated in other sections, education is indisputably a service. It certainly does not involve the commercial transfer of property rights to physical goods. Services involve outputs that can change the physical, mental/emotional, legal, economic, "knowledge" or other conditions of the consuming unit. [60] Understanding the education "product" requires a grasp of the education "service".

A service is an intangible commodity because it cannot be: physically possessed, transferred or returned after purchase; legally owned (certain service outputs can be e.g. intellectual property); sensed or stored; or the subject of exclusive sale or ownership. Service benefits are self-evident if a buyer is willing to pay for them.

Education products change the knowledge and skill conditions of the consumer. The hope may be for future employment and business success, but the service is narrowly targeted because the service provider must, to be practical and sound in business and management terms, focus on what is doable and achievable by them, what can be promised contractually and what can be done to keep those promises and live up to vested obligations. Regulation must be equally practical and do what it can in its separate and legally distinct way to ensure that this happens. Again, institutions cannot guarantee or promise that conditions will change because students do the learning, but they can promise to provide a service that provides the environment that will allow the student to learn.

It follows logically that a quality education product is one that is (in classical commercial terms) "merchantable" and "functional" in the sense that it does what it is supposed to do. The only logical way to think about the education product is that it is that collection of product factor inputs that are contractually promised (Outcome 1) and paid for collectively and that create an environment that allows a student to learn and to achieve the set learning outcome objective which is not promised because the student controls that outcome. It helps the student upgrade their knowledge conditions.

8.5 Promised Content Systems, Information Resources, Teaching Methods and Technologies Are Product Features and Not Quality Measures

An education product strives to help a student achieve a learning outcome objective or state of knowledge. That requires that program specific content or information resources be systematically organized and delivered onsite, online or in any way possible to the student. This is not always the same as teaching methods and technologies although there are overlapping elements. Grade-one content differs from grade-two content. Computer science courses are different from law school or medical school courses. Content matters. Carriage and content are distinct.

These resources are among the product factor inputs or resources that are assembled as part of the product that is sold to and delivered to the student (Outcome 1). The student contract must have some reasonable specificity about content and also allow for ongoing changes to be made to ensure that the product is continually updated.

The way a program is taught and delivered is a key feature of the product and a product factor input and not a quality measure. Teaching methods are business systems. These systems are key parts of that collective set of inputs that constitute the education product promised by the institution to the student and that helps the student achieve the learning outcome objective which itself is not promised because the student controls that outcome.

They may not be, but they can be considered business systems that are subject to legal protection. For example, they could be considered trade secrets in other circumstances, but because the education process is so publicly shared those protections are not practical given that trade secrets must generally be kept secret. Intellectual property laws could also apply.

These input factors are key elements of the assembled product factor inputs and the education product because without them nothing can happen. They are part of the bargain. The student contract must allow for some level of change, but there are limits. Arguably a student cannot be promised an onsite and class based system and then have it arbitrarily replaced with an online system. Again, change provisions must always allow for institutions to make reasonable changes to allow constant improvements and updates provided they contribute to and do not derogate from achievement of learning outcome objectives.

The specific technologies would normally not be promised in the same way most specific inputs are not promised, but there are exceptions. If a student, for example, wants to learn and is promised they will work with specific software or hardware then that specific promise must be satisfied unless the change is expressly or constructively agreed to. As technology changes how education programs are conceived, developed, offered, operated and delivered the nature, purpose and content of student contracts inevitably must change and adapt. The consumer must be served and the contract performed.

It must be clear whether the institution provides all necessary hardware and software or expects students to have their own technology. The assumption and contract default should be the former. Even if labs do not exist and "Bring Your Own Device" systems are in place it must be clear who owns devices used and who is responsible to provide and pay for them. If cloud based systems are used and access payments are required then the same issues exist. If freely available or open resource systems are used then the question lies more with how they are used and applied. Student expectations must be considered and contracts should be clear. People expect to work, learn, socialize, and play whenever and wherever they want to and those expectations can easily be expressed or implied contract terms.

The point here is not to distinguish pedagogy and andragogy. The point is to illustrate the kinds of systems and features that could be contractually promised and expected. Subject to reasonable and contractually allowable changes, there must be some common agreement regarding how a program will be taught.

The terms andragogy and pedagogy are different. The latter deals with adult education and the former with younger students, but given new technologies and the aptitudes, abilities and inclinations of younger students the two systems of learning are becoming less distinct.

Pedagogy traditionally was focused on absorbing broadcasted content in class and recalling it on exams. This is becoming obsolete. Many students of all ages do well without lectures. Students are choosing alternative models for education including online and international products. There is a rise in informal learning as individual needs are redefining schools, universities, and training.

Traditionally though pedagogical systems meant the learner was dependent upon the instructor for all learning and the teacher instructor assumed full responsibility for what was taught and how it was learned. The teacher instructor evaluated the learning. The learner usually came to the activity with little experience that could be tapped as a resource for learning. The experience of the instructor was highly influential. Students were told what they had to learn in order to advance. Their orientation to learning was more of a process of acquiring prescribed subject matter and content units were sequenced according to the logic of the subject matter. Learners were primarily motivated by external pressures, competition for grades and the consequences of failure. These are classical views and new technologies are changing this at the level of the classroom and in virtual forums.

Andragogy principles traditionally and by definition relate to adult learners, but in reality they now apply to many non-adults. Here the learner is more self-directed and responsible for their own learning. Self-evaluation is characteristic of this approach. Learners bring more of a volume and quality of experience to their education and each adult is a rich resource of knowledge, experience and diversity for themselves and other students.

In terms of their readiness to learn, students in this format are triggered to learn when changes occur. They know they need to know in order to perform more effectively in their life and work. They are able to assess gaps between where one is now and where one wants and needs to be. The adult's orientation to learning is focused more on performing a task, solving a problem and living in a more satisfying way. Learning must have relevance to real-life tasks. Learning is organized around life and work situations rather than subject matter units. Motivations for many adult (and increasingly many non-adult) learners focus on self-esteem, recognition, better quality of life, self-confidence and self-actualization.

8.6 Quality Assurance Efforts Must Focus on Merchantable Products (Outcome 1) That Help Students Achieve Learning Objectives (Outcome 2), Subject Matter Content, Levels of Complexity and Expertise

The second outcome is the achievement of a Learning or State of Knowledge "Outcome" or objective. This is not a contractually offered or promised "product" or outcome. The institution promises to provide a product that will help the student reach the objective, but it cannot go beyond that. Institutions cannot promise it because only the student can achieve it.

Students do not promise achievement of the objective because: such a promise cannot practically be made; it is not necessary to induce the institution into the contract; and the student's failure could not be considered a breach that causes a loss for the institution. Students are not protected from the risk of their failing the course unless the quality of the product (collective inputs) is so deficient that achieving the learning outcome was impossible.

In the current environment, some change even to the learning outcome objectives may be necessary during the program. Unlike changes to the program itself that can just involve new ways of achieving the objective, changes to the learning outcome objective itself go to the heart of what the contract and product are about. That means notice of these changes may require a greater level of notice or mutual agreement. Some institution discretion is often required, but unilateral action could give the institution too much leeway in terms of redefining the learning objective it commits to helping the student achieve.

The concept of attaining a learning objective or state of knowledge encompasses two core elements. First, there is the area of knowledge or subject matter content (the object of "knowing" or area of "study"). Labels are attached and often changed as knowledge expands. Physics is not biology. Each area has countless sub-categories, details and complexities. Linkages and distinctions between subject areas exist.

Secondly, there is a person, learner and "knower" that learns and gains knowledge and levels of expertise and ability depending on what they study and learn. The level of difficulty depends on the nature of the subject, the level of detail and complexity pursued and the subjective capacities of the learner. The level of knowledge and expertise gained depends on the capacity of the learner and the level of detail and complexity of study pursued and mastered.

In terms of contracts, regulations and quality education, this is all relevant for two reasons.

First, quality programs can exist with any type of program or subject area and at each level of detail or complexity. Courses on bartending may not be as inherently difficult as a program on astrophysics, but both programs can be of quality. In all cases, admissions and assessment systems reflect the product and learning outcome objectives as they relate to content subject matter and the expertise sought and achieved.

Secondly, quality should be confined to the commercial concept of determining whether a product is merchantable. A quality product is a merchantable product. It is of merchantable quality.

The term "merchantable" is used in the way it is normally used in commercial environments. A merchantable (quality) product is one that is reasonably fit for the ordinary purposes for which it was produced and sold. Education firms (institution) should be and are, like other sellers or producers, required by law to make and sell products of merchantable quality. The ordinary purpose for an education product is to help a student learn and to achieve a set learning objective (Outcome 1). [61] That is what the parties intend contractually and that is all that they as parties can control. The institution also promises an assessment system that validly and credibly validates achievement of learning objectives.

What the student may then do with the knowledge and skills gained in terms of life, jobs or business is a subsequent matter that the product producer has no control over. No one would tell Ford that its trucks were not merchantable and of quality because a buyer failed in the construction business they bought the truck for. Any services that go beyond teaching and assessment to help an ex-student find work or develop a business would be separate and there again nothing can be guaranteed (Objective 4).

This allows, as is advised, for quality assurance to capture or encompass any level of difficulty, complexity or expertise. If a person or authority needs to do more than just determine if a product is of quality and able to help a student achieve a learning objective then they should look beyond quality. For example, a product could be quality assured, but perhaps - because it does not lead to the level of knowledge and expertise required - still not be one that a lender wants to lend for, that an immigration authority wants to admit a student for, that a profession does not want to use for admission purposes or that another institution does not want to give credit for.

9

Student Assessment As Contract Product (Outcome 3), Innovative Assessment, Credentials and Credit Transfer

9.1 Assessment as Contract Promise and Product, Credentials, Credential Evaluation and Agents of Change

The disruptive innovation now here and gathering steam in the education sector will impact the future of assessment systems. Innovative assessment will impact everything that happens in education. The reason for this is simple. Holding to the definition adopted, education is about the systematic delivery of pre-defined content for a pre-defined learning objective and the assessment of whether that learning objective was achieved.

The way education is delivered, how learning objectives are pursued and met and means of assessment are all subject to change, but if assessment systems change that facilitates the diversity of delivery that is possible without sacrificing the validation of learning and its recognition in the world.

A credible assessment system (Outcome 3) is part of the contractual promise and product because it validates if a learning objective (Outcome 2) was met. The student expects this (while also disliking exams) because without it the credential is of questionable value. The student contract should make this promise clear. Conversely (See Plagiarism), the student must contractually promise to not engage in activities that abuse or manipulate the assessment system and that could distort or exaggerate their academic achievements and bring the assessment system and the credential into question. This is necessary to protect the student, other students, the tradable currency of the credential and the general integrity of the institution and its education and assessment products.

9.2 Assessment As Contract Product, Limited Nature of Credential Which Is Not Bought and Sold

Judicial deference cannot be justified on broadly stated and vague grounds that something is "academic" and therefore beyond judicial reach. Students should not be able to march off to court every time they get a grade they don't like, but assessment matters can be the basis of a valid contract or tort claim that courts say they will rule on. Money is spent, time is invested and futures can be on the line and both parties have legitimate expectations.

The non-availability or unreasonable nature of assessment, credential granting, credential evaluation and credit transfer systems can unreasonably restrict a person's freedom to pursue the education they choose and their dreams and potential. If one gets the required grades they should be able to go to the program and down the path of their choice and not that chosen by governments that do not fund programs directly or allow privates to provide them. [62]

The education product (Outcome 1) is an assembled, aggregated or intermediated collection of inputs that help the student learn. Assessment and credential systems may use the samc or other factor inputs to create a parallel and contractually promised product that validates learning. The learning and achievement of the Learning Outcome Objective means little if there are no assessment and credential systems that will be credible and recognized in the world beyond education. Plagiarism is a serious matter (See Issues Management) because it can destroy the currency of the credential.

The credential is not a product that is bought and sold on its own, but a declaration of fact—the fact of the academic achievement. The paper document is documentary evidence of the declaration. The institution only promises to award it and make that declaration if the student meets academic standards. A degree is still not the product even when the term is used to describe not the final achievement, but a set package or bundle of credits that is pre-defined as acceptable for "degree" purposes, that is, for the purpose of the achievement declaration. In that context it is more closely part of the pre-determined learning objective. The product helps the student to achieve that recognized bundle of credits.

The assessment product determines whether a student achieved academic standards and indirect if the education product was capable, as promised, of helping the student attain the learning outcome objective which is not promised because the student controls that outcome. Assessment products may be integrated with the education product, but they are also separate. That integration increases with new technology. Step by step systematic learning and then verification of progress to date can be hard to distinguish, but both must exist so that education can be distinguished from reading a book or listening to a radio. Assessment aids learning because it inspires diligence and establishes where one is academically, but its key purpose is to validate learning.

A credential is not a legal declaration about student contract performance or regulatory compliance. It is not a contract promise or representation made to any person who may receive it or rely on it in the future. It is not a promise in most cases about future credit or credential evaluation, recognition or transfer. It is not a promise about common (uniform) content, learning objectives and states of knowledge. This series of "non-promises" could be modified by expressed or implied contract terms, but in most cases that is unlikely and not advised. It could be evidence that the product was merchantable and worked as promised to help the student achieve the learning objective and possibly evidence that such a product was also made available to classmates or others that were not successful or that try to claim product deficiency.

The quality assurance regulator for career training in British Columbia defined a credential as a formal "qualification" that includes an evaluative component and results in transcript credit and not just a certificate of attendance. This definition is helpful to the extent it reflects the need for assessment, but it falls short in other ways. A credential is not in many cases a declaration about a specific qualification. You are normally qualified "to do something". With most credentials the student only has the right to state they have the credential. This definition fails to capture the reality that a credential only declares that specific courses were taken and passed or recognized for credit purposes.

9.3 Two Assessment Elements—Assessment Process, Award of a Credential Which Itself Is Not a Product

Assessment systems involve two steps. First, there is the awarding of a mark or other means of recording that specified learning occurred in a specific program, course or lesson. Testing is used to determine the extent to which students have mastered a body of material and if they are ready to progress. It is also used to compare students one against the other. The former is more important from a valued credential perspective because with the latter you could just have a group of weak students with the top of the class still not having a high level of knowledge.

Secondly, there is the award of a credential that serves as evidence of and a declaration of fact, that is, that a broader program learning objective was met—normally involving multiple courses or parts. The credential is only promised if the student achieves academic standards and fulfills other contractual obligations (pays tuition). It is not a property asset that is bought and sold. This illustrates that the program was sufficient (a contract promise) to help the student achieve the learning outcome objective (not an institutional contract promise because the student does the learning).

9.4 Features of Credible Assessment Systems and Credentials, Assessment Targeted At Subject Matter Content and Level of Difficulty and Expertise Associated With the Learning Objective

To be credible, fair and reasonable and in accordance with what are likely implied contractual terms, internal and third party student assessment systems must have certain features. Not all of these features need be contractual. Students and institutions have reasonable expectations about assessment. A contract cannot list them all. Most are destined to remain unexpressed or implied because they would likely be intended by reasonable parties.

Assessment must be conducted by competent persons and be systematic, objective (not subjective for each student), predictable, fair, consistent, impartial and unbiased. They must be focused on academic standards only and not business, humanitarian or financial considerations. Systems should cover the entire program and not only specific modules or elements. They should serve students that may be weak at exams or other assessment methods (A policy point). Transcripts should be a full and comprehensive record of academic achievement and be issued quickly after graduation. Transcripts should refer to incomplete grades and credit or advanced standing given at the time of admission. Students should have notice of academic standing while they are still eligible for partial refunds. Most importantly, assessment must focus on reliable evidence that the student achieved set academic standards.

Quality programs that do what they promise to do and help the student achieve a set learning outcome objective combined with a credible means of assessment lead to a credible credential. The credential must come from a party that has substantial authority with and the respect of the persons that later assess what the credential declaration means in real terms.

Again, assessment (Outcome 3) determines if the learning objective (Outcome 2) was met. Other sections observed that learning objectives encompass subject matter content and multiple levels of difficulty, detail and complexity (the object area of study). They also encompass the expertise or state of knowledge sought and achieved by the subject learner and that the product helps them achieve. Assessment must be suited to and reflect both. The education product is of quality and "merchantable" if it is sufficient to help the student achieve the subject matter expertise associated with the set learning objective. The assessment product is of similar quality if it properly and credibly assesses the student and validates that the targeted expertise was achieved.

There are contract and regulatory issues with assessment. It must be in tune with admission standards and product promises. If the assessment is too difficult that could have contract importance. If it is too easy then the student may be happy on one level, but not well served on the other because weak assessment institution wide weakens the credential. The facts of each case are the key.

9.5 Permanent Beta and the Need for New Credential Systems to Authoritatively Declare Learning Achievement and States of Knowledge In An Age of Continuous Learning

New forms of credible and authoritative credentials or declarations of academic and learning achievement are needed to capture the reality of and to encourage the pursuit of lifelong learning, professional development and continuing education. They are needed because providers and programs are more diverse than ever before.

Steve Jobs called Apple the "biggest start-up on the planet." Reid Hoffman (LinkedIn Founder) and many others say people must apply the same mindset to their careers and lives.[63] A student is a consumer in relation to an education service provider, but the same person is a "product" and service provider in workplace and business markets. Hoffman points to Apple, Google, Gmail, LinkedIn, Amazon and other firms that keep their product in "permanent beta" and subject to continued improvement and innovation.

These entrepreneurs consider "finished" to be an F-word. Everyone and every firm and product is a work in progress. The business professor Clayton Christensen (also cited in this work for his book Disrupting Class) once told graduating students at Harvard Business School, "If you study the root causes of business disasters, over and over you'll find (a) predisposition toward endeavors that offer immediate gratification." At the same time, though, Hoffman points out, persons must not do the opposite and think too far ahead because "you will change, the world will change and the competition will change".

All persons must plan to develop skills and experiences that are broadly useful in many business and workplace contexts. Writing skills, general management experience, technical and computer skills, people smarts, and international experience or language skills are examples of skills that have "high option value" (Hoffman's term) because they are transferable to a wide range of possible options. On top of those general skills, people must also re-invent themselves and develop new expertise from time to time.

In both cases, these learning, work and business realities dictate the need for institutions, programs, assessment systems and credential systems that reflect these realities and allow the person to reasonably accurately and authoritatively communicate or declare their current state of knowledge and competencies to others. The idea of a degree, diploma or certificate can, for some, imply "Finished". That was fine in an era where you received a degree and traded on it for much of your life. Today, things change fast. Many degrees can be of limited use on their own (Emphasis Added) upon graduation let alone five years down the road. That does not mean they are not of value. They just have to be quickly supplemented.

People commonly get these credentials and then rely on resumes to communicate what they have done and learned in the post credential period. That is not enough. Learners must be able to validate their achievements and state of knowledge, no matter how it was gained, with formal, authoritative and credible assessment systems and credential declarations. Innovation is required.

Post-secondary work does not have to just be Bachelor, Masters or Ph.D. It can be PSE 1, PSE 2 or PSE 25. The label is immaterial. It must be a reasonable and accurate description of real states of knowledge and skill as credibly assessed and validated and authoritatively declared. As noted below, saying one has a degree in something is not really very descriptive or informative.

9.6 Assessment, Credentials, Prospect for New Accredited Systems for Declaring Learning Achievement, Third Party Assessment, Limits of Declaration, Innovation Suited to Change

The institution contractually promises to provide an education product (Outcome 1) or learning environment that has the features that can help the student achieve the set learning outcome objective (State of Knowledge). Achievement of that learning objective (Outcome 2) is not contractually promised by either party because the student controls it and failure would not constitute contract breach by either party.

Assessment systems are also contractually promised so the student is assured that the learning achievement will be validated in a credible way. The credential granted is a declaration of fact by the institution that a learning objective was met and it is documentary evidence of that fact. It is not a legal declaration about student contract performance or regulatory compliance. It is not a contract promise or representation made to any person who may receive it or rely on it in the future. It would be evidence that the product was merchantable and worked as promised to help the student achieve the learning objective and possibly evidence that such a product was also made available to classmates or others that were not successful or that try to claim product deficiency.

Possible liability could lie in tort law with parties that intentionally or negligently declare untrue facts as true where parties that could reasonably be foreseen or expected to rely on that declaration do so to their detriment. Credentials are not property assets that are bought and sold by students and institutions.

The asserted facts go beyond the label "Degree" or "Diploma" in Discipline X or Y. The factual detail, often set out in transcripts or even more detailed records, varies, for example: credit hours and course topics (majors, minors), marks and grades or reservations on the declaration. It is not a declaration that every person that holds a credential with the same label in the same subject area and even from the same institution and class cohort has a common state of knowledge because of variations that may occur on the detailed facts asserted and with each learner.

The credential is not a declaration that it has resulted from any compliance with common content or credential standards required by law or any agreement (e.g. with a professional body) unless that is in fact the case in the particular circumstances. If uniformity or transferability is promised then quality regulation can encompass it on the grounds that a quality product should do what was promised. As noted in sections on articulation and credit transfer, however, such promises are generally not made and must be cautiously made because of third party involvement.

Future assessment, credentials or declaration of learning achievement may not come in traditional forms. As people learn in more diverse ways from more diverse providers and in more diverse fields of study a new type of declaration may be required. The traditional "degree" or "diploma" was perhaps more suited to a time where you earned a credential and then traded on that declaration of fact for much of your career.

Today lifelong learning is the reality and it is common and often necessary for people to extensively list a range of professional and personal development activities—those that involve formal assessment of knowledge and skill and those that do not. This gathering together of information about what a student has learned and their declared state of knowledge is not much different in reality from the traditional degree or diploma declaration that also involved gathering information about courses taken and credentials issued for successful completion of designated groups of courses.

These new forms of declaration will have to have some measure of authority behind them so that third parties can reasonably rely on them. That authority often comes from the nature and authority of the party making the declaration. The learner alone would not have the needed authority because of perceived self-interest. Institutions traditionally had by and large a well-deserved level of social and commercial trust build up over time because of recognized reputations surrounding past ability to teach and assess knowledge and issue reasonably reliable credentials in an impartial and objective way. They could continue to do so for courses they teach or for others they do not teach. What is clear is that the monopoly that institutions have over credentials and the authoritative declaration of learning achievement is coming to a close.

As diverse learning occurs and third party (beyond the learner and institution) assessment systems make declarations about learning the authority of the declaration and assessor will grow and become more trusted through reputation, recognition of work and possibly through regulated accreditation. Many third party systems already exist. For example, professional or vocational organizations often assess credentials from disparate institutions (or from non-institution or self-taught systems) and many have common assessment systems that new members are required to satisfy. ESL schools generally teach to common third party exams. More industry and vocational groups are likely to develop these capacities and dedicated assessment firms are also likely to become more numerous. At some point, how you learned it and how long it took you to learn it becomes less relevant. Technologies will expand the reach of these third party systems. Internal and external systems could co-exist.

Third party assessment systems referred to could be driven by institutions, groups of institutions, individual students or groups of students. For example, a group of institutions that offer visual effects programs nay want to counteract charges by regulators or others that their programs are not of high quality. They could go beyond their current industry advisory councils and internal assessments to work with industry studios and firms and other institutions to create a common third party assessment system that operates independently. Teaching assistants or outside exam invigilators are not third party assessors because they act for the institution that provided the program.

Employers, service consumers, education institutions accepting transfer credit, immigration authorities or professional groups are interested in results and ultimately they will make practical decisions and not automatically defer to tradition. Accreditation of these new third party assessment systems would again arise on the noted principle that if an institution can be accredited then so can some of the individual functions that it exercises.

Again, contracts promise assessment systems and credentials when academic standards are met. Contracts must also make it clear that credentials, where awarded, are also not declarations about any common standard state of knowledge for the purposes of credit transfer or comparison with others unless that is in fact the case. The default must be the former. Regulations could require that contracts include some of these qualifying provisions.

9.7 Digital Badges, Open Source Credentials, New Models for Declaring Learning Achievement

The emerging open source credentials movement is one example of how traditional education systems are losing their monopolies and grip on sector power structures. Much of that power comes from the perception that traditional institutions are the only place to get credible validation of your state of knowledge. Open source systems won't be the only manifestation of this movement. Possible systems of accreditation for new and strong systems of assessment, learning declaration and credential evaluation are another example.

The following is the entire text of an article in The Chronicle of Higher Education. It bears printing in full because it makes similar points to those made above, but in the context of real examples and a growing movement.

> April 8, 2012, A Future Full of Badges,
> The Chronicle, By Kevin Carey
>
> In the grand University of California system, the Berkeley and UCLA campuses have long claimed an outsized share of the public imagination. It's easy to forget that the state system has more than two great institutions of higher education. In the heart of the Central Valley, UC-Davis has grown in a hundred years from being the "university farm" to becoming one of the world's most important research universities. Now it's part of a process that may fundamentally redefine the credentials that validate higher learning.
>
> Throughout the 20th century, scientists at UC-Davis, a land-grant institution, helped significantly increase crop yields while leading research on plant genetics, water conservation, and pest control. When the present century began, Davis leaders knew the times called for not just production but conservation and renewal. So they created a new, interdisciplinary major in sustainable agriculture and food systems. Many different departments were involved in crafting curricula that range across life sciences, economics, and humanities, along with experiential learning in the field.
>
> The university also conducted a detailed survey of practitioners, scholars, and students to identify the knowledge,

skills, and experiences that undergraduates most needed to learn. The survey produced answers like "systems thinking," "strategic management," and "interpersonal communication." They sound like buzzwords—and they can be—but if taken seriously are nothing of the kind. Simultaneously understanding the intricacies of hydrology and plant DNA, the economics of federal agricultural subsidization, and the politics of community development is a high order of systems thinking. The first students enrolled in the program this past fall.

Meanwhile, across the mountains, in Silicon Valley, the Mozilla Foundation was also thinking about the future. Mozilla, a non-profit organization built around the ethos of the open Internet, created the popular Firefox Web browser, which anyone can download, free. Along with the John D. and Catherine T. MacArthur Foundation, Mozilla is sponsoring a competition for the development of digital "open badges." The first winners were announced last month, and one of them was the UC-Davis sustainable-agriculture program.

What is a digital badge, exactly? The MacArthur foundation says it's "a validated indicator of accomplishment, skill, quality or interest," which calls to mind the colorful pieces of cloth that Girl Scouts sew onto their sashes. But that's a simplification that borders on meaninglessness. The winning Davis entry describes something far more sophisticated and important.

Instead of being built around major requirements and grades in standard three-credit courses, the Davis badge system is based on the sustainable-agriculture program's core competencies—"systems thinking," for example. It is designed to organize evidence of both formal and informal learning, from within traditional higher education and without.

Say you're an employer considering a job candidate. Under "systems thinking," the applicant's badge portfolio would include some of the UC-Davis courses he's passed, along with grades. But it would also include evidence of the applicant's specific skills, like "integrated pest management," which he might have learned working on a farm. Other badges would describe workshops attended, awards won, and specific projects completed. Each badge would allow the employer to click through to more detailed levels of evidence and explanation—documents, assessment results, hyperlinks, video, and more.

The badge system, moreover, isn't just a transcript, CV, and work portfolio rolled together into a cool digital package. It's also a way to structure the process of education itself. Students will be able to customize learning goals within the larger curricular framework, integrate continuing peer and faculty feedback about their progress toward achieving those goals, and tailor the way badges and the metadata within them are displayed to the outside world. Students won't just earn badges—they'll build them, in an act of continuous learning.

Why does this matter? To start, consider that the sustainable-agriculture badge framework was designed with great care and purpose, based on what experts, employers, professors, and students believe is most important for the world we live in today. Can most existing department-based academic majors say the same? Many appear to be based on the "some combination of vague distribution requirements and whatever the faculty want to teach this year" system.

The majority of the badge competition winners, moreover, don't come from traditional colleges or universities. They include Disney-Pixar, NASA, the U.S. Department of Veterans Affairs, Peer 2 Peer University, and the National Oceanic and Atmospheric Administration. The badges movement is based on the idea that people should be able to gather useful, verifiable evidence of everything they learn, not just everything they learn while attending an accredited postsecondary institution.

Finally, the badges movement is open. The top-flight educators at UC-Davis may develop the first widely used badge system for sustainable agriculture, but they won't, in the long run, control it. Over time, farmers, students, civic groups, companies, professional organizations, and individual scholars will all contribute to a continuing process of helping people organize critical information about their lives.

Compared with the new open badge systems, the standard college transcript looks like a sad and archaic thing. Its considerable value is not based on the information it provides, which is paltry. What does a letter grade in a course often described only by the combination of a generic department label and an arbitrary number (e.g. Econ 302) really mean? Nobody knows, which is why accredited colleges often don't trust that information for the purposes of credit transfer, even when it comes from other accredited colleges.

Instead, the value of the traditional degree comes mostly from the presumed general authority of the granting institution—and the fact that traditional colleges have a legally enforced near-monopoly over the production of credentials that are widely accepted for the purposes of getting a job or pursuing advanced education.

Open systems tend to blow such lucrative arrangements apart. The doomed effort of for-profit academic publishers to maintain their grip on prestigious scholarly journals is one example. The imminent demise of the physical textbook market is another. Open badges won't be controlled by incumbent institutions with a vested financial interest in limiting the supply of valuable credentials.

Many of the first badge systems will fail, of course. They won't be designed well enough or properly connected to communities of interest. But some will take root and thrive. More users will beget more users. Employers will gain facility in the use of badges and confidence in those who bear them.

When that happens, it will create hardship for traditional institutions that now use the revenue generated from their undergraduate-credential franchise to subsidize the cost of graduate education, administration, scholarship, and other activities. But society as a whole will benefit enormously. The store of human capital will be more broadly and accurately represented by credentials that are useful in a mobile, interconnected world. Separating the credentialing and teaching functions of higher education allows organizations to specialize in one or the other.

Open systems make the world more egalitarian and less expensive. Higher education is in serious need of both.

It's not surprising that a land-grant university would be among those at the forefront of this movement. Such institutions have traditionally maintained an admirable balance between serious research and a broad commitment to distributing useful knowledge beyond the campus walls. The open-credentials movement will allow some colleges and universities to extend their reach to unimagined lengths.

Kevin Carey is policy director at Education Sector, an independent think tank in Washington.

9.8 Content and Learning Objectives, Quality Is Not Uniformity, When Uniform Standards Are and Are Not Desirable

Contrast the above innovative ideas that target expanding the ability of learners to pursue and validate diverse learning experiences with public policy that can potentially do the opposite. In April 2012, the BC government announced a possible new Quality Assurance Act for the entire post-secondary education sector.

The target of the proposed Act and discussion paper was a multiplicity of agencies and standards involved with education quality assurance. With respect to multiple agencies we favor Higher Education Commissions that would be broadly based with real power. They are considered separately in other sections.

Student and institution relationships are governed not only by quality assurance regulation, but by contracts between parties. Here the focus is on regulated standards that arise because a contract exists and creates risk and the need for regulation to mitigate that risk separately, but in parallel with the parties' contract enforcement efforts. Common standards and systems are desirable in some cases, but they are not a magical solution in an age of great program and institution diversity. The substance of standards is the key. There are procedural standards and substantive standards. Substantive standards can focus on operations or content.

Common standards are suitable where there are similar non-content substantive or procedural features. Recruiting and admissions rules are often needed. There is often a need for systematic curricula that drives content delivery and for assessment of whether set learning objectives were met. Credentials should only be issued when they are earned. Faculty qualifications are in most cases required. Safety standards for facilities are needed. Records should be kept. These elements in most sectors could be regulated by common agencies and standards.

Regulation imposed content should not be imposed under the guise of quality regulation.

9.9 Quality Is Not Uniformity Unless That is A Promised Product Feature - Quality Regulation Should Not Impose Uniform Content or Learning Objectives—Industry Parties May Agree to Uniformity

Programs do not have to be the same in order to be of high quality and that point is potentially overlooked in the noted BC discussion paper. Ford and Chrysler cars do not have to use the same design and blueprint in order for both to be of high quality. To suggest that two institutions and their programs must be the same in terms of content, learning objective, targeted competency, assessment and credential before they can operate as quality assured institutions would be extraordinary.

The BC paper was of concern because it said diplomas and certificates should have to reflect common competencies. It said there are often no agreed upon standards on what many credentials represent or what the learning outcomes are. There is a difference between quality and the kind of uniformity posited by the BC report.

There are three contract issues involved here. First, individual students and institutions should not have specific content, learning objectives, targeted competencies and assessment and credential systems imposed on them under the guise of quality regulation. Contracting parties should be able to strike their product bargain. Secondly, the student and institution may agree in their contract that a product is to feature common content, learning objectives, targeted competencies and assessment and credential systems. In that case quality can involve uniformity because a product should be as it was promised to be and do what it promised to do. Thirdly, there could be agreements involving institutions, industry groups, professional groups, employers or other private parties that also target uniformity and transferability. In this latter case, for example, two visual effects trainers could decide on their own or with employers and industry groups to structure this kind of uniformity, but it should not be imposed under the guise of quality assurance regulation.

Again, quality must focus on whether the product was merchantable, that is, on whether it did what it promised to do and that normally relates to a learning environment that helps the student learn and achieve a set learning objective. Regulation works separately from the parties' contract enforcement efforts, but they do target a common risk.

Transferability can be important, but it is not the most important thing and it can be accomplished in diverse ways without central government imposition of common standards.

Credentials are not valuable just because they are uniform, but because they are a declaration that certain learning objectives were met. There is great variation with degrees aside from credit hours required or faculty qualifications. The idea of there being common competency levels or states of knowledge at the degree level in specific disciplines is fantasy. The state of knowledge resulting will never be the same. They are what they are.

Ultimately, uniformity, equality or the lack of it depends on what you measure. If you measure the actual state of knowledge of grads there can be great variation. If you measure credit hours, faculty qualifications and course names there may be equality, but it would not be a comparison that would be helpful in assessing real states of knowledge. Even within groups of public institutions and one jurisdiction not all degrees are treated the same. Many Universities will not recognize degrees in which any part of the degree was offered by an institution that is not a member of associations it recognizes. [64]

9.10 Imposed Uniformity Can Stifle Innovation, Enshrine Mediocrity and Restrict Adaptability and Change

Moves to impose common curricula on widely diverse education providers could enshrine poor quality and mediocrity or stifle innovation and the movement to more diverse providers and products that respond to diverse needs. Rapid adaptation to changing conditions would be retarded if changes could not be made without broad based consultations and efforts to continually enforce commonality. Students at the PSE level are adults and able to assess differences. Regulatory and business requirements that institutions and programs "constantly improve" would be hampered if changed could not be made with the constant approval of regulators or collaborators. Institution integrity is hard to maintain if control over program content is lost. Adaptations should be by agreement.

It is not realistic to expect that the contract and its product will not change during the term of the contract. Regulators cannot require that there be continuous improvement and then not allow change. We have had regulators tell institutions that what exists on day one must not change. Failing to change when improvements are likely to enhance the program would be an abdication of the responsibility to do what is best for the student. The product again is the guide. Change is acceptable if it enhances achievement of the learning objective. Requirements to adhere to externally imposed content and credential requirements can make it hard to adapt to change. The contract should state what can change and why and what cannot change.

9.11 Quality Standards Don't Focus on Employer Needs, Distinguishing and Blending Education and Workplace Markets

The BC discussion paper noted above referred to a need to have common program standards that focus on employer needs. Quality assurance systems protect students from contract product (the object of quality) consumption risk and not employer risk. The student wants in many cases a program that will help them fill a need for an employer, but policy expressions should reflect student consumer protection and not employer needs.

The problem is real. Many countries have jobs without people and people without jobs. [65] The problem can't be solved, however, unless reality is clear. Too many people of policy influence avoid reality—a commercial market between student consumers (Demand) and institutions (Supply). They see education as a government, social and economic mechanism to "supply" trained persons to satisfy the "demand" of workplace proprietors "consumers". They talk as if there is a market and demand and supply dynamic between institutions and workplace proprietors. [66] This is discussed in sections on outdated industrial age education models (Part 4, Product Performance, Quality, Stephen Covey).

Students are not products, outcomes or outputs. They are consumers. If industries say they need a number of workers and then do not hire them the institution and students can't sue them. If the institution does not produce enough workers then workplace proprietor can't sue the institution. Employers have contracts with employees and other service providers. Students have contracts with institutions. Good policy and law build on that reality.

Institutions must listen to the workplace and they must listen to students that also listen to the workplace and their own research about current and future prospects. The danger is that governments, public (government funded or as otherwise defined) institutions and workplace proprietors try to micro-manage supply based on what they see as the "demand" from workplace proprietors. It is the old central planning (some would say Stalinist five year economic plan) model where technocrats forecast demand and build an infrastructure for supply and control supply to meet that demand. Student demand is more complex than that. They want jobs or business prospects and they want to learn about all sorts of things. They want transferrable skills and do not just want to be cogs in someone's machine. They may see future markets differently. Business intelligence about future demand should consider what tens of thousands of researchers (future students) say and not just what workplace proprietors or isolated public servants say.

The central planning model puts too much power in the hands of those that determine which programs are needed, how many positions will be offered and, at the admissions level, who gets the prize. Those that do not make the cut need other institutions or disintermediated and unbundled product providers to provide the same programs or program type results that will allow them to compete for those available positions and they may want other programs.

9.12 Quality Products and Credible Credentials Depend on Learning Results Credibly Assessed and Not Brands

The credibility and true benefit of a credential does not lie with a "brand", but with the effectiveness of an institution to help students learn and achieve a learning objective and state of knowledge. As noted, the achievement is not promised by the institution, but systems that can help a student learn and systems that credibly assess and validate learning are promised.

A credential is evidence that a learning objective was met. It is not property that is bought and sold and that can be transferred to others. It is only valid and credible if there is an assessment system that reliably determines that the learning outcome objective was met. If it was met then it follows that the product was merchantable and functional and did what it was supposed to do and helped the student achieve the objective because the objective was met.

It is not branding and reputation that drive this. Don Tapscott observed in Macro Wikinomics that the virtual monopoly that universities have to grant degrees may or may not be challenged, but he correctly observed that the value of a credential and the prestige of the institution that grants rely on its effectiveness as a learning institution. If it is eventually shown to be inferior to alternative learning environments, their capacity to credential will diminish. Reputation and brand will only go so far. Tapscott asked: Will a Harvard undergrad degree, taught through lectures by teaching assistants in large classes, be able to compete in status with the small class size of liberal arts colleges or the superior delivery systems that harness the new models of learning?

A comparable statement would be: If it is clearly and empirically established (e.g. through third party assessment) that the learning achieved in alternative environments (less well branded) is equal to that in high reputation and well branded environments then systems of credit transfer should acknowledge that and market recognition should justifiably follow. This is harder to do if those in charge of regulatory and credit transfer systems have vested interests that could suffer with this acknowledgement and recognition.

Ultimately, credible third party assessment, credential evaluation systems and similar systems that validate the learning occurring in diverse settings will be a test for traditional institutions. There is no reason a student in high school or a private university prep college should not be able to take a course or pursue self-directed studies that results in the same state of knowledge as that attained in a university program and if that is done they should be recognized for it in credit, credential and credit transfer terms. Learning is learning and it should not matter where it occurred and how it occurred.

9.13 Object of Quality is the Product that Helps Students Achieve Learning Objectives and Not the Learning Objective Itself

The BC discussion paper cited above referred to quality assurance repeatedly, but it did not define the object of quality or define what is meant by quality. It talks about quality learning objectives, but it is not the learning objective that is quality or not, but the education product that is of high quality if it is merchantable and does what it is contractually promised to do, that is, help the student achieve the learning outcome objective. References to quality learning outcomes implies government setting standards that the objective must live up to. This kind of content control is unwarranted and an unjustifiable intrusion into the freedom of learners and providers to construct the program of choice.

The key is not that the learning objective be the same no matter where the learning took place (as the paper stated), but that the student's achievement be recognized when it is the same no matter where it was learned.

The paper's references to measuring learning outcomes were also open to question. Measuring them implies measuring them against some standard imposed by government. Government should not be imposing content or standards that require a credential to declare common states of knowledge. That is part of the contract bargain and maximum freedom is necessary. If standards are imposed by industry or other institutions by way of agreement and agreed to by students then that is fine, but centralized government quality assurance regulator control of content and credential declaration must not exist.

9.14 Law School and Legal Profession Example: Uniformity Distinguished From Quality Assurance

Law programs illustrate some of these points. Any law program in Canada that wanted its students to be eligible for admission to a provincial law society (the "Bar") would have to satisfy the "common law degree" requirement of most provincial legal professions statutes. There is variation from province to province. Until recently, law societies never attempted to articulate what competencies they expect graduates of a Canadian law school to possess. Because of a growing number of candidates for admission to the Bar who have been trained outside Canada the Federation of Law Societies of Canada established a Task Force to review the standards for approval of the law school degree. They published these criteria.

Law societies depend on law schools. They regulate entry into the profession in the public interest in accordance with provincial legal professions' statutes, regulations, professional rules and codes of ethics. The accreditation or licensing of lawyers in Canada generally has three elements - graduation from an approved law school, successful completion of a bar admission course and a period of articles. A student can also pursue a foreign law degree and approach the Federation of Law Societies of Canada to write a series of exams set for foreign grads. If they pass they can apply for membership with provincial law societies as if they had graduated from a Canadian law school.

In the US, the American Bar Association sets standards for law schools.

In both countries it is not (as we recommend) uniformity that is imposed on institutions and programs at the quality assurance regulation level. New law schools would fall under the universities statutes or degree authorization laws, but these standards would come from the private legal profession. Government quality assurance regulators should not dictate content and learning objectives. Quality is not about sameness and uniformity. Again quality standards should focus on facilitating contract performance (separately from the parties' contract performance efforts). If an institution wanted to offer a law program that did not target meeting law society admission standards it could still be of quality in the sense that contract and product expectations were met.

9.15 Third Party Credential Evaluation Systems

Credential evaluation services within institutions, organizations of various kinds or free standing service firms have multiple purposes. Credentials provide students with evidence of their academic accomplishment. They are not property bought and sold. Credential evaluation protects the student's ability to have their credential more broadly recognized, but they also are used to protect our borders, the consumers of professional services, credit transfer systems and the admission standards and integrity of existing programs. They allow disparate institutions and programs to be knitted together into some semblance of a common standard.

Credential evaluation is not part of the assessment system and does not involve the awarding of a credential. Technically an institution also evaluates credentials when they engage in admissions or credit transfer systems.

Credential evaluation services within institutions or free standing service firms assess an already awarded credential (based on reliable assessment systems) in reference to other credentials or standards set by third parties. Third parties would be parties that are not the student or institution involved with the initial assessment and credential award that occurs under a student contract.

Credential evaluation systems are useful if there are no uniform standards for institution accreditation, program content and learning objectives, program assessment or credit transfer and that is often the case—and the preferred case because of arguments given about separating regulation imposed quality standards and uniformity initiatives. Because of the already extreme and growing diversity of institutions, programs and sought after learning outcomes any meaningful uniformity at the institution, program and learning outcome level must be left to inter-institutional standards, industry standards or professional group standards.

Institutions, employers, professional organizations, lawyers and other professionals, immigration authorities and other government agencies or private parties use these services. Canada's Minister of Immigration, [67] Jason Kenney, announced plans in 2012 to hire outside companies to assess the credentials of newcomers before they arrive in Canada. Simply having a degree in a particular field will no longer be enough for an individual to get points toward acceptance as a skilled worker. Kenney said visa offices don't have the time or expertise to do a qualitative assessment of every applicant. He said this was an opportunity for specialized assessment of credentials by experts. He said, unlike immigration officers, experts know what the standards are to be licensed as an engineer or as a physician in Canada. It is not yet clear, but Minister Kenney may be talking about more than just a traditional credential evaluator. He may be focused on that model with greater direct involvement of industry, professional and vocational experts.

The users of credential evaluation services are ultimately accountable for that final decision. Evaluators give opinions. These evaluation firms [68] use conversion guides, publications, profiles of countries' education systems and translation services. They claim to provide accurate and reliable evaluations of international academic credentials. They say they aim to help integrate internationally educated persons into the employment and education environment of their newly adopted country. They verify documents from institution or via direct correspondence with authorities.

Credential evaluator competence cannot be taken for granted. Associations are attempting to guard against scam operators and it is too early to know if some form of regulation is required. This sector could, because of its growing importance and potential value, be a candidate for the new type of targeted and non-institution based accreditation systems that we propose in other sections.

9.16 Articulation, Credit Transfer, Exclusion of Institutions Often Unjustified, Inclusion Must Expand to All Providers Meeting Standards, Rights Based Credit Transfer

Along with assessments, the issue of articulation agreements, arrangements between institutions and credit transfer will be even more important in the future. It is not a justifiable position that a student with the same level of knowledge as another person is denied the legal right to have that recognized. Credit transfer issues have contract elements. Contracts should state that no promises regarding credit transfer are being made unless in fact those promises are being made.

Fair and equitable credit transfer systems (bi-lateral, multi-lateral, public or private) must focus on real states of knowledge no matter where the credit was earned or validated or where the learning occurred. Many new systems of articulation, credit transfer and credential evaluation could become subject to accreditation on the principle that if government can accredit institutions it can accredit those that provide the individual functions that institutions traditionally exercised.

This does not mean all products need to be the same in terms of all factor inputs, including curriculums, and learning objectives because it is never true to say that persons with common states of knowledge emerge from programs that share the same or similar inputs and learning objectives. It is also true to say that persons with some variation of states of knowledge or that come from different programs may still be capable of success in the program, profession or workplace where credits are assessed and accepted.

A lack of recognition for credits earned at an institution or for learning and possible credits earned outside institutions, but verified by emerging third party assessment systems can exist without any risk based justification for that lack of credit recognition. Two institutions or parties may not have an agreement or multi-lateral credit transfer agencies may limit the involvement of certain parties, institutions and learners for reasons that have nothing to do with risks to academic standards. That is no longer acceptable.

Standards must exist, but all institutions or assessment systems, on behalf of their students and learners, or students and learners directly must have the right to meet those standards and to enjoy the benefits of participation. Standards should be disclosed, concrete and fairly and uniformly applied to all. As always, they should be based on specific risk mitigation. Blanket exclusions that have nothing to do with real risk cannot persist. Where risks do exist, standards can and must be set to mitigate that risk. Again, all should have the right to meet those standards. As with most other accreditation systems—if standards are met the agency should have to grant the right participate.

Current systems generally afford no legal rights for students, institutions or assessment parties. Even multi-lateral systems that use terms like "agreements" ultimately refer to their systems as "guidelines" that any participating institution can choose to override without any need to justify it on academic grounds.

There are at least two options to build credit transfer systems that afford at least some legally enforceable rights. The first deals with the above noted multi-lateral credit transfer agencies. Legal rights of participation by institutions, independent and third party assessment systems and learners directly should exist and only be denied if standards focused on real risk are not met. Current exclusions are often not based on objective assessments of risk. Too often they are based on bias, preconceived notions and unjustified conclusions and assumptions. Agencies often do not even try to assess the risks. Multilateral systems are often controlled by traditional vested interests that have nothing to gain from broader inclusion.

In the same way accreditation often "must" be granted when standards are met, inclusion in transfer systems should have to (Must) be granted if standards are met. Alternatively, other properly accredited transfer agencies (general or sector focused) must be allowed to emerge and then required to provide for broad participation based on real risk. Again, the principle would be that if institutions can be accredited then some of those individual functions can be the subject of accreditation.

The second option would focus on contract rights. Articulation agreements between two or more institutions or parties may be enforceable, but often they are not because consideration and contract intent are unclear. Students are not party to these agreement and have no enforcement rights. They could argue they have those rights under third party beneficiary laws because the agreement are written primarily for their benefit or separate contracts could evolve involving the students directly as parties and the institutions involved. This is perfectly possible.

Again, third party assessment and credential evaluation systems can work hand in hand with articulation and credit transfer systems to ensure students are not dead headed and denied the right to have their credits and state of knowledge recognized. There need not be any sacrifice of academic standards. Vested interests, however, control current systems and that will retard innovation. Currently, if junior college credit can (not legally) be transferrable to a senior university the student must still be admitted at that university. If they are admitted (there is no right of admission) then the senior body may, but is usually not legally bound to accept those credits. If they would use them as credit upon admission then there is no reason why they could not or another independent body could not take those credits and apply them to later credentials even without admission. The senior body is not the only party that is capable of aggregating credentials and making declarations.

If it is empirically established (e.g. through third party assessment) that the learning achieved in alternative environments (less well branded) is equal to that in high reputation and well branded environments then systems of credit transfer should acknowledge that and market recognition should follow.

9.17 Articulation or Sub-Contracting Services Do Not Involve Indirect Provision of Programs

Despite what some governments suggest, there can generally be no such thing as indirect provision of a program because an institution must have a contract with a student and credit transfer arrangements or agreements do not make the other institutions party to those student contracts. Direct provision of a program occurs where an institution provides a program directly to a student under a contract. A degree grantor does not "provide" or indirectly provide the programs that may be articulated to it. The party that has the legal obligation to provide the program provides it and not the party receiving the credit later or allowing for the credit transfer.

A non-degree program articulated to a degree program is still not a degree program and a non-degree granting institution is not legally allowed to provide a degree program directly or indirectly.

If a credential granting institution has a contract with students and hires others to provide the program to students on its behalf this is still a direct provision of the program by the credential grantor because they are the contract party that has the legal obligation to directly provide the program under contract. The sub-contracting service provider has a contract with the institution providing the program and not with the student. The institution contracting with the student just hired a sub-contractor to deliver the program much like they would hire a teacher. Regulations may require that instructors be employed by the credential grantor. The sub-contractor does not provide the program to the student directly or indirectly. There is no real collaboration either—just a commercial arrangement between two parties.

If a non-degree granting institution enters into contracts with its own students to provide a program of a degree grantor then it must have program approval from the education regulator and permission or a license from the degree grantor to use its programs for that purpose unless it buys the copyrighted works. It could still not provide a degree program because it would not be permitted (licensed) to by the regulator.

If the original degree grantor also provided directions (not just intellectual property) and complete business systems as to how the entire institution and program should be managed then that looks like a franchise (it may still not be a franchise), but still the program is provided by the new party under its own regulatory approvals and student contracts and the original degree grantor is not involved. There is again no indirect provision of programs.

9.18 Non-Degree Programs Are Not Programs Leading to Degrees Or Parts of Degree Programs, Institution Integrity, Separation and Parallelism

If a non-degree program is articulated to a degree program it is still not a degree program. Regulators have made the mistake of equating the term "leading to a degree" with "degree program". Programs leading to a degree (via articulation) are not degree programs and do not have to be approved as degree programs. They do not automatically "lead" to a degree.

Non-degree programs are not degree programs by virtue of an articulation agreement, but the term "program leading to a degree" [69] is misleading. Governments have been known to include under this heading actual degree programs offered by authorized Degree Grantors and certain non-degree programs that may be the subject of articulation agreements between degree grantors and non-degree granting institutions. This latter approach is misleading and legally unsound. Degree grantors are responsible for the equivalency of academic standards, but this can be done via agreements as to standards and the degree grantor need not have to control the sending institution.

It is also not legally the case that non-degree programs are "part of" degree programs or that any articulated program is part of the other programs articulated. Students must be clear about who the parties are in student contracts and what contractual product is offered. At one time BC's Degree Authorization Act administrators adopted an integration approach and suggested the standard should be that the Degree Grantor should treat the Non-Degree Grantor as if it was "part of" itself and this included the idea that it should have the authority to approve all faculty members hired at the level of Non-Degree Granting Institution. This is not legal reality unless agreements and applicable statutes allow for it.

The programs are not "part" of a whole that is offered under contract to a student. Again, unless two or more institutions are party to a student contract and grant a credential jointly, the term "joint" programs or degrees or references to two elements being "part of" something larger must be avoided.

In certain jurisdictions, a collaborative arrangement was defined as an agreement or partnership between a degree granting institution and a collaboration partner where the partner provides all or part of a degree program. This is not correct in legal terms. Unless two or more institutions are party to a student contract and grant a credential jointly, the term "joint" programs or degrees must be avoided. Institutions should not say the Institution A and Institution B Program unless that is the legal reality. With most articulation agreements, no party offers the programs or grants the credentials of the other party in the name of or on behalf of the other. They do not do so under any form of contract of or for service with the other party or under any form of license or assignment of rights granted by the other party.

Governments often have confusing approaches to articulation. They will say each institution must have its own academic integrity and then suggest that "separation" and "parallelism" of the two institutions is not acceptable because of a lack of oversight by the receiving institution. The legal fact is that the two articulating institutions are separate legal entities. No new separate legal entity is created in most cases with articulations. No partnership or agency relationship is intended for legal reasons because one does not empower the other to enter legal relationships for the other. Institutions can't maintain their academic integrity if they do not have the requisite level of separation and control over its hiring or business systems. The two can enter into agreements that limit discretion and freedom and give the other party veto power over decisions (e.g. the hiring of faculty), but this is not required or advisable for most articulations. It is possible to promise that a certain standard for faculty, instruction, admission and graduation will exist without giving the other side veto power over them.

9.19 Student Contracts, Credit Transfer Promises, Representations and Institution Liability

Students are often misled into believing that they have a legal right to credit transfers because of statements made by the sending or receiving institutions involved. Students have sued institutions successfully regarding this form of misrepresentation. In Canada, there have been students that successfully sued institutions not on the basis that the student was a beneficiary of an articulation contract, but because an institution induced the student to enter the student contract with a representation about credit transfers.

If a university represents that taking certain pre-requisite programs will entitle students to transfer to other universities in senior years those students can treat it as a contractual representation and seek damages if it proves to be untrue. In Olar v. Laurentian University [70] the calendar said: "Students having successfully completed the first and second year programs may proceed into the third year in specified courses at Laurentian University or may transfer into the third year of other Universities in Ontario, if they wish to pursue Chemical, Civil or Mechanical Engineering." The student proceeded with the claim in damages against the university on the basis of the statement, his reliance upon it, the fact it was a misrepresentation and the claim of damages which included an extra year of tuition, textbooks, living expenses and the loss of a year of professional income. He was eventually successful and received a large sum of money in the form of compensatory damages.

The student contract should say as a default position that no such representations are given, but that can be subject to other express agreements. Institutions should not expressly or impliedly state that students have some form of legal right to a transfer of credits either coming in or out of the institution unless that is the legal reality and normally it is not.

9.20 Pre-Approval of Foreign or Other Credentials

In general, the recognition of foreign credentials is a process that focuses on post credential periods and this means persons can invest years of time studying in programs without knowing whether their credential will be accepted or not. Immediate changes by professional organizations and others that accept credentials should be made so that the acceptance is given before the student commits to a large investment of time and money.

For example, foreign trained law students (some who study at a distance from Canada), including some Canadians, can apply to the Federation of Law Societies of Canada when they graduate and if they successfully pass several exams set by the FLSC they can apply to provincial law societies for membership just as if they had graduated form a Canadian law school. There is no practical or substantial reason why judgments could not be made in advance. The same logic can apply to any credential. There is no real rational reason why pre-approval is not possible.

9.21 Institution's Assessment Promise, Student Promise, Plagiarism As Contract Breach, Theft, Counterfeiting and Credential Abuse

Plagiarism is one example of a credential being abused or brought into question. Plagiarism is partly about theft and partly about counterfeiting, but primarily it is about denying another the right to claim that something is their sole creation. Some argue that an action is only stealing if you deprive the owner of the thing stolen. This is not the case. Even if the true creator is not deprived of the works in question they are, by the act of plagiarism being deprived of the right to be the only one able to claim that this is their creation.

The problem with plagiarism is not just the "taking" element, but the "passing it off as your own" element. In this sense it is more counterfeiting than stealing, but it is still stealing. Counterfeiting of money is a serious crime, not because it steals money from the government, but because it undermines the monetary system. The ten dollar bill only has value because it is presumed to be genuine. If everyone could just print their own money it would cease to have value.

Counterfeiting undermines monetary and economic systems. Similarly, an act of plagiarism or other action that results in a person having a credential that was largely unearned can seriously undermine the credibility of the institution and its credential and the surrounding systems of credential evaluation, credit transfer and formal institution articulation. Course credit only has value if the student worked to earn it. If the credential is not earned it has less value for all who hold it and the system falls apart. Immigration officials, articulated (credit transfer) institutions, professional organizations, student loan lenders, employers and others that rely on the integrity of the admissions, program operations, assessment and credential systems lose trust in the credential and institution.

There are two elements to plagiarism or actions of credential manipulation—the action itself which is generally a violation of an expressed or reasonably implied contract term and the action to give credit for unearned benefits.

The first is an action by the student that attempts to garner for themselves an unearned benefit. Even if credit is not given for the work, the action is an attempt to garner an unearned benefit and is deserving of penalty. The second is an action by the institution to grant credit for plagiarized work or work that does not otherwise meet academic standards. Both actions weaken the credential if credit is given for bad work so issues of dismissal, assessments and failures and institution reputation must be considered and balanced.

As noted, a credible assessment system (Outcome 3) is part of the contractual promise and product because it validates if a learning objective (Outcome 2) was met. The student expects this (while also disliking exams) because without it the credential is of questionable value. The student contract should make this promise clear.

Conversely, the student must contractually promise to not engage in activities that abuse or manipulate the assessment system and that could distort or exaggerate their academic achievements and bring the assessment system and the credential into question. This is necessary to protect the student, other students, the tradable currency of the credential and the general integrity of the institution and its education and assessment products.

A strong student contract has provisions regarding intellectual property, but these are not the key plagiarism sections. Intellectual property provisions say students must respect the IP rights of the institution and third parties. Any alleged legal violation must be established by the institution or third party. It is not up to the institution to protect third party rights. It is not in a legal position to even know if the third party rights are as claimed. If that violation is established that would be evidence that the student contract provision was violated. This could then be cited as plagiarism if any work, protected or not, is passed off as one's own creation.

A clear provision in a contract is preferable to a provision lost in a sea of policies and regulations that may or may not find their way into contracts. The provision should make it clear that plagiarism itself, even if no credit is ultimately given for plagiarized work, is a prohibited action that could result in specified disciplinary actions including, but not necessarily dismissal.

A good student contract refers to prohibited actions and grounds for termination and dismissal and plagiarism is on that list. This makes it clear the offence is of legal importance. The legal issues surrounding dismissal can be complex. Even if the contract says plagiarism is a prohibited offence and can result in dismissal this does not mean that dismissal can or should automatically occur or that it will even stand up to a legal challenge. Students may challenge whether the dismissal was proper give the entire context. For example, in a one year program it may not be reasonable to dismiss someone for one instance of plagiarism. There may be scores of other assignments yet to come or in the past.

If instances of plagiarism are alleged and admitted to or established and a student is not dismissed then they must be informed about how that may impact their final result. They must not be misled. Before the time for possible refunds is over the student must be told that they may not graduate as a result or that their grades will reflect the matter.

Rules should define the offence. Plagiarism can encompass everything from using un-cited work and passing it off as your own and that could simply involve failing to use quotation marks. It can also encompass other forms of cheating. Whether it rises to the legal standard of plagiarism or a contractually prohibited action depends on the facts. If a person cites the fact that they have borrowed ideas then it is more difficult to claim plagiarism because the passing off element is not there. There can still be a violation of IP rights, but that must be proven and that is largely a matter between the offender and the IP holder. The school then must focus on whether the academic standard is not being met.

Policies and contracts should make it clear that only authorized persons can make dismissal or disciplinary decisions. This should not just be the program head. It should involve the President or other senior manager and ideally even legal counsel because the decision has serious legal implications.

10

Other Contractually Promised Services and Benefits (Outcome 4) and Not Promised Services or Outcomes (Outcome 5)

10.1 Promised and Not Promised Services

An institution may, to attract students and support primary education and assessment services, provide a range of services that can support the two main and contractually promised services or operate and be contractually promised separately. There may be some overlap with the education product inputs, but these services could include the student pub, copy machines, housing, daycare services, food services, career planning offices, entrepreneurship (e.g. mentorship, venture capital or incubation) services and other auxiliary enterprises.

These would likely only have serious contract impact if they truly induced a student into the contract and if the parties expressly or implied intended that the institution was legally bound to provide these services. No doubt many of these services are not intended to be contractual in this way, but that may not be universally the case. As is always the case, the parties must be clear as to what is exactly promised. If a career planning service or business development service is promised that does not mean that a job or a successful business is promised.

Cost controls often require that difficult changes be made to services. If contract promises are made then they cannot be unilaterally changed unless the contract expressly or impliedly allows for it. Contracts should make it clear that the institution can make any reasonable change on its own (with stated exceptions) provided the ability to facilitate the set learning outcome and other primary outcomes is not compromised. It should also include specific provisions to create a legal default where no or minimal additional services are contractually offered and promised.

Regular news from the education sector makes it clear that institutions are cancelling programs and other services. The question is whether these services were contractually promised and if contract breach exists at all or if a breach worthy of a legal remedy is warranted if the service is cancelled or modified. There is no one simple answer. The facts of each case are the key. The issue may again be one of real, factual and reasonable reliance on a representation or promise by a party claiming breach of that term. In other words, the question is whether they actually relied on it and reasonably relied on it when they decided and were induced to enter into the contract.

In some instances, this case can likely be made. If a business student is promised that a business incubator will exist in order for him to help commercialize a business product then it is quite possible that this was a primary factor that reasonably induced him to go to university business school A as opposed to school B. A grad student might be induced to enroll because of a representation or promise about a corporately financed research project. It may not be possible to fall back on the fact that overall the institution was able to help the student achieve the learning objective if in fact something more than that help was actually promised.

As indicated in other sections, institutions are competing hard for the best students and often promising the moon. They must start looking at that in terms of what they are or are not legally bound to deliver.

10.2 Cutbacks and Contracts

Again, the product factor inputs that make up various promised products are not offered and paid for individually. If services support primary education and assessment services then cancellation of other services may not have contract impacts if the delivery of those primary services was such that the institution was still able to help the student achieve learning objectives.

The facts are always the key. It may not be enough to have an office with a name on the door saying "Career Planning Office" with one staff person for 30,000 students. What exactly do they do or did they promise to do? Can the service be cancelled at any time without contract impact when finances are tight? We have faced many students that have based claims on these factors.

The issue of austerity measures and cutbacks are addressed in more detail in other sections, but the parties cannot avoid the legal and contract realities. If a service was emphasized and used as means of inducing a person into a contract and does induce a person into a contract then legal issues can arise if it is unilaterally withdrawn because of austerity measures or other reasons. Usually institutions give this no thought and just assume that students will do nothing about it. In the future that may be less the case.

These services are often not academic programs in the sense that they may not relate directly to the program of study, program operations and the assessment of academic progress. Students often articulate complaints around the lack of career or business planning services or even the lack of a job. It is common for universities to highlight "Career Services" or "Business Services" on their website. If this was an inducement to enter the contract and reliance existed when contracts were entered into then that could mean a cause of action exists that a court would consider if the service was not provided or not provided to the level of quality expected. Again, it may not be possible to always fall back on the argument that overall the institution helped achieve learning objectives if in fact something more was promised such as specific help in getting a job or getting a business started. The actual job or business would not be the key, but whether the help promised was provided. The key is what was promised.

10.3 Faculty Research, Corporate Projects and Other Activities Are Generally Not Part of Student Contracts

Modern institutions, especially larger universities, are beehives of activity. Faculty members teach and do research. Corporations or governments support research projects that may or may not involve teaching faculty. In some cases, especially with post grad work, these projects are an important inducement for a student to choose one institution over another. In cases like that the matter can be contractual and disputes can arise if contract terms are not precise.

In many cases, these activities would not be considered contract warranties that emerge from pre-contract representations or contract promises for all students because they are not directly related to the primary function of the program which is to help the student achieve a set learning outcome. Most students are not even aware of the research projects going on around them let alone induced by them when they make an enrollment decision.

The government or corporate money provided for a research or corporate project is part of a relationship (often contractual) between the institution and the government or corporation and the student is not normally party to it as either a regulated subject or benefitting object. In some cases, they may be. Each case is different.

Institutions or students should be careful to address specific cases where a student may be strongly induced to attend because of these more peripheral activities. For example, if a grad student is attending because he was induced to come having been told that a corporately funded project was going ahead and that turns out not to be so then there could be contract consequences. There are real life examples. Not only tuition would be involved because the student may be on scholarship. A contract could still exist even without tuition because consideration could take another form. With gifted scholars, the opportunity cost for a grad student can be significant. Delays in their academic and professional development could involve large sums of money. Other sections cite case law examples.

A business student may attend an institution because they are told that a business incubator on campus will help them develop a business idea. Is that a contractual promise? Markets should be clear. What if the incubator is cancelled for financial reasons or it is not very good? These questions are often ignored by institution managers that still do not see or respect the students as contract parties. The service may only have peripheral reliance to the actual education product itself where the student is taught, learns and is assessed, but that does not always mean that the matter is not significant and worthy of attention. The separate expectation and promise could rule the day.

10.4 Contractually Un-promised Contract Period or Post-Student Contract Period Outcomes, Education Systems, Time Limits for Institution-Student Relationships and Regulator Jurisdiction (Outcome 5)

These Outcomes are generally not contractual and therefore of limited relevance to direct education quality assurance regulation because of—as argued - the link between contract performance and regulation. They can arise during the contract period or the post contract and post consumption risk period. These Outcomes may relate to a job, professional services and business results or anything that the student hoped to accomplish with the training. They will often have nothing to do with the primary education and assessment products or other promised services. The contract should address this.

Job or business results, professional memberships or credit transfers are not direct education outcomes or objectives and generally they are not promised and cannot be promised because of regulatory prohibitions against making related claims or because such representations or promises would be effectively void. You cannot promise or represent or reasonably believe that another is promising or representing something that clearly lies outside the control of the party making the promise or representation.

These are economic outcomes that depend on a multitude of personal, social and economic conditions. Such hoped for results cannot be cited as "legal standards" that a school can be expected to achieve as a condition of overcoming legislated prohibitions (See Standards). Again, a standard is something that can reasonably be accomplished in an effort to mitigate specific risk. Impossible requirements are really new absolute prohibitions and would generally not be allowable. These issues are explored more in other sections and especially in relation to how quality assurance regulation and workplace and business regulation must be regulated and addressed separately while maintaining needed linkages to ensure that the objectives of each are met.

11

Contract Period Is Key to All Outcomes, Regulator Jurisdiction, A Product Feature and Not A Quality Factor or Measure

11.1 Contract Period Relevant to All Outcomes, Products and Quality Assurance

The student enrollment contract generally has a beginning and an end. It has a period or term. Sections on indeterminate contracts are found below and those can in some cases be unenforceable.

The contract period is relevant to all outcomes and products and therefore to quality assurance. It distinguishes pre-contract representations from contract terms that may or may not include or incorporate pre-contract representations. It is the period where the education product (Outcome 1) is delivered and where the assessment product (Outcome 3) validates if the learning outcome objective (Outcome 2) was achieved. It determines what other services are delivered under contractual promises during the contract period or that perhaps may exist or continue after the enrollment contract ends or after its other education and assessment elements are performed.

11.2 Contract Period, Product Feature and Not a Quality Feature or Measure, Not Imposed by Government

The length of a program is a key feature of what a program product is. A student may be induced into a student contract because of the length. Two year MBAs are now less attractive than one year programs because students want a quick post-baccalaureate degree that provides practical skills with the same credential.

This can be contrasted with an attempt in BC Canada by the career training regulator to make program length a quality issue by making a bylaw stating that the length must be sufficient to achieve the learning outcome objective which is targeted at that required for initial employment. [71] There are two things wrong with this. First, they cannot impose the learning outcome objective. That is part of the contractual bargain.

Secondly, the learning outcome objective must be adjusted to the program length and not the other way around. Clearly, the student and institution intention and bargain is that the academic expectation or graduation standard is set in accordance with what one can reasonably achieve in terms of learning objective in the time set.

This faulty regulatory approach suggests the program is not one of quality unless it is long enough to achieve the learning objective that a regulator has somehow set and determined to be appropriate for initial employment for an undefined position. This is not possible because they cannot impose that on the bargain and because they have the power to set quality standards for the institution and program and not impose what the program is in the first place.

The second element of this bylaw was that the institution had to justify having a program that was longer or shorter than other comparable programs. This is even a worse provision than the one above. It is built on a completely false assumption that institutions are required to somehow teach to a common standard or learning objective when no such standard has been established by collective institutions, government or any other party.

If a common standard and program length is agreed and imposed (e.g. credits for a degree) then it would have to be the subject of specific regulations (strongly not recommended and likely not lawful in most cases) or multi-party contracts and not a general provision as was the case with this BC example. The bargain between the institution and the student should prevail and it should have an expressed or implied provision that the learning outcome objective is achievable in the program period given the student's determined capacities as judged by application and admission procedures.

11.3 Regulatory Jurisdiction Over an Institution is Limited by the Contract Period of Consumption

Regulator jurisdiction over an institution normally arises from the need to protect a specific consumer or class of consumer from risks associated with a type of transaction and contract so it follows logically that the regulator's jurisdiction over that specific or class of institution and student relationship is limited by the contract period of consumption. Like the contract, that jurisdiction and power has a beginning and an end.

That regulatory trigger does not give and the regulator does not have the mandate or obligation to protect past students from statutorily undefined risks for an indeterminate period of time in the period following the student contract period of consumption. No consumption risks exist and the regulator is not tasked with protecting these persons or class of persons from every conceivable type of economic and social risk that lies beyond the contract period of consumption and outside the contemplated purposes of the student protection statute.

This point relates to the issue arising from some regulatory efforts in BC, without statutory authority, to hold regulated institutions responsible for and punish them for what may or may not happen to past students in the distant future after graduation. It relates to efforts to confuse quality education focused on providing a product capable (the contractual promise) of helping a student achieve (not a contract promise) a set and desired learning outcome with quality careers and lives. This is discussed in depth in other sections.

The triggered jurisdiction does not extend beyond the product itself to include everything done or potentially done with that product or that one hopes to achieve with the use of that product. These points are addressed again in section drawing generally legally unsound and unwarranted links between education quality and employment or business results.

11.4 Without Statutory Mandates Regulators Cannot Limit Or Impose the Term of a Student Contract

Again, because program length is a key feature of the product itself and not a quality measure, regulators cannot, without clear statutory mandates to override contracts and impose essential contract terms, limit the term of a student contract.

A BC regulator tried, but could not disguise a length of contract provision that restricts program length with an attempt to force multiple resigning of documents. The BC agency [72] had a provision that said no enrollment contract could be for more than 18 consecutive months. It then also said that notwithstanding the 18 month rule and for multi-year programs the institution could have the student enter into a contract of up to 12 months duration for the first year and each subsequent year. That made no sense and was internally contradictory. If a contract is entered into for an 18 month or 12 month period and the institution only promises to provide training for that period then that is all there is. There is no multi-year program offered, promised or provided. If a school can only enter into a contract for the 18 or 12 months that is all they can offer and promise to provide and all they are required to contractually provide. If each 12 month contract promised a multi-year program and contracts renewed automatically or by requirement then there is no need for multiple contracts. A truly new contract would normally require new intent exercised volitionally.

There was also a contradiction between two sections with the latter saying the contract must state the commencement and completion dates for the program. If the contract cites these dates as the program and promised dates for the full multiple year program then it is not a separate year by year contract. If it states this duration to be only one year then it is not technically a multi-year program that is promised.

If the institution is only contractually promising to provide one year at a time then it could choose to not provide the subsequent years because it made no promise to provide them. If the subsequent years were not provided for any reason the student may claim they were misled and demand their first year tuition back because an "orphaned" year is of no credential value. They could claim that they were promotionally promised a multi-year program that would result in a certain credential. The institution could change the terms (if both parties agree) for subsequent contracts.

The alternative is to not promise a multi-year program, but only a series of one year programs that can be knitted together in a form of internal articulation program, but if no promise of a multi-year program is possible then that would have to be a conditional promise. In other words, the institution would offer a one year program now and if it offered additional one year programs they could then put them together to earn a credential in the future.

Again, education and quality assurance regulators have no jurisdiction to dictate program duration unless they have specific statutory power to do so because that has nothing to do with program quality and everything to do with defining the product itself that it is the object of quality. It is determining what the program is at its very heart.

There is huge potential here to mislead students. Promotional materials may talk about a multi-year program and students may rely on that instead of what the contract says. If they use a poor contract that does not have a strong and enforceable entire agreement clause both parties would unknowingly be exposed to risk and uncertainty. The school could choose to not offer future years, raise prices in future years (if both parties agree) and make whatever changes they want in future years (again, if both parties agree) and the student would have no legal recourse because the school would not have contractually promised anything beyond the one year program.

The contract could say that if multiple contracts are required that each future contract has the same terms unless the parties agree otherwise. This bylaw also creates problems with refunds. If a student attends under a one year contract then the program period that is used for refund calculation periods is shorter, but each subsequent year would have its own new refund period. Put together, the available refund period for the student would likely be longer. In the BC case, the intended objective—to protect students—was accomplished with another bylaw that said no student had to pay more than a one year payment in the event of a multi-year program.

The same regulator had approved the multi-year program and then it essentially said you cannot promise to provide it. The statute in this case defined the prohibition (no provision of the defined program type without registration) and regulated body of programs as those being over $1000.00 and over 40 hours in length. There was no reference to any kind of maximum. The agency had no power to create new prohibitions or to set minimum or maximum lengths for a program.

11.5 Contract Period Relevant to Institution Performance, Student Rights and Duties and Product Price

Many student contracts still stipulate that the program must be completed by a set date. This element of the bargain should be clear because otherwise the institution could find itself facing a never ending relationship with students that feel entitled to just continue studying until they get it right. Even where set ending dates do exist it is not uncommon for students to ask for more time—especially if tuitions are high and time investments are extensive. The institution must use its discretion and carefully balance its interests with the interests of the student and the other students in the class—if a class exists.

Often without students being aware, certain institution and student contracts (especially calendar contracts) may allow universities to increase tuition fees at any time and some courts have upheld their ability to do so even when the increases were extremely high.[73] The ability to make the change is one issue. Another legal issue is whether a student signs a four year contract for a four-year degree program (our view) or a year by year contract. The latter is unworkable in most cases and not in tune with most student expectations. A student can argue that they paid a set price for a set product—a program that would go on for four years. The issue of a contract provision allowing for the institution to unilaterally make any kind or size of price change during a contract term is a separate issue.

11.6 Indeterminate Program Length Could Make Contract Unenforceable, Academic Standards Possibly Impacted

As distance and online learning become more common and programs are not just tied to one place at one time an issue arises concerning the ability to enforce an indeterminate contract. In most cases where students are given great leeway in terms of completion time there is still a requirement that they finish within a set number of years or other period. If no limit exists it may (Emphasis Added) make the contract invalid and unenforceable because it could be impossible to define when performance is complete.

This may be less of a factor now with more emphasis on programs on demand and less emphasis on programs that always start and end on set dates with learning objectives and academic standards having to be met by graduation day, but the issue often still remains. If one student completes the program in one year and another takes five years some would argue that competency and ability judgments could be made, but clearly that depends on the facts.

11.7 Case Studies: Power to Regulate Products With Set Durations and Features Is Not Power to Regulate All Regulated Firm Products, Short Duration and Corporate Training

There is no principle in Canadian, US or UK common law or statute law that we have uncovered that stands for the premise that if a regulator regulates one of a firm's products that they can automatically assert jurisdiction over all of the firm's products even if those products do not fall within prohibitions and regulated product definitions.

Many education regulatory systems limit their reach to a certain type of training with restrictions often focused on a specific type or quantum of risk to student consumers. Regulators normally cannot unilaterally extend that reach. Again, we have the BC example where regulators unilaterally expanded their reach to education program products not defined and not prohibited by law to be offered without regulation and registration. In BC a person (institution) is only required to "register" and only regulated and required to adhere to quality standards if they offer to provide or provide career training as the term is specifically defined. Only career training is prohibited.

The right to have categories of institutions existed, but there was no power to create new categories of programs, new prohibitions (and thus new registration requirements) or new categories of protected students with the same or varying rights (short program students and corporate training students were given fewer protections). An agency cannot define its own jurisdiction.

With this example, career training was defined as training or instruction in the skill and knowledge required for employment in an occupation defined in the regulations. This definition leads to the conclusion that quality career training provides training that develops the knowledge and skills required (prepares them) for employment in defined fields. It is also defined as training that exceeds a length and cost prescribed. The word "and" is used so all three elements had to exist. The agency focused the first introductory phrase and ignored the time and cost factors when it tried to redefine what it had jurisdiction over. Without any power to create new powers, prohibitions or student classes the regulator tried to create four classes of programs: 1. Full CT programs (to replace the existing CT definition). 2. Short duration CT programs. 3. Corporate training programs. 4. Programs that do not fall under the other three categories (not subject to regulation). [74]

When the law sets a definition, generic or common use meanings do not apply. In this BC example, the agency originally (later they said "all programs offered") said it only asserted jurisdiction over programs not falling under the statutory definition of if they are what they still define as career training. An email dated May 22, 2008 said: I do not believe I said that once an institution is registered all its programs must be registered whether they involve "career training or not". We exact this requirement in order to ensure that all students enrolled in career training programs in a registered institution are provided with consumer protection. They have no mandate to protect everybody regardless of risk. Career training was statutorily defined and they tried to modify that without the power to do so. Eventually they cast this position aside and passed a bylaw that said the opposite - that if the school was registered because one product was subject to regulation that then all of the school's products were subject to regulation. Amendments to the Act and Regulations redefining terms did nothing to change the core issues.

The BC career training agency also arbitrarily - and (ostensibly) without legal authority - tried to expand its reach over corporate training programs provided by institutions that were already subject to regulation because some of their programs fell under existing prohibitions and regulations. They did so even though the corporate training programs would not otherwise fall under legislated prohibitions and regulations. Corporate Training normally refers to cases where an internal or external trainer provides a program to managers and employees. If it is only an internal program then regulatory issues do not arise and even when an external party enters into a contract with the company there are no regulatory issues because there is no education provider contract with the student. The contract is with the corporation. If the outside trainer has a direct contract with students then that would not be corporate training, but a direct education service for students in a corporate environment.

When institutions that directly offer regulated products to student consumers also enter contracts with corporations under which the institution provides an instruction service to the corporation that indirectly benefits the corporation's employees those corporate programs are not regulated programs in most cases. If they were the work of regulators in most countries would multiply exponentially.

Assuming employees are not individually contracting with the institution as facilitated by their employer, in these cases there is no student contract and where student risk exists it arises only under the employment contract. Students are not privy to (and not bound or protected by) the institution-corporation contract and because they are not paying the institution the student is not at financial risk. The corporation is not a student that learns during a program and the corporation-institution contract is not a student contract.

Funds should not be payable under that corporate training contract to assurance funds (or bonds) where they exist because intended beneficiaries of those funds are students. Students could not make claims because they would not have paid. Corporate employees do not submit applications and would not be subject to the protections afforded by the application of admission standards and bylaws regarding applications, admission standards, assessments and other matters. In the BC context, bylaws say the institution and student can't waive admission standards, but this is common with corporate training. Assessments are rare.

Corporations are also not paying on behalf of students (as certain definitions required) because students are not required to pay the institution in the first place. They can't pay on behalf of someone else if that other person is not required to pay because they are not fulfilling the obligation of another. They are not paying "on their behalf". They are paying for themselves under a contractual obligation. The corporation can't enter into a student contract on behalf of an employee and effectively bind the employee to that contract without the consent of the employee and without the various elements required for the proper formation of a contract being satisfied. Contracts cannot bind third parties that are not privy to the contract.

In the BC context, the term "corporate training" does not appear and is not defined in the Act or regulations and does not fall within regulated categories. The section set out what contracts for corporate training must include. One reference to a "corporation purchasing training" made it clear corporate training is provided by an institution to a corporation under a contract between the institution and the corporation. The agency again had no jurisdiction to create new categories of programs, students and prohibitions.

12

Public Law and Regulation, Private Law and Contracts Give Rise to Regulation

12.1 Interacting Public Law and Private Law

Again, public law is common law and statute law made and enforced to protect the public interest as opposed to specific private rights. It addresses relationships between private individuals or corporations and government. Private common law or statute law (contracts, tort or property law) addresses relationships between private parties—individuals or corporations. Public and private law can interact and address the same parties or relationships while retaining their own nature and remaining separate and distinct. The education sector, and particularly the student and institution relationship, is an example.

12.2 Contracts Are The Primary Mechanism To Govern Student and Institution Relationships

The volitional contract and the law of contract that governs its formation and enforcement are the primary mechanism for governing the student and institution relationship. Contracts and contract law are one social response to a need for relationship and risk governance. Regulation can target the same relationship, but the two mechanisms are different and legally distinct.

The contract comes first because its features will determine if regulation even applies. When the contract has certain features the jurisdiction of the government and its delegated agency arises (See other sections). Only certain training is usually prohibited by the statute. Jurisdiction then arises for a set contract period in relation to those contract parties.

12.3 Regulations, Contracts and Business Policies Target the Same Relationship But Public and Private Authorities, Parties, Tools and Methods Are Distinct and Operate Separately

Enrollment contracts, business policies and education regulation often target a common relationship so their provisions or targets may be similar even though the processes of creation, application and enforcement are separate with separate parties, rights and duties. A contract is made by its parties. Laws are made by constitutionally empowered lawmakers or by their delegates that are empowered to make subordinate legislation. Business policies are created by persons authorized by the firm to set policies.

Regulatory or administrative actions are not prosecutions. The objective is usually not sanction, but prevention of recurrence. The concern is with adherence to standards. Attention is directed not so much at individual offenders as at the category or industry to be regulated. The objective is to identify the main risks of antisocial conduct and to take action to minimize offensive behavior by publicizing standards, requiring proof of competence and compliance.

Regulators govern the regulated relationship that is also governed by contract, but they do so with the use of different tools. They use public instruments, that is, laws or regulations that exist or that they are empowered to establish or other assigned adjudicative and administrative powers. Regulation can mandate behaviors that may increase the chances of contract performance, but again their job is not to enforce the contract. Only the parties can enforce the contract.

The student contract is separate from regulation and public statutory duties involving regulators and regulated parties are separate from private contract duties involving contract parties. The student contract is often the trigger for regulator jurisdiction and the type of regulation required. A distance education program is different from an onsite program. Because public statutory duties that institutions owe to regulators are separate from contract duties institutions owe to students, non-compliance with public statutory duties does not create private rights and duties. Non-compliance with private contract duties does not create public rights for regulators or third parties (unless third party beneficiary laws apply).

The student contract should make it clear the institution only represents they are compliant with regulations regarding institution and program approvals so they can lawfully provide the program and claim that regulatory status. It should be clear this does not include representations about any specific degree or type of compliance with public statutes and that any non-compliance with those statutes has no contract significance. This is the law as it stands in most jurisdictions, but it is a good idea to use the contract to affirm it. Students often fail to understand the distinction. They may file complaints that have nothing to do with the contract and yet claim contract breach.

A BC example is a good illustration. A section of the statute allowed students to seek a tuition refund from an assurance fund. The Act empowered an agency to award a tuition refund if the institution had, in the opinion of the agency, misled the student about its operations. The agency's subordinate bylaws minimally referred to contracts and asked the student to state which provisions of the Act, regulations and bylaws had been violated. We successfully defended against student contract actions that tried to claim that bylaw violations vested private rights. With public duties the institution makes no representations to students and cannot be held to have misled them. The public duties are owed to government and not the student. Evidence of a breached public duty could be relevant to claims of contract breach or misrepresentation only if a similar term of contract existed.

Here is another example. In most jurisdictions, if a person flies on an airline under a contract with that airline and then finds out that the airline failed in a duty owed to a government transportation regulator that failure does not create a private duty and legal cause of action for the passenger.

In this BC case, there were two grounds to establish that the bylaws could not stand. First, there was the issue of jurisdiction. The statute only granted certain powers or jurisdiction. It stated that the statute can lead to and the agency can find civil liability, but that power is confined to the expressed words of the section that focused on the term "misled". Anything that tried to go beyond that was ultra vires the statute. The statute only provided limited scope to find civil liability i.e. to find that the student was misled by the institution about any aspect of the institution's operations.

Secondly, the case law was clear that no civil liability flows automatically from the violation of a statutory provision. The public agency was given no power to hold that civil liability flowed from the violation of its bylaws, the Act or regulation. That would have had to be expressed clearly. The court held in the key case that the breach of the statutory obligation did not create a civil cause of action. Here the BC agency tried to create a civil liability beyond what the Act provided for. The Act says the board can determine if a student was misled. If they were then civil liability can exist. The agency went beyond its jurisdiction and against Canadian law by holding that a violation of the Act, regulations or bylaws constitutes a case where a student is "misled". [75]

Regulation must address the risks associated with that contract, but that is not the same as enforcing the contract which only its parties can do. Non-compliance with public statutory duties does not create private rights and duties. Non-compliance with private contract duties does not create public rights for regulators or protected parties. The exceptions are few and far between.

Regulation vests or imposes rights and duties on regulatory and regulated parties (subjects). Third party objects may be protected by the law, but they (e.g. the student) have no direct rights vested in them that they can enforce. The rights of enforcement are held by the regulator. The contract vests rights and obligations in its parties and only they enforce the contract.

Regulation can mandate actions that may make contract compliance more likely. Without express power to do so it does not govern the Lis Inter Parties or disputes between contract parties. Any power to settle or rule on a dispute would have to be triggered by a contract party because a regulator could not force a party to enforce a contract against their will.

12.4 Regulators Do Not Enforce the Contract Unless Special Statutory Powers Exist

The government does not enforce the contract because only the parties can lawfully do that under privity of contract doctrines. Government could not force a contract party to take legal action. Regulation can mandate actions that may make contract compliance and performance more likely. Government may deem certain terms to be included or require that certain terms be included, but that power is limited without clear statutory mandates.

Regulators cannot in most cases declare that a party was in breach and if they had that power that would be the power to adjudicate a dispute or Lis Inter Parties and go beyond the normal regulatory power where an agency enforces and acts pursuant to statute to enforce that statute or its subordinate legislation. If regulators are tasked with some form of dispute resolution involving students and institutions they would be using the contract instrument and applicable contract laws (or other laws) to settle that dispute. They cannot re-invent these laws and must comply with them as the law of the land in order to avoid making errors of law that are judicially reviewable.

12.5 Governments Cannot Impose All Contract Terms, Corporate Objects or Business Plans

In most jurisdictions, governments cannot violate the parties' freedom of contract and impose detailed and substantive terms of contract unless they are expressly given that significant power by statute. They can often require that certain types of provisions be included, but it cannot dictate the entire content or form of the agreement. This was tried in BC, but in the face of strong opposition and several legal opinions it was withdrawn. They then presented a "recommended" contract which is followed by too many schools either because they feel intimidated or because they wrongly conclude that they are safe if they use it. The contract in fact creates problems for both parties because of what it says and more importantly what it fails to say.

Similarly, education regulators are not given the power to limit the objects of a private corporation. Most corporation laws today allow corporations, for profit or not for profit, to act as natural persons and to engage in any activity that a natural person can engage in or to set for themselves any objects they choose to be limited by. Natural persons can act and offer and provide products without restriction unless restricted by law. A university board of governors is limited jurisdictionally to the powers granted it by legislation or charter. For example, it often cannot take decisions without following the required consultation process.[76]

Many regulators seem to view themselves more as headmasters than commercial industry regulators. Others seem to think that they are the CEO of the company. It is not necessary to regulate the business's mission statement and general business plan as some have done. When a federal transportation regulator sits down with Air Canada or Delta Airlines they do not tell them that they must update their mission statement and goals or even require that they have them. It is none of the regulator's business and not necessary to protect the consumer from risk.

12.6 Registration, Accreditation, Prohibitions, Permissions (Must Be) Granted If Standards Are Met, Granted Rights Generally Not Assignable Property

Institutions are the targeted regulatory subject only because they offer products to consumers and because they are legal entities that can act to protect consumers, but it is what they do that matters and that creates risk for student consumers. If they do nothing there is no risk and no reason for regulation.

Registration or accreditation or similar terms have specific legal meanings, purposes and consequences that may vary by jurisdiction. As is the case with many regulated industries, education registration or accreditation may involve "permission" or a "license" to engage in an otherwise prohibited action such as offering a type of program or they may grant a right to claim a status as evidence of meeting set standards.

In some jurisdictions there is no real line between registration and accreditation. In others while registration leads to a right to operate and to overcome that operational prohibition, the accreditation process is voluntary. The institution can operate without accreditation status. If accreditation quality standards are met and accreditation is granted (it often must be granted if standards are met) the institution has the right to claim that quality assured status in relationships with and representations to students.

In BC, the features of career training (cost, duration, degree, vocational) offered and provided under contract to the student trigger the application of laws and the jurisdiction of agencies. [77] All three elements of a career training definition must apply before the program falls under the definition of career training and before the action is subject to the prohibition and the need for registration and consumer protection. The prohibition is a means of managing risk. Jurisdiction is triggered by the prohibition which is contractually focused and that jurisdiction gives the regulator the power to take steps to address specific risk.

In addressing risk, unlike contracts, regulation vests no private rights in the protected object of regulation (the student) and the regulations do not focus on specific transactions, but on classes of transactions.

With the BC (common elsewhere) example, a prohibition states that the person cannot [under contract] offer to provide or provide career training to students unless they register under the Act. The program must be provided or offered under contract because if there is no contract there is no legally enforceable promise or duty to provide it.

Registration removes the prohibition and constitutes a license or permission to engage in otherwise prohibited activities (like entering certain types of contracts) and that license and the specific registration do not involve or extend to activities that were never and are not prohibited. You can't be granted permission to do something that you were not prohibited from doing. The right to freedom of contract and to engage in non-prohibited activities never ceased to exist. Jurisdiction over the institution is confined to what it does and what falls within the purpose of the Act which is to protect students of only specific programs that carry the highest risk.

In many cases, again with the BC example, [78] registration and accreditation must be granted if standards are met. This follows the need for registration in the prohibition section that creates the platform for protection. Then statutes or subordinate regulations or bylaws kick in to set specific requirements for the granting or maintenance of registration or accreditation. Many jurisdictions use the words "must" or "shall" or other terms, but the legal effect is the same - the benefit must be granted if the standards are substantially met. The Act usually only allows for specific types of bylaws and primarily those relate to quality standards.

The choice is not really there for governments. To state that the government "may" grant approvals would give them the authority to override freedom of contract despite all criteria being met and all risks being addressed. This would be highly arbitrary, an unjustified limit on personal liberty and contrary to cherished legal and economic traditions. Charter or Rights or Bill of Rights issues could arise. This is especially true with education.

A slight variation is found in BC in the Degree Authorization Act (DAA), but the result is the same. The Minister "may" give consent if satisfied that an applicant has undergone a quality assessment process and met criteria that the Minister "must" establish. The word "may" is used with the consent, but the word "must" is used in relation to setting criteria. Normally this means they must adhere to the criteria that they must set. They can't just be constantly moving the goal posts. The interpretive assumption is that the legislature intended them to follow the criteria they must set. They do not have the discretion to ignore that mandated criteria. Any existing discretion still has to be exercised in accordance with the statutory purpose which is normally consumer protection.

Permissions or rights granted under statute generally do not carry with them and form of assignable property rights. Certain elements of property ownership (a bundle of rights) may apply, but such application is limited. Comparisons to the ability to assign contract rights (a species of property) are limited. Certain public permissions or licenses can be bought and sold in the absence of prohibitions, but new holders often still have to meet legal requirements and be approved. The key is to understand that a registration, accreditation or program approval cannot just be bought and sold like other property assets. The regulatory scheme they are granted pursuant to is the key alongside the general principles of administrative law.

12.7 Program Approvals (Must Be) Granted, Condition Precedent to Student Contract and Not A Declaration by Regulators of Content Suitability for Workplace Markets or Any Purpose

The student contract should state that the institution represents and warrants that they have program approvals at the time of execution of and that the approvals are a condition precedent to the student contract. This would overcome any possible ambiguity about non-approvals not nullifying capacity and would mean that an absence of approvals could result in the contract being nullified. The contract should stipulate that this is only if the institution was aware of any non-approval when they entered the contract. The lack of approval may tarnish the credibility of a credential awarded.

One US case [79] in part held against a student because the court held that the student was not sufficiently aggrieved by paying tuition to receive instruction in an unaccredited program and no remedy was given. The focus there was more on a state consumer protection statute and the court held there was no real reliance by the student on the program accreditation element.

This is needed because in addition to being legally able to enter into contracts generally the institution must be able to legally provide a certain type of product under a specific contract with a student. For example, in BC Canada, the law requires that to enter into contracts under which specified types of training are provided the institution must have institution and program approvals. This suggests that without it the party is non-compliant with the law and an arguably an expressed or implied term of the contract. Approval is never a declaration by government about the quality of the content or its ability to achieve any specific result in the workplace or other forums. It is a declaration that the institution can legally offer it.

In jurisdictions like BC (and Ontario) where registration and accreditation must be granted when set standards are substantially met it follows that individual programs that must also be approved as part of general quality standards requirements must (if laws are vague) also be granted if set criteria are substantially met. The impact of the word "must" and the right to registration or accreditation mean nothing if a regulator can disapprove of programs for reasons not related to quality and protecting a student consumer from consumption risk.

Registration and accreditation relate directly to the provision of "programs" because they revolve around the prohibition section which relates to the provision of training—a prohibition that "must" be lifted if quality standards are substantially met. Institutions are the targeted regulatory subject because they are legal entities that can act to protect consumers, but it is what they do that matters and that creates risk for student consumers.

Regulators generally do not and should not dictate program content, but they do often have requirements for program approval. They can rightly require that some form of expert advisory council help develop a program curriculum. The standard is not set normally to determine good or bad in terms of market need or other factors and regulators normally are not out to approve or disapprove it, but to establish a standard to ensure that the school will have a systematic guide for delivery.

12.8 Contract Period of Consumption and Regulator Jurisdiction

The length of a program is often a key element of the product itself and not an element of quality. Given that regulator jurisdiction over an institution arises from the need to protect a class of consumer from risks associated with a type of transaction and contract it follows logically that the regulator's jurisdiction over that class of institution and student relationship is limited by the contract period of consumption. Like the contract, that jurisdiction and power over specific parties has a beginning and an end and the end is the end of the contract.

That regulatory trigger does not give and the regulator does not have the mandate or obligation to protect past students for an indeterminate period of time in the period following the student contract period of consumption. No consumption risks exist and the regulator is not tasked with protecting these persons or class of persons from every conceivable type of economic and social risk that lies beyond the contract period of consumption.

12.9 Regulatory Best Practices and Smart Regulation

The three core functions of government are often said to be to: address conflicts and create and maintain or restore an order or equilibrium (a norm); provide public goods; and promote equality. The order sought and achieved must reflect set ideas and values, legitimately different views and political compromise and balance.

The terms Regulatory Best Practices or Smart Regulation are used in many contexts and come from numerous sources. [80] Some principles are legal in nature and others are based on ethical ideas or ideas of balance and fairness.

Smart regulation should: be innovative and open to and adaptive to change; be fair ; balance diverse interests; promote fair, effective, efficient, intelligent and competitive markets; reduce administrative burdens for regulated parties and regulators; use effective and balanced enforcement tools; be based on comprehensive and expert knowledge of what is regulated; be fair, impartial, predictable and clear; and be transparent, accessible and evidence based.

Smart regulation minimizes the risks of regulations and only addresses real, primary and serious risk. President Obama said: "We should have no more regulation than the health, safety and security of the American people requires". [81] Principles often state that policy should be consistent within and between departments, governments and across domestic and international jurisdictions. This avoids needless fragmentation and the costly tyranny of small differences. Regulation must, of course, adhere to the rules of administrative law.

12.10 Quality Standards, Meaning of Quality and Meaning of Standards

If a regulator is given the ability to set and enforce quality standards under a statute then the focus should be on the quality promised under the contract or perhaps set certain minimum standards. It should not dictate the bargain or the quality that the parties are prepared to bargain for given the price negotiated.

Education regulation often revolves around the term "quality standards". The concept of "quality" is addressed separately, but in summary it must relate to whether the product is merchantable, that is, whether it does what it was promised to do and with education that would be to help the student achieve a learning objective.

A standard is a threshold set or accepted by authorities (law makers, contract parties, managers setting policy) that, when met, establishes that a person, thing or action has qualities or features that make it suitable or appropriate for them to be awarded certain rights of action or class description. Qualities or features may relate to: risks mitigated if standards are met; the qualifications, fitness or capacity to perform a task; a quality or quantity of a tangible or intangible thing; or a certain inherent nature. In terms of prohibitions and permissions, it means suitable or appropriate to perform an action that is otherwise prohibited.

Standards (whether legally required or optional) must be distinguished from measures of standards compliance and certainty must exist. The benefit can relate to being able to act and perform otherwise prohibited actions. Adherence to a standard can be judged or measured through tests, rules, criterion, principles, models, examples or comparisons. The adherence method or measure is not the standard. For example, an employment rate might be a minimally important (we argue it is often irrelevant and not causal in nature) way to "measure" program quality, but it cannot be a definite legal standard for finding quality because that would mean that quality goes up as economies and unemployment rates fluctuate.

Technical violations of standards should not carry penalty risks if the real risk or loss is minimal. The penalty should fit the crime. Deminimis rules apply to contracts and in regulatory contexts depending on statutory provisions.

The standard requires behaviors that lower the targeted risks of protected (objects) persons. Performance that meets standards minimizes risk. The agency has no authority to set standards beyond what is required to address risk. Tribunals can generally not erect new prohibitions. If an agency demands something that is impossible to achieve that is not a standard. It is a new prohibition and even if they had the power to create new prohibitions (rare) they would not do it in the guise of a standard and those too would have to address risks targeted by the governing statute. A requirement that you achieve an industry average rate of employment or a set income rate for students would be an example (real life examples). It is impossible to do and not a standard.

Another example relates to debates surrounding the term "employability". The appropriate use of the term relates to being ready to work because the program, as promised, helped the student achieve a learning objective. In BC career training is defined in terms of cost and time and as instruction in the skill and knowledge "required" for employment. In the US the federal Higher Education Act and Title IV regulations refer to "preparing" a person for work. Quality education then would be that which helps a student become "employable" because they are "prepared for" or have the skills and knowledge required for employment. Employability is a valid legal standard. Having to be employed is not a valid legal standard because it is not something the regulated party can control or achieve.

If an agency has authority or discretion to allow a party to act and overcome a prohibition if standards are met and then it says they cannot do that it acts outside its authority because it created a new prohibition it had no authority to create. This would fetter discretion and fail to give the individual circumstance its due weight. If a tribunal rests the conferral of a privilege on a criterion of achievement the question is whether the statute permits that condition and it often will not. If it is ambiguous, the ambiguity should be resolved in favour of the regulated party if the criterion of achievement is not within their control because the legislature would not intend to rest the conferral of the privilege on matters outside their control. If the criterion is outside their control and even impossible to achieve the criterion looks like an absolution prohibition that the tribunal generally cannot create.

As a final note, a standard can also be viewed as a requirement set by law or consensus so that isolated systems can communicate and interact effectively. A legal or other standard could require that jurisdictions make some standards uniform with those in other jurisdictions. Uniformity issues are addressed in other sections. Uniform operational standards are often acceptable, but governments should not dictate content. Quality does not mean uniformity. Private parties can and often negotiate uniform content and credential systems.

12.11 Separate Regulatory Regimes and Different Statutes, Mandates, Purposes, Rights and Duties

In the same way it is important to keep different contracts separate and contracts separate from public instruments it is also important to keep the public bodies, roles and relationships involved with different and separate regulatory regimes separate from each other. Separation is needed because each has its own set of purposes, objectives or targeted risks. Education quality assurance systems are separate from public student loan systems, quality assurance designations or immigration and border control systems. Violation under one regime is not automatically violation of a related regime. Any public action must be grounded in law and questioned in terms of what law it is taken pursuant to.

Lenders and work permit grantors naturally want to lend to and grant permits to the students of "quality assured' institutions, but their criteria must relate to other factors (Quality Assurance Plus) because product quality concepts cannot encompass the kinds of criteria needed to address every kind of lending, immigration, border control or other risk. This has become an issue in BC and other jurisdictions and the concept of quality becomes distorted. It must stay focused on what is necessary to protect student consumer rights and expectations.

Each regulator or public authority must distinguish what they are tasked to do from what others are tasked to do in terms of risks, regulated parties and non-regulated, but protected parties, objects or beneficiaries of regulation. It must be clear what risks exist, what standards and duties exist to address that risk, who owes the duty and who the duty is owed to.

13

Administrative Law and Legal Constraints on Regulators

13.1 Constitutional Law, Lawmaking and the Delegation of Powers

This is a very cursory look at complex law, but it is relevant and important context for any discussion about how commercial sectors are regulated and how that regulation relates to commercial and contract realities. As noted, regulation is often triggered by features of contracts with certain regulations targeted at specific contract risks. Other sections establish how volitional contract instruments, governed by the law of contract, and regulation targeted at contract parties and relationships operate separately, but often for common purposes. Administrative law makes sure that public actors comply with the law.

Constitutional law comprises the rules for determining which public authorities have the right to make laws for the governing of a society. These public authorities include constitutionally empowered legislatures, parliaments and houses of congress. Constitutionally empowered lawmaking authorities can then pass legislation that delegates some of that legislative power to subordinate agencies of government. They cannot delegate all of or abdicate their legislative power. These subordinate laws made by subordinate agencies may be called regulations, bylaws or policies or given other labels, but the name does not matter. The awarded power must be exercised properly.

13.2 Administrative Law, Courts and Judicial Review, Anomalous Use of Judicial Review in Education Sector

Administrative law ties in with regulation because regulators, as parties with delegated powers, must act within the confines of their governing statute and with the common law (or statutory) principles of administrative law.

The contract is a volitional instrument created by the parties to help them govern their relationship. A regulatory statute for the education sector or any other sector is normally targeted at specific parties or subjects and attempts to modify behaviour that can mitigate risks to and protect benefitting objects or parties (students).

Administrative law is not substantive in this sense. It is not regulatory law. It has more to do with ensuring that regulatory bodies behave in a certain way. It is not about enforcing laws that govern regulated parties, but about the enforcement of legal rules that apply to those that make and enforce laws via powers delegated to them by law.

Again, administrative law deals with the actions of administrators to whom legislative, adjudicative or executive and administrative powers have been granted (delegated) by laws which have been validly enacted under the constitution.

It deals with legal limitations on the actions of government officials exercising powers delegated by statute and impacting on a person's legal and economic interests. Administrative law deals with the remedies available to those affected by transgressions of these limits. In general, courts can quash decisions or order their reconsideration, but they cannot substitute the tribunal's actions and decisions with judicial actions or decisions because they cannot exercise rights only granted to the delegate tribunal.

Delegated powers may include the power, as specifically delegated by statute, to make subordinate law that is as binding as statutory law, to administer (execute) law and to adjudicate, that is, set policy and render decisions with consequences for individuals on the basis of preset policy and law. All of these functions are now subject to judicial review in Canada. The law of other jurisdictions has not been researched in depth on this point.

Courts may be created constitutionally or by statute (varies by jurisdiction). Common law systems, with their principles and rules regarding courts adhering to precedent set by certain other courts, effectively give courts the ability to make binding laws. Courts cannot delegate their powers. Courts can review the actions of primary lawmakers under constitutional provisions (e.g. Canadian Charter) and the actions of their delegates under administrative law principles.

Judicial review in the education context has an added complexity. Normally, judicial review under the principles of administrative law deal with parties that are given the power to make laws in relation to regulated parties. Because of the unique role of the traditional academy and education institutions it was often the case that courts would review decisions of institutions as they would regulators under administrative law rules rather than under the law of contract. Arguments in favor of ending that practice are explored in other sections on the historical anomaly of judicial review for institutions.

13.3 Grounds for Judicial Review of Delegated Powers, Jurisdiction Exceeded, Unreasonable Exercise of Discretion, Bias, Errors of Law, Lack of Procedural Fairness

Grounds for the review of decisions and actions of a body given delegated powers by a constitutionally empowered legislative body could exist if: granted powers were exceeded; if granted discretion was exercised unreasonably; if procedures were unfair; the agency was biased or could be perceived to be biased (a form of unfairness); or if the agency made an error of law. Examples of all of these are given in other sections.

The common law (case law or judge-made law) tends to favour individual rights and freedoms when they conflict with state interests. British common law said the King and his officials had no powers other than those granted by law. The law included royal prerogatives and statute law, but the courts successfully asserted the power to determine the existence and extent of the prerogative power.

Another way of saying that delegates must act within their jurisdiction (granted or delegated powers) is to state that, with few exceptions, actions which infringe the liberty of the subject require the authority of a statute. Every official act must be justified by law. If an official acts outside statutory authority they enjoy no more powers than a private individual.

When it is said that delegates cannot make errors of law that means that if the exercise of their statutory powers involves the consideration and application of other laws they must adhere to the law of the land. They cannot remake the law. The law is a unified whole and does not mean one thing in court and another thing at a tribunal.

Procedural fairness rules deal (not in all jurisdictions) with matters like: notices regarding the nature of proceedings; pre-hearing disclosures of evidence to be used to prove allegations; the opportunity of the alleged wrongdoer to present a case and to respond to the case made against them; the right to counsel; the right to interpretation; legitimate expectations regarding procedures; lack of bias; institutional (decision maker) independence and impartiality; unreasonable delays; those hearing a case having to decide it; reasons for decision having to be given.

13.4 Discretion

Abuses of discretion are just one of the grounds for review noted above, but the topic warrants special attention because it is commonly misunderstood. When the actions of regulators are questioned, it is common for them to say that they have "discretion" to do what they did. This is sometimes the case, but it is common for them to overestimate their discretion and to confuse discretion with some kind of unlimited and arbitrary power.

Discretionary powers are different from clearly and expressly delegated powers. They exist if they are necessary to carry out the purpose of the statute and granted powers. Too many regulators confuse the concept of discretion with arbitrary and unlimited power which does not exist in our systems of law and government because of our focus on the rule of law.

In Canada, these limits on discretion are set out in the Roncarelli case that [82] made it clear that agencies must act in good faith and carry out the law according to its intent and purpose. That case made it clear that in public regulation no Act can, without express language, be taken to contemplate an unlimited power. It said discretion implies good faith in discharging public duty and that requires administration in accord with the statute and its line and objects. The Act must be interpreted, applied and administered in accordance with the purposes and intent of the Act. One common way to view discretion is as the power to make a decision that can't be determined to be right or wrong or perhaps that can't be seen as being in violation of some rule or outside a set reference point.

When discretion is involved you must also consider the possible ways that discretion can be abused. A finding that an abuse of discretion occurred can mean that the exercise was unreasonable and that jurisdiction was exceeded. It can't be that a legislative body would delegate the power to abuse discretion.

Common types of abuse of discretion are discretion exercised: with an improper intention, unauthorized purpose, in bad faith (dishonesty, fraud and malice) or on irrelevant considerations; on the basis of inadequate material, including where there is no evidence or without considering relevant matters (or giving unreasonable weight to one factor over others); where there is an improper result, including unreasonable, discriminatory, retroactive or uncertain administrative actions; on an erroneous view of the law (not the same as errors of law; by adopting a policy which fetters an agency's ability to exercise its discretion (adopts inflexible policy) and to consider individual cases with an open mind. Relevance is governed by the governing statutory framework. If criteria exist and must be followed, but they still have discretion to consider other factors that can override the more set criteria then all factors must be consistent with law and policy.

14

Future Markets, Diverse Providers and Products, Disruptive Innovation, Disintermediation, Demassification, Less Scarcity, Global Markets and the Pursuit of Education Ideals

14.1 The Pursuit of Ideals and Solutions to Problems Depend on Innovative and More Diverse Education Providers and Products

The preceding sections set out core ideas about systems thinking, outcomes and products. This was done because of what is a common lack of legal and commercial discipline about how these terms are used in the education sector context. The following points set out just a few of the ways that disruptive innovation is impacting education markets, products, contracts and regulation.

The successful pursuit of education ideals depends on innovation. Problems of access and equity, education cost and affordability, student debt, constrained public finances, lifelong learning, economic development, worker shortages and greater education and business or workplace integration can all be substantially addressed by innovative and more diverse education providers and new education, assessment and other service products. The way these products are assembled and provided is open to great change and students can drive that change if they embrace their consumer and market power. Unions are normally formed by service providers and not consumers. Students could form new kinds of consumer groups to influence product development and public policy.

14.2 Diverse Education Providers - Public and Private, For Profit and Not For Profit - Integrated At Market, Contract, Contract Law, Medium of Communication, Learner and Regulation Levels

There are only slight and illusory differences in legal terms between so-called public (private—non-government—government funded) institutions and private institutions and the two are unified at various levels making erratic and unequal treatment at the legal and regulatory level untenable. On the private side there are distinctions between for profit and not for profit institutions, but at the student level these differences generally mean little.

All modern institutions, public or private, for profit and not for profit, are unified at the market and legal level through the mechanism and application of contracts and applicable contract law and other laws. No one can argue that student or provider rights can reasonably, justifiably or practically vary under the law because of differences in corporate structure. The applicability of contract law and other laws, statutory and common law, is not going to vary because of slight differences in how and why institutions were structured corporately and legally.

They are unified at the media level because the learner accesses both onsite through similar means and now often through common technology and media. They are unified at the level of the learner because it is the same learner that interacts with them and that experience of learner and provider product (learning environment) does not vary just because of corporate structure. Often the same factor inputs are assembled—just by different entities. If they did not know most learners would not know or care. Most students give these matters no attention and often they should not. The term public means different things legally and culturally in different countries.

Education regulation should be targeted at education products and consumption risk. Regulation operates separately from, but alongside contract law to ensure students receive what was promised to them and that products satisfy legal standards focused on mitigating consumer risk. Students in all sectors should have the same protections and different regulations can only be justified where risks differ. No group of institutions should be elevated beyond the same standards and given elitist special privileges unless that is justified on the facts. Regulations and contracts operate separately because parties to the regulatory relationship are the institution and public agency while the parties to the student and institution contract relationship are only those two parties. The rights and duties of the parties are distinct, but they target a common relationship and risk set in most instances.

14.3 Institutions Are Aggregators and Intermediaries and Subject to Disintermediation, Trends From Similar Innovated Industries to Greater Numbers of Diverse Suppliers Is Arising In Education

Earlier sections distinguished education from other media content industries, but nevertheless education still is a form of media content industry. It has always used and reflected information and knowledge resources and used print and multi-media channels. Now and into the future, digital technologies and the Internet are becoming the primary platform and dashboard for accessing education content and systems. Physical spaces are common to all.

If education follows the trend of other dis-intermediating and demassifying media content industries - and there is every indication it will—the reality of the future will feature greater numbers of education providers because of demand and the ability to provide supply. Traditional institutions may remain dominant because of brand and market position, but more providers will be players either in competition or in collaboration with them.

These providers will not just be like traditional institutions. They may provide individual parts of the broader product offering—individually or with other service providers - directly to consumers that assemble the parts as they find necessary. As noted, the entire contract offering of an institution to a student involves the education product (a collection of input factors that creates an effective learning environment), the assessment product and then finally the other services and benefits promised.

Institutions pull together, intermediate or aggregate (for a student) various input elements (faculty, curricula, equipment, real estate, assessment systems) to create that learning environment where a student can learn and achieve a state of knowledge or learning outcome objective. What can be pulled together can be pulled apart and re-assembled or offered independently and that is what disintermediation or disaggregation is about. The process (along with lower technology costs that facilitate dive… …olutionized recording, movies, publishing and… …ucation is already in the early stages of…

…ne ability of a supplier (musician or … or student) to jump around interme… …itution) and to contact their sought after …t they offer directly.

…emand, changing views of traditional au… …ve this. Greater information access and com… … possible with technology flatten hierarchies …d dispersed players. They remove boundaries. …uppliers can jump around traditional intermedi… …ovide what others supply and demand respectively. …ave to be cost effective, more than the sum of the …t all the parts are needed and wanted. [83]

… about consumer demand. Just like independent film mak… …ans now go around traditional intermediaries and deal directly wit… …eir consumers in markets, certain education input factors or those that control them (faculty, curricula providers, reference publishers or assessment and credential systems) can seek out buyers on their own. They have the right to commercialize their knowledge and service. Universities can't claim how great their grads are (and they are) and then suggest that they don't have the ability or right to teach in private institutions or to deal directly with student consumers without institutional intermediation, public or private.

Like automobiles and other products that are now assembled in different parts of the world from parts around the world, education elements are already being assembled in the same way and not just in one spot although the traditional institution will prevail if it can continue to be more than the sum of its parts. An institution can break out input elements and sell them individually, but that is different from disintermediation. They are just choosing to sell individual elements instead of the entire package.

If and when these processes become well branded, credible, market recognized and lower priced (because input costs may drop or not all consumed) the major changes will be hard to stop. Universities continue to draw students because of the brand and the perception that the degree credential is all important, but it is not because it is not possible to attain similar levels of knowledge in other ways. [84]

If knowledge holders approach students on their own without institutional intermediation then that relationship changes fundamentally. Faculty or staff members do not normally contract with students. They contract with and are legally responsible only to their employer institution. Employing institutions are vicariously liable for the actions of their faculty and staff. If an instructor works as an independent (non-employment) contractor they still do not contract with the student, but their duties to the party hiring them are different than they were for employees. Only in rare cases would a teacher be liable in tort or contract to students. This changes if they contract directly with the student because of disintermediation.

14.4 Demassification, Production and Delivery Diversity

The mass audience is no longer the key to everything. Mass media could bring one product to millions efficiently. It could not bring a million shows to one person when that one person wants them. Modern systems can and the same is true with education. Hits now compete with niche markets of any size. The era of one size fits all is ending and in its place is a market of multitudes and a multitude of markets.[85] Niches always exist, but the cost of reaching the niche has fallen. Niches are a force. Underlying all of these elements is a move to greater openness. [86] This relates to earlier points about monopolies and their breakdown.

Demassification is different from disintermediation although there are linkages. There was a time when everyone only had a few TV channels and a few programs to watch. They had one or two newspapers and magazines to read. Options were limited. Technological change allowed greater producer, production, product and delivery system diversity. Increased numbers of providers were enabled to reach smaller and more specialized markets not via disintermediation, but because of access to new and affordable technology. Specialty TV channels, demographic targeted radio stations, independent film makers and interest focused magazines (physical and virtual) dot the landscape and serve dedicated niche markets with customized content.

With past education systems, a few institutions offered a few programs because knowledge was not as vast. Specializations within disciplines and sub-sets within those specializations are now common. Many university Presidents freely admit that they cannot do and be everything. [87] There are debates within university circles with regard to the role of different types of institutions so that duplications are avoided and areas of expertise can be developed. Within every vocational or professional group it is necessary for post-grad institution work, professional organization professional development programs and ongoing corporate training to address the fine points of knowledge needed for practical work. It is commonly said that what we learn in first year may be outdated by fourth year and fourth year topics may be outdated by the time the person hits the office. In some cases diversity can be encompassed within existing institutions, but in many cases it cannot because of available expertise and funding.

14.5 Institutions Aggregate Programs, Disciplines and Small Groups

Traditional education institutions aggregate production factors and create contract products or learning environments for students and they also aggregate or bring together various schools or disciplines. It is a collection of schools and student cohorts and often these cohorts are small.

This collection of disciplines can be a good thing because students are able, within a confined space, to access and experiment with a range of disciplines and help them have a rounded education, but often they specialize quickly and that benefit is not realized. It can also make the institution hard to manage. [88] Often individual faculties or departments march to their own beat and not that of central institution executives. [89]

This reality is relevant to the overall point about the need for and the ability to dis-intermediate and diversify and change how education is done and who does it. Large institutions are not going to die, but they may not be quite as large and diverse because (again it bears repeating) traditional institutions cannot do everything they are asked to do by governments and students. [90]

14.6 Scarce Program Positions, Diverse Supply Needed, Demand Hard to Predict, Opponents of Diverse Providers and Trade Accept Limited Positions and Limited Opportunity For Those Not Admitted

Traditional economics was largely about managing scarce resources in the face of often unlimited needs and wants and deciding what commodities were to be produced and in what quantity. The refrain was what, how and for whom? Scarcity is still a reality in many areas and sectors and in others there is much less scarcity. The discussion must focus on the specific object that is either scarce or not. For example:

1. There are more knowledgeable people around inside and outside of academia that can help learners move toward a desired state of knowledge. They should be encouraged to do so and the learning should be validated and transferrable. Despite some traditional thinkers that insist most instructors should be full-time it is increasingly possible for persons active in the world to actively teach at the same time.
2. This does not necessarily mean that all potential teachers and mentors are world class academics and researchers, but those persons are not always necessary and to the extent those world class academics are scarce they can expand their reach through technology and reach more people. Again that learning, whether it occurs within traditional institutions or not should be validated.
3. Buildings may be scarce on campus, but a modern institution has to be more than one address.
4. Computers may be scarce if you think about traditional computer labs, but increasingly these are not necessary as more schools buy computers for their students or "BYOD" prevails (Bring your own device).
5. Bandwidth is no longer scarce and this is having an impact on education. It allows not just for content delivery, but for teacher-student interaction, student to student interaction and for dispersed third party assessment and evaluation systems.
6. Public funds are scarce and that forces difficult supply decisions as they relate to resulting scarcity with programs and positions in programs or other services, but private funds may be available and that supply can be provided by others willing to do so if the prevailing business, financial and market constraints can be met. Tight finances and price points force innovation at the product and price level.
7. Profits may be scarce or hard to come by, but social businesses and investors may be willing to provide services with nominal or no returns beyond initial investments.

8. Time is always scarce and working women and men are often at the forefront of education change because they want and need flexibility in order to balance work, studies and family. Local programs may not be available in the same way local work may not be available while distance programs and work are available. [91]

Admissions officers can only admit someone if there is an available position. This is particularly the case with onsite classes where there are only so many "seats", but even some online and distance learning systems have constraints because unlimited numbers of students are hard to serve. Technology can change that to some extent.

This constraint becomes less of a factor if only certain elements of the "product" are offered. If instruction is all that is offered and it can be offered online then the sky may be the limit as evidenced by the Stanford Computer Science Prof that quit his job to teach courses online to hundreds of thousands of people at one time (at least that was his hope).

In many cases, however, even if a student is qualified for admission they cannot be admitted if the number of applicants exceeds the number of available positions. This is a major gateway obstacle and one that we cite repeatedly as a reason to allow diverse providers. This can be a factor with professional schools and any program where demand exceeds supply. Available positions and funding, public or private, can result in gateway doors being slammed in the faces of persons that are qualified, that could succeed in the program and that could compete for and win opportunities in the real world. Funders and admissions officers should not have the power of God over applicant futures. They must live within the restrictions they have, but the system as a whole must create other opportunities for those applicants if they decide to continue in pursuit of their goal. That decision to continue should be a properly informed one.

There are persons and groups (not surprisingly they tend to represent or work with current dominant institutions) that oppose education trade (See that section) and the prospect of open markets that feature diverse education providers limited only by the requirement to meet common quality standards. The same parties tend to also believe that programs and especially professional and graduate programs should limit the number of seats to the number that governments, professional organizations or institutions determine are needed to "stock" the workplace. [92]

There are two obvious problems with this. First, it is hard to predict short term workplace and business needs let alone longer term needs. As outlined in other sections, many governments have commissioned reports that tell them exactly that. As a result, governments usually get predictions wrong resulting in shortages or surpluses. The other problem is that even if they got it right it would be those that make admissions decisions that would have the power of God to decide who had a chance to compete for those scarce positions. Other sections argue that informed buyers and sellers should make those decisions and all persons should have a chance to enter programs that give the opportunity to compete for future opportunities. Decisions are more intelligently made when they are decentralized and made by more informed persons. The market will decide who succeeds and not gateway minders.

It is hard to understand how these parties can claim that they seek social equity (as many do) and also claim that persons should not have the right to voluntarily enter commercial contracts with parties of their choice to enhance opportunities. Positions in institutions and programs are often limited and without other options those unable to access institutions and scarce programs or positions have to go without. How does that enhance social equity?

14.7 New Producers—Large, Small, Private, Public, Foreign, Domestic, Institutions and Non-Institutions - Must Be Free to Provide Programs and Serve Learners

As more persons produce and deliver quality education products there must be better regulation and better management of them to make sure they are not needlessly blocked or restricted unless that can be justified because of specific consumer and consumption risks.

The borderless Internet and other digital technologies will continue to put pressure on traditional systems for creating, marketing and delivering education program content. Like Video On Demand on TV (VOD) there is often no need to wait for a course to be offered at the discretion of a specific institution at a specific place and time. People can just order it online and have it now. The same can be true for all product input factors and assessment and service systems.

The Web, as a means of digital content delivery, has a relatively low cost of entry and new digital technologies have also made content production costs lower. Distribution is now a commodity. There have never been as many potential ways to distribute content. There are over-the-air broadcasters, cable broadcasts, specialty cable channels, satellite systems, direct broadcast satellites, phone systems, wireless cable systems, video tapes, DVDs and the Internet.

These producers do not have to be or look like traditional "institutions" that are aggregators and intermediaries and they do not have to be regulated in the same way. They could include a law firm, an accountant, an engineer or a corporation that has expertise. Anywhere and any environment where knowledgeable people exist and where knowledge can be found can be a form of producer. The assessment element does not have to be wrapped up with the production of content.

Private sector options can be expanded. It is already actively involved with K to 12, vocational training, degree and post grad training, professional development, corporate training and professional designation systems that rely often on trademarked designations. Corporations like Microsoft, Cisco, Novell and many others set requirements for training, often provide materials and courses themselves and allow others to teach to their standards and toward a corporately awarded designation. Many industry associations do the same and many such corporate and industry credentials are influential with employers. In Canada, actuaries [93] and many other groups (including health care workers) studying at various public and private institutions can write a common exam.

Size does not matter. Small providers can provide perfectly good education. Most providers start small. Large institutions are collections of small groups. Research also shows in Canada that small colleges have better satisfaction ratings than larger institutions. [94]

Again, credible and possibly regulated third party assessment and credential evaluation systems can be used to validate new kinds of training. If governments can regulate and accredit institutions there is no reason why they cannot do the same for individual elements or functions of institutions like assessment and credential evaluation.

14.8 Constrained Public Funding, New Technology and Social Change Force Supply Side Innovation

This need for diverse providers relates to, but is not just about constrained public finances. Just because public money is scarce does not mean that the demand is less. Stories abound about how governments in the US, Canada and the UK are being forced to cut back or drastically reconfigure their program offerings because of constrained public funding. [95] In Ontario, Canada, economist Don Drummond [96] presented the government of Ontario, at its request, with a report about the province's economic and fiscal challenges. He said the fiscal response must reform the way the government delivers virtually every service and education did not escape his attention.

Most jurisdictions are facing similar pressures. The solution can no longer be seen as just pouring more taxpayer money into the top of the funnel so that public (as we understand that term) institutions can expand to meet all of the needs. The reality is that they can't even come close to meeting all projected needs.

The trend at universities over the past decade has been to pack in as many students as possible, but in some cases enrollments are now being reduced or growth is being restricted.[97] In some cases, higher priced graduate programs are being maintained while undergrad programs are being cut. To the chagrin of many, business and computer science may take precedence over humanities because of perceived workplace opportunities even though demand is strong for the axed program. [98]

Technology, innovative supply and program systems and increased private sector investment can help fill that gap and even without public sector funding issues these solutions must be allowed to play their role in building capacity on a level playing field that is not weighted toward public (government funded or as otherwise defined) institutions. Profit for many businesses is important, but increasingly private firms do have social objectives and are prepared to limit returns for the sake of achieving those objectives. [99] Too many assume that money is the only thing driving private business and that includes private education. There is also nothing wrong with profit or the pursuit of it.

14.9 Customized and Commoditized Products, Information Engineers and Providers, Professional or Institutional Delivery

Again, some education providers won't look like old style institutions. Richard Susskind articulates how technology is impacting the legal profession, [100] but his observations and predictions relate to education also. He sees information systems or markets as a left to right continuum. With law, legislation and case law, usually free for the reading as primary sources of law, are at the left. Then come journals, raw legal data, text commentaries, information services or agreement precedents. At the far right you have specialized legal practitioners providing advisory and legal project services at high rates on a one to one basis where each product is a new product.

With education you can have public domain information or non-structured sources of information at the left. As you move right you have increasingly structured, specialized or privately controlled texts and information. Further to the right come academics, professionals or knowledge workers that provide at first more generalized and then increasingly more customized education products to large or small groups or individuals.

For education or legal services you have, from left to right, more value added analysis, more work and information engineering, a more customized, structured and usable product for a consumer and more liability for the information provider that applies more input themselves at a higher cost. The key is to access the higher levels of expertise at the right without having to pay the high associated costs. Designed information services and products can function along the right side and be utilized, recycled or reused by many clients. If every consumer goes to a provider at the right side the cost to individuals and the economy would be unacceptably high.

Information engineers in education (writers, academics, professionals) served institutions (aggregators and intermediaries) with special products through the medium of information providers (publishers). The writer of a text was not generally the instructor for the class. Information engineers and providers were traditionally distinct. New technologies allow information engineers and new kinds of publishers to move along this continuum from left to right—often in competition with each other - and provide direct services to consumers at rates below what traditional service providers would charge.

The ability to identify and gather together individuals with common needs for the purposes of delivering targeted group services means these individual services at the right of the continuum can become group services. In addition, technologies allow diverse products to be produced for and delivered to individuals and small groups more easily and can to some extent undermine the point that the far right is always a source of higher cost.

A related phenomenon is illustrated with a Harvard example.

Exasperated by increasing subscription fees charged by academic publishers, Harvard University now encourages faculty to make their research freely available through open-access journals and to resign from periodicals that keep articles behind pay walls. Harvard says it can no longer afford the price increases imposed by publishers. [101]

One simple example to illustrate these points would be to have an information engineer, publisher or institution all directly making information available directly online with distance learning formats and software combined with non-institutional instruction, mentorship and assessment systems.

For the foreseeable future, information will always come from people and require people to interpret and apply it. These engineers and providers will often not provide one on one or one to group advisory work, but information products may be customized. That one on one or one to multi-point work will still be necessary in many cases because information products can't address all circumstances or anticipate all situations or exceptions. Machines will not develop moral judgment, natural language capabilities, common sense or high level reasoning abilities any time soon. Education at a high level still requires that. The question is where the line is. Where it is necessary it should be paid for and where it is not that cost should be avoided.

14.10 Case Studies: MIT Open Resources, Major US Universities and Massively Open Online Learning, Minerva, Outsourced TAs, Stanford Prof Steps Out to Serve Students Directly,

Introduction

These examples raise questions. If credible online or innovative courses cost less (not a given) they may result in a different credential so there is a distinction from programs costing more even if knowledge gained is the same. What do institutions offer for higher fees? If course content is freely available (curricula, recorded lectures, texts), what do students pay for - interactions with faculty and students, well branded credential (not a purchased contract product, but value perceptions can exist)? Why pay high fees for a poor lecture if you can watch world experts online?

MIT and Harvard Open Resources

MIT and Harvard have both put much of their curricula, instructional materials and notes online for all to see and access (ocw.mit.edu or edX). Many other institutions are following suit. A student could access these materials, but normally that would not result in a recognized credential. It now offers related courses online that could result in a certificate. There is nothing to a stop a person from approaching a third party assessment firm to assess the student's state of knowledge gained in this way. If a student wants international exposure then a local college is hard put to compete with MIT. There are already a number of outsourced teaching assistant firms to help these students and students at institutions (e.g. Instructional Connections).

Major US Universities, Innovative Assessment and Massively Open Online Courses

Princeton University, the University of Pennsylvania, and the University of Michigan, Stanford, UC Berkeley and other top-tier US universities are embracing massively open online courses as the logical extension of elite PSE in an increasingly online, international landscape. They join others as partners of Coursera, a company founded by Stanford engineering professors and buoyed by $16 million in venture capital.

Using Coursera's platform, the institutions develop free online versions of their courses that anyone can take. The courses will be interactive, with potentially hundreds of students completing exams and assigned work that will be marked by intelligent software or their peers. The universities will not offer formal credit through Coursera courses, but some might give students the chance to earn certificates bearing the names of both the institutions and the company. There is no formal credential, but some university officials indicate that tangible recognition of non-enrolled learner achievement is a goal. Third party assessment systems could play a role in that. [102] Digital badges (Above) could come into play.

This Coursera initiative parallels what Harvard University and MIT are doing via a new non-profit partnership, known as edX. They will also offer free online courses from both institutions. Harvard's involvement followed MIT's announcement in December 2011 that it was launching MITx, an open online learning project. EdX will be overseen by a non-profit organization governed equally by Harvard and MIT, each of which has pledged $30 million toward the initiative. [103]

Purdue has also unveiled an ambitious international online-education project. It will be aimed at a global audience. PurdueHUB-U will serve up modular online courses with video lectures, interactive visualizations, and tools for students to interact with each other and their instructor. Leaders hope the project will improve face-to-face classes and bring in revenue by attracting students worldwide. [104]

Teacher Leaves Stanford and Serves Students Directly

A knowledge holder may seek a teaching opportunity and have it denied to them. They may have a top level faculty job and find they don't like traditional models. The sections on disintermediation illustrate that evolving systems of education may open up new opportunities for these persons. Those with knowledge and that can help others expand their knowledge can and must be allowed to increase their knowledge and free to teach those who seek them out and in ways where the learning that results can be validated. Knowledge seekers must be free to seek out and work with persons that can help them develop the knowledge and skills they want and need. Large universities can only hire so many people and many other qualified people are turned away. Blocking private schools is just another way of limiting their freedoms.

Knowledge holders may not need an institution to intermediate their services at all. Third party assessment systems can validate the learning. One example was Stanford computer science professor Sebastian Thrun. He left the institution to launch Udacity, a start-up offering low-cost online classes. Thrun said his move was motivated partly by teaching practices that evolved too slowly to be effective, concluding that he could not continue teaching in a traditional setting. One of Udacity's first offerings was scheduled to be a 7-week course on "Building a Search Engine" for persons with no previous programming experience. Thrun hoped for 500,000 students to enrol and he had 200,000 first time around. If students can get credit then the incentive to stay within the university circle is lessened. Final results are unknown, but the case is still illustrative.

The big question is this: If his teaching and program were good enough to warrant the high level credibility and credential worthy and transfer status given when he was at Stanford then why should this new course not also attract a credible credential that is equally as accepted and transferrable? Surely it is what happens inside the box that matters and not whether the box is government or publicly initiated, owned or funded. The contract parties change, but the student and teacher dynamic does not.

In general, evidence that the big change is coming can be found with the rapidly growing amount of money being invested by venture capital in education technology start-ups. [105]

Minerva, Different Form of Intermediation, Onsite and Online

Backed by a $25-million investment and a star-studded list of advisers (including former Harvard University president and President Obama economic advisor Larry Summers), the Minerva Project wants to create "the first elite American university to be launched in a century." Ben Nelson, the CEO of the photo-sharing site Snapfish, says Minerva plans to define "elite" differently from Ivy League and other selective institutions. Lower prices are a goal. Students will be admitted through a rigorous process based on academic credentials and an interview to test an applicant's drive, analytical skills, and goals. Factors like money will not be considered.

Minerva aims to hire top professors to develop their own online lectures and course materials and students will also sift through that material in twenty-five student interactive seminars led by instructors. A residential option will allow students to reside in dormitories in major cities worldwide, where they can experience the same kind of peer encounters that enhance the education at liberal arts and other residential institutions. [106]

14.11 New Community Education Capacity and Economic Development

The rural villages and urban slums of the developing world and the rural and economically under developed areas of the more developed world need education development as part of their economic development plans. Education supports all industries and all persons and is itself a huge economic generator.

In many cases, communities, rural and urban, can create their own community based and private for profit or social business based institutions or education firms to meet targeted community needs. They do not need to wait for the big State U to set up a branch campus after years of senate meetings. The learning facilities do not have to look like a campus. As one associate said one time, Stephen Hawking could come and give a lecture at Starbucks. In every community there are lawyers, accountants, industry experts and people with all kinds of knowledge and skill to share. They do not have to ship money to other locations or they can supplement programs offered online or onsite at other locations. The key is to make sure learning is achieved, validated, recognized and suited to local needs and opportunities.

14.12 Education Is Not Geographically Contained, Markets No Longer Have to Start Locally

As with TV, music, film and other content industries, it is difficult to create and contain education content delivery and other aspects of education within the confines of national boundaries and national models. [107] Education consumers can seek out quality and specialized programming and they don't care where it comes from provided the learning occurs and the assessment and credential processes are credible and recognized.

Vancouver BC students are studying law at centuries old law schools in the UK by distance learning and they will be able to write special national exams set by the Federation of Law Societies of Canada to meet standards that will allow them to apply for admission to provincial Law Societies.

Education can occur across borders with online and digital processes or students and institutions can move to other jurisdictions. Product factor inputs or different elements of the education product (faculty, instructional materials, administration, assessment or services) may exist in various jurisdictions. It is not rare to have students in various locations, teachers in other locations and administrators in even other jurisdictions with all interacting in real time or via recorded processes. Ultimately, education content is "consumed" and learning is done where the student is. They do not always have to go to where the producer is. Student-teacher interaction can occur online or onsite throughout a term or in focused short term sessions.

In the global economy, traditional distinctions between domestic and foreign markets are eroded. International trade has existed for thousands of years, but for most of that time it was distinct from local trade. There was a time when you needed a large market and full employment at home to create a market for a product. International business just built on that. That is no longer the case. Competition affects jobs because more firms can compete in markets and because global markets can encourage large companies to outsource from small suppliers. Global markets, when truly efficient (not a given), encourage competition and scale. Larger markets are still often (not always) needed for product and enterprise viability, but they just don't have to be in one place.

Global scale is often needed for competitiveness so a roll-out into as many major global markets as possible is often advised. International education is no exception. Even large public institutions in Canada and the US have recognized these realities and that is why they are aggressively marketing world-wide. It is in part about wanting the best global students and in part the need to get the needed scale. Scale is needed for some functions and programs, but not for all. Large research institutions are different from teaching institutions. Small public or private firms can compete perfectly well in many markets.

Global education corporations can also transcend national boundaries and operate in global markets. They too can seek efficiency as a means to achieve global competitiveness. They can break down barriers to the free movement of people and ideas. Global education markets are, but are not just composed of many local markets. Groups of student consumers with common demands may be assembled across borders. All of this can help bring costs down and increase access to quality education products—if regulators do their job.

There is greater interconnectedness and inter-dependence [108] between trading nations because of a greater international flow of goods and services (trade), direct investment, technology and capital transfers. Few industries face domestic markets that are still protected from international competition. Firms, including education firms, must compete head to head in all major markets to succeed.

14.13 Trade Principles Distinguished from Immigration, Four Types of Cross Border Service Trade Flows, Contracts and Trade Principles, The GATS and Education

Trade principles cannot be confused with immigration although the two may relate. Students or workers moving across borders are not "products", but the services they seek or provide may be and may be subject to trade law. Immigration and border control authorities ultimately control borders by awarding study or work permits to students and workers meeting the necessary criteria. Other sections discuss the need to distinguish laws targeting border security and economic development risk from laws targeting education quality risk. As risks vary standards must vary.

In most cases, immigration and trade authorities cannot avoid having to have their own criteria because education quality assurance must be focused primarily on enforcing standards that relate to risk arising from a contractual relationship. To do more can result in distortions of what quality means in a commercial and education context and what can be practically achieved by contract parties or quality regulators.

The General Agreement on Trade in Services (GATS) and other trade agreements distinguish between four modes of supplying services globally:

1. Cross-border supply refers to services flowing from the territory of one member into the territory of another member (e.g. banking or architectural services transmitted via telecommunications or mail). This could cover distance learning where the provider and student remain at a distance in distinct legal jurisdictions.
2. Consumption abroad refers to situations where a service consumer that is a citizen of one member state (tourist, patient or student) moves into another member's territory to obtain a service.
3. Commercial presence implies that a service supplier based or resident in one member state establishes a territorial presence, including through ownership or lease of premises, in another member's territory to provide a service (e.g. domestic subsidiaries of foreign insurance companies, hotel chains or education institutions).
4. Presence of natural persons consists of persons of one member entering the territory of another member to supply a service (accountants, doctors or teachers). GATS members remain free to operate measures regarding citizenship, residence or access to the employment market on a permanent basis. What some opponents of global education forget is that opportunities for individual teachers, working within one institution or many or

on their own, can greatly expand if they can access a global market for their services.

Clearly, immigration and the movement of teachers, students and managers are involved when some of these modes are utilized and not involved when others are utilized. The same is true of international trade rules. Careful attention to the facts of each case and the laws that apply to the facts are, as always, the way to face difficult challenges.

The inescapable reality of education commerce and contracts can trigger trade and immigration laws. This is nothing new. Canadian Trade authorities have made this clear. For example: "Education is now an industry. Canada needs to approach the international marketplace for educational services with the same discipline and commitment that we bring to other sectors." Sergio Marchi, former Canadian Trade Minister, former Canadian Ambassador to the WTO and former Chair of the Council for Trade in Services. [109]

The General Agreement on Trade in Services (GATS) is a treaty of the World Trade Organization (WTO). It came into force in 1995 after the Uruguay Round negotiations and extended the multilateral trading system to the service sector, in the same way the General Agreement on Tariffs and Trade (GATT) targets merchandise trade.

All members of the WTO are signatories to the GATS. Basic trade principles (Below e.g. Most Favoured Nation status) apply to GATS. Upon accession, members may introduce exemptions. Before the Uruguay Round, public services such as health care, postal services and education were not included in international trade agreements. Most were considered to be domestic activities and hard to trade across borders. Many services - for example, international finance and maritime transport - were open for centuries as needed components of merchandise trade. Foreign participation in domestic services existed in many countries prior to GATS.

The world has changed. Many sectors, including education, have undergone fundamental social, technical and regulatory changes, opening them to private commercial participation and reducing barriers to entry. Information technologies and the Internet—and transportation systems that make persons and firms, including students, teachers and institutions, more mobile - have expanded the range of internationally tradable service products to include commercial activities like medicine, education (onsite and online), engineering, architecture and advertising.

The reality is that educational services have been exported for as long as universities have had international students. Many western institutions have long had linkages with foreign institutions or their own satellite or subsidiary firms and campuses around the world. Many more are now pursing international students and establishing a commercial presence in foreign markets because they realize their survival and competitive position may depend on it.

The GATS eases international trade in services and that does involve reducing barriers to competition. A barrier can be a tariff (border tax), or non-tariff (law, practice or policy). With education, trade barrier issues revolve less around tariffs and more around other possible obstacles to trade and that includes standards barriers regarding foreign institution accreditation, [110] program or professional admissions and other standards or even visa barriers (See above distinctions between trade and immigration standards). Standards for institution accreditation can block foreign schools from setting up domestically or even from offering distance education if they restrict advertising or take other steps to block them (See section below on education trade opposition).

International trade law principles can apply to education, but specific treaty provisions are the key. Most Favored Nation principles (Article II of the GATS), where they apply, require that a nation give no less favorable treatment to a nation's products than they do to the products of any other country. National Treatment principles state that once goods (or services) enter a market they must be treated no less favorably than the equivalent domestically produced goods. The same expansionist and protectionist instincts found with physical goods trade also emerge with regard to services and education services. National treatment is a general obligation in goods trade and not negotiable. It is negotiable to some extent under the GATS.

Obligations under the GATS fall into two groups: General obligations (e.g. MFN, NT above) apply directly and automatically to all members and services sectors. Then there are commitments concerning market access and national treatment in specifically designated sectors set in individual country schedules and the scope of those schedules may vary between members.

Private and public education are generally covered by the North American Free Trade Agreement and the GATS, but reservations may exist so that governments can continue to discriminate or distinguish between public and private and continue to favor and invest in public education. Similar measures are likely in future free trade agreements between Canada and Europe and Canada and India. The details of these trade agreements are not pursued here. This is a general introduction to principles only.

The GATS applies in principle to all service sectors. One key exception is in Article I (3) which excludes "services supplied in the exercise of government authority". These are services that are not supplied on a commercial basis or in competition with other suppliers. Cases in point are social security schemes and any other public service, such as health or education that is provided at non-market conditions. To be excluded, a country's education system may have to completely publicly financed and administered and that is rarely the case and never desirable in our view. The reality (see other sections) is that so-called public institutions are generally government funded (often in decreasing amounts) private corporate entities and not government as such and do compete with other suppliers.

Education trade critics blame that commercial reality and the resulting lack of trade deal exclusion, even in the public post-secondary education sector, and anything short of completely free education from cradle to grave, on lack of government funding, but in many cases people will choose to pay to get what they want even if free services are available.

These critics also argue that the commercial reality—and the lack of GATS exclusion, exists because of the growth of private for-profit companies in Canada that (in their words) sell diplomas for profit. This again, is false reality. As noted in several sections, no one sells degrees and diplomas. They are awarded if a student achieves a learning objective as a result of a product they produced. The problem is that this is a reality these critics try their best to avoid. They say education is not a product or commodity, but a public service and as argued repeatedly that is just not economic reality in the absence of a totalitarian government that bans that kind of commercial transaction.

It is hard to argue that common domestic treatment of all providers is not warranted if they are treated largely the same for international trade purposes. In relation to the GATS (other sections), it boils down to what the phrase (required for GATS exclusion) "supplied in the exercise of government authority" really means. To many it means not in competition with other suppliers. The reality is that so-called public institutions are often not government as such and do compete with other suppliers. Even if trade agreement exclusion can be justified the exclusion would normally exist to protect domestic students (e.g. protection of subsidies). Exemptions from common dispute resolution methods or quality standards are harder to justify.

14.14 Trade Opposition and Vested Interests, Trade Agreements Acknowledge Commercial Reality, Opposition Based on Fear of Lost Exemptions From Regulation Rather Than Lost Citizen Control

Faculty, student and other education unions are often at the forefront of opposition to education being tradable across borders. [111] They argue that the GATS treaty turns public goods and human rights into commodities and products that can be bought and sold in markets. They believe education should be excluded from these markets.

Education International (the world's largest representative of education unions) and its union members insist that education is a human right and a public good and not a commodity that should be commercialized. It says it is the responsibility of all governments to provide all women and men, boys and girls, free quality public education. It generally opposes education services being covered by commercial trade agreements. It says it is an advocate for equity in society and that it challenges discrimination on the grounds of gender, sexual orientation, socio-economic status and racial or ethnic origin or characteristics. All of these positions are easily critiqued.

What they essentially say is that even in a knowledge economy no one other than government or government funded private firms should engage in education transactions. Not only is this extraordinarily impractical, it runs counter to their supposed goal which is to serve students and enhance social equity. The idea that the State can serve all diverse education needs from cradle to grave is outdated and backward. The position is founded on the false reality that trade agreements commercialize education and ignores the true reality that persons with knowledge and persons that seek knowledge have the free right to contact and enter contracts together for the purpose of helping the learner achieve a learning objective. This is true even for those so-called public (government funded private) institutions that also enter contracts. The commercial reality pre-exists the trade agreement.

It is hard to understand how these parties can claim that they seek social equity (as many do) and also claim that persons should not have the right to voluntarily enter commercial contracts with parties of their choice to enhance opportunities. Positions in institutions and programs are often limited and without other options those unable to access institutions and scarce programs or positions have to go without. That does not enhance social equity.

Many of those that oppose foreign institutions - or even other institutions from other parts of the home country -coming to their jurisdiction to do business and compete physically or virtually will at the same time encourage their home jurisdiction's institutions to have branch campuses abroad and to recruit international students so that local tuition rates can stay low or so that the institution remains economically viable. [112] The hypocrisy can be striking. You cannot expect to access foreign markets if you do not open up your own market. In many cases, their opposition exists because this form of disruptive innovation can upset the status quo and their market dominance, power base and dominant public policy influence.

Trade agreements that encompass education are doing nothing more than acknowledging reality and setting out some rules for how these education providers (public or private) and consumers can connect across borders. In many cases (e.g. money laundering, personal information) it has taken international treaties on specific subject areas to force domestic legislation. International industry groups that want to expand to global markets can pressure governments to create common standards that can give firms legal access to new markets. Traders cannot expect global access without opening doors at home.

Some of these opponents argue that trade deals like GATS or NAFTA take away the government's power to regulate domestic commerce and cede power to business interests ahead of the interests of citizens. There are exceptions built into GATS and other treaties that address many of these concerns, but it is generally factually untrue. Home countries can regulate—they just cannot discriminate and what is wrong with that. It is fear of competition and the fear of losing regulatory protections that favor them that drives the critic's argument.

Some opposition seems to be based on the fear of regulation and not the fear of the lack of regulation of others. Canada has no quality assurance standards for public (government funded or as otherwise defined) institutions and when provincial standards are set for various sectors they are often exempted. As noted in other sections, this becomes less tenable where institutions work in and serve common student markets and where students deserve common rights and the enforcement of common quality standards. That does not mean standards are completely lacking in the public sector, but the lack of recognized and formal national or regional multi-institution standards has prodded some Canadian institutions to seek accreditation in the US so they have greater international recognition and standing. [113]

Forty three European nations [114] agreed on EU wide quality assurance standards so the EU could be globally competitive in education markets. The US has regional accreditation systems that are approved by federal authorities for student loan and other purposes and that national link creates a form of national standard or at least a mechanism for their development. EU standards targeted development and facilitation of: EU and national brands; attracting and retaining domestic and international students; student, professor and worker mobility; integration between university and college systems; credit transfer and credential recognition; dependable statistics and analytical systems; movement of institutions into global markets where larger markets and scale are possible; growth and development of trusted online and distance learning programs; and loans for foreign students in domestic programs.

15

Collaborations, Capacity and Caution

15.1 Term Collaboration Has No Inherent Legal Meaning, Not All Collaborations Are Legal Partnerships

Collaborations can be fraught with legal, liability and business dangers. The upside can be great or minimal. The issues usually revolve around unclear purposes and objectives, ineffective methods and inadequate contract substance. The term collaboration has no inherent legal meaning in the say way the term joint venture has no inherent meaning. In this context the term will be used, but you could just as easily use the terms "joint venture", "partnership", "twinning", "tie-up" (a favorite word in India) or "strategic alliance". The name is immaterial. The key is what the parties agree to do together and what each party promises to do or represents as fact.

In some cases, legal partnerships will be formed and that again depends on what the parties are doing together, what their intentions are and how third parties are impacted. Legal partnerships may exist if two or more parties provide capital to a joint venture or if net income is shared. If it exists then an agency or principal and agent relationship will likely exist and that would mean that the parties would be legally responsible for the actions of the other.

No new legal entity is created with a legal partnership and that can be a simple or general partnership, a limited partnership or a limited liability partnership. Each is distinct, but we don't elaborate here. A partnership can exist even if the parties don't intend it. What they call it does not matter. The key is the nature of the relationship and the likely reliance that third parties may place on it and that can create the need to protect that third party. For example, a third party may purchase something from the partners as they act together.

15.2 Two Means to Create Collaborations—Corporations With Contracts and Contracts With No Corporation -Distinguishing Collaboration From Commercial Services, Sales, Leasing or Licensing

You can only understand these terms in the context of the two methods that can be used to give them legal life. First, two parties can create a new corporate legal entity together through which they can act together. Any corporation with multiple shareholders is a form of collaboration, joint venture or strategic alliance. A contract exists there in the form of constating documents and articles or a shareholder agreement.

Secondly, they can enter into a contract that will set out what they intend to do together and how their relationship will work, but no new corporation or legal entity is created. The individual parties, partners, collaborators, joint venturers or strategic allies act together as individuals.

It is crucial to understand the difference between collaboration and commercial services. If one party, an individual or corporation, just hires another party to do something for them in return for payment of a fee or other consideration then that is all there is - just one party hiring someone else to do something for them. They are not collaborating or doing something together for a common purpose. The relationship is just commercial in nature.

Intellectual property, personal property or real property licenses or purchases would generally not be considered collaborative in nature. The contract is more one of purchase and sale, lease or license. A lease or license is just permission to use something for a period of time under specified terms. A franchise may seem collaborative, but in essence it is not.

Collaborations are marginally commercial in the sense that promises are given by each party in exchange for the other's promise, but the exchange is not one party's service for a fee from the other or one party's service for another party's service that benefits the first party directly, but rather a promise from each to do something that will contribute, along with the collaborator's promise, to a common purpose. In other words, each party makes their promise to contribute to the common purpose because the other party makes a similar promise and not because they each receive the others promise in return for their own promise because of immediate personal benefit. Again, this can be contractual or a new corporation (legal entity) could be formed.

It may be common to refer to employees as collaborators and team members and that everyone is working together for a common purpose, but in legal terms the nature of the employment contract is commercial. A fee is paid in return for a service performed. Specific collaboration terms in an employment could modify that essential reality. The same is true of most non-employment independent contract agreements.

15.3 Distinguishing Collaboration and Outsourcing, Neither May Change Consumer Relationship

Outsourcing is usually just a case of service provision occurring outside the normal boundaries of an operating legal entity. Even hiring an external lawyer or consultant—instead of asking an employee to do the work—is, to some, a form of outsourcing. The term is also used in cases where employees are used, but they are hired in another jurisdiction so that those that normally do the work lose that work to other workers and employees. The employees assigned the work could have employment contracts with a related or subsidiary company or entire unrelated firms.

With outsourcing organizations have a need for services and they choose to have that work done outside the normal boundaries of the entity needing the work or outside the normal process of task assignment. The term never has just one meaning. When students go overseas to study they are not and the foreign school is not outsourcing. The student is not engaging a service they would otherwise do themselves. The two parties are just selling and buying across borders.

Cases of collaboration or outsourcing can involve almost any element of an enterprise or operation of the entity from marketing to production and from operations to delivery and fulfillment, but they often only involve contracts between the operating entity and those parties that help the operating entity provide its core service to a consuming unit under a contract to which only the operating entity and the consumer are party to.

The operating entity (education institution) has a separate contract with its consumers (e.g. student consumers). Unless the collaboration involves the two parties acting together to enter contracts with consumers jointly or jointly and severally or unless they create a new entity or institution to do the same the student will still just have their contract with the original institution and operating entity.

If the joint purpose is not just to enhance the enterprise of each party as they serve their respective consumers (Above), but to jointly serve an end user in some way then the relationships changes because that end user may rely on the fact that both joint parties are involved. For example, two parties could work together on some kind of joint or co-marketing or production initiative, but they still have their own customers or they could work together and serve a consumer with some kind of common service.

Failure to make these contract distinctions has resulted in big problems for institutions in our case files. Consumers (e.g. students) must know who they are contracting with and it must be the party that has proper regulatory approvals to do so where that regulatory approval is required. Collaboration and outsourcing must involve clear agreements or it can be very easy to mislead consumers.

15.4 Collaborations Are Distinct From Articulations

Collaboration agreements are not the same thing as articulation agreements (which themselves are often not enforceable) between two or more institutions although collaborations could involve an articulation element. One institution may work with other institutions or non-institution parties to enhance their respective marketing, admissions or program operations capacity, but students do not generally contract with the other institutions or firms. They contract with the firm that has the approval and legal capacity to offer the contracted product. In our experience, most problems arise because of confusion students have about who they are dealing with contractually.

Articulations (See Separate Sections) do not involve collaboration - working together for a common purpose. It is an agreement to do something in the future (grant credit or admission) if conditions (graduation and request for admission) are met, but the student is not usually a party to the contract and thus cannot act to enforce it without the use of complex third party beneficiary laws or other awkward legal mechanisms. In addition, the multi-lateral or bi-lateral agreements or arrangements are often said to be "guidelines" and include terms that give the receiving institution full discretion about their future actions. This brings into doubt the enforceability of the agreement because no real promise is made. Institutions must not mislead students into thinking they have legal rights of credit transfer unless that is the legal reality. This is addressed more in other sections.

15.5 Reasons for Collaboration Similar to Retaining Services, Collaboration Keys and Regulation

Collaboration is different from commercial services provision, commercial sales or outsourcing, but the reasons for using each of these ways to get things done are often similar. Some of these reasons are: to access needed skills and capacity that otherwise cannot be accessed because of firm size, market orientation, strategic objectives or corporate culture; to access capital in debt or other forms with the help of a more profitable and financially stable partner; to enhance competitive advantages and market position; to command and control scarce resources or production facilities; to increase knowledge of local markets; to access specialized market and product skills; to access complementary skills and knowledge so both benefit; to reduce and share risk and costs; to focus on core competencies and solve problems rapidly; to improve economies of scale; to access new markets without new production facilities; or to manage foreign ownership restrictions.

Successful collaboration requires: common vision; a roadmap; clear vision of desired outcomes; effective process; individual metrics to measure goal achievement; and communication. A clear legal agreement should exist to govern the elements of successful collaboration. The real key is to plot out visually who the contract (collaboration) or corporate parties are and then follow the trail to what they are undertaking to do together and what each will do for that purpose. Again, if the nature of what they are doing is not so much what they are each doing in pursuit of that shared purpose, but what they are each doing to help the other meet their individual goals then it is more commercial in nature rather than collaborative.

Collaboration can unfold in more than one way. Two partiers can work together to accomplish a common purpose that does not involve a third party end user or they could work together for the purpose of jointly serving an end user. With the contract only (no corporation) option there is no new entity so each collaborator is responsible for that service and likely jointly and severally liable. They may also collaborate to help each other for the purpose of combining strengths to build capacity that both can use to serve their own individual clients. If a new corporation is created by the collaborators then that corporation will often (not always) be used to serve end users or conceivably each collaborator could also continue to have their own clients.

These contracts should address: management and control; how money comes and goes out; how separate entities, functions and identities are blended coherently; how to assess contributions and assign compensation; dispute resolutions; confidentiality and privacy; competition law and the avoidance of collusion; division of powers and exclusivity of rights; taxation; integration with existing operations; dependency; commitment and consensus; accountability for individual commitments and joint activities; financial and legal liability; active and silent parties; buy-out and exits; liquidity of invested funds; use and approval of resources; nature of relationship (agency, fiduciary or legal partnerships); authority for decisions; intellectual property; or regulatory compliance responsibilities.

Collaboration normally need not trigger regulatory or contract attention because students would normally not be directly involved. Students do not have to know about the various business relationships that exist in the product factor world in most cases.

15.6 Institutions May Or May Not Be Or Involve Collaborations, Student and Institution Relationships

As noted, an education institution is an aggregator or intermediary. It pulls together product factor inputs to create products that serve consumers. In most cases this intermediation will involve commercial service or purchasing contracts, intellectual property licensing agreements and other similar commercial and contractual relationships. The corporation itself may be collaborative if there are multiple owners, but formal collaborations involving multiple parties do not exist unless those parties enter contracts or form new corporations to pursue common purposes.

Most instances of collaboration or cases where the term is used involve two business firms working together for and toward some common purpose. In many cases these arrangements are more commercial than collaborative, but each case must be judged on its own facts. If a consumer—like a student consumer—has an innovative kind of relationship with a service provider then those facts also must be carefully scrutinized before it is actually labelled as collaborative in nature.

If a student has a student contract and then also works on campus as a teaching assistant or in any kind of position to try and reduce tuition charges or to receive subsidiary income in most cases the relationship is not really collaborative even though the parties may talk about being part of a team. The individual facts are the key and the nature of existing contracts must be scoped out and in that process an accurate legal picture starts to emerge.

The legal nature of all of the relationships involved must be sorted out or the system will crash because of disputes or because a lack of clarity and multiplicity of interpretations stifles or incapacitates management.

Part 3

Contracts, Recruitment, Admissions, Dispute Resolution

16

Education Marketers Induce Persons to Enter Binding Contracts and Must Manage Related Risk

16.1 Sales and Marketing Is By Definition the Inducement of Persons to Enter Contracts, Pre-Contract Representations, Tort Law, Not Everything Said Is Contractual, Actual Inducement Is Key

Marketing, including education marketing, is about inducing persons to enter binding contracts. What is said and represented will in many, but not all cases, with or without later modifying terms, have contractual importance. Many institutions, education marketers and regulators lose sight of this fact. The student contract is performed over time and is instrument that can see terms added, imputed and implied over time so it is possible that representations or promises made by non-marketing and sales persons can also have contract importance if the contract does not restrict it.

Prospective students are not students yet because they have not entered a student enrollment contract. Some regulatory statutes involve the protection of "prospective students" and this can, for example, justify measures to control misleading advertising.

What marketers say or represent about the institution and its products to induce the contract can also result in an institution being liable under the law of tort where duties to adhere to a standard can exist when the nature of a relationship warrants it and even if no contract results—for example, if a prospective student relied to their detriment on a representation. For example, an overly zealous admissions officer may say something that is relied on. For example, it could lead the person to quit their job prior to definitive acceptance.

If a contract eventually does arise then the representation could be incorporated by implication as a contractual warranty. This could happen even if the contract has terms that try to limit those inclusions although having limiting terms is still a good idea. If it does not arise then liability can still exist in tort if the elements of tort exist i.e. loss and damage, a relationship that gives rise to a duty of care, violation of the standard of care that exists and related requirements.

Not everything said or represented prior to or during a contract for promotional or operational purposes is contractual or subject to tort law. There is what is called "sales talk" and operational materials are constantly evolving. As noted, there are related relationships in the education realm that can result in a student mistakenly assuming that they have some kind of associated legal right and that the institution is on the hook for it. Examples would include credit transfers, professional membership, jobs or immigration status.

The test is often focused on what actually and reasonably induced the person to enter the contract. The student may have to prove they were in fact induced into the contract by what was said. Courts would likely apply a reasonable person test to make that determination, that is, would a reasonable person have been so induced given all of the factors involved.

16.2 Marketers Can Still Do Their Job, Incentives Are Not Always A Problem, Records of Materials

Marketers can still do their jobs even while they pay more attention to the legal elements of what they do. An institution wants to illustrate that it is distinctive and that it stands out from the crowd. Fundamentally that involves setting out what it promises (contractually) to do and the representations of fact that it wants the prospect to rely on. [115] This can be done without undue liability resulting. The key is to know the product promised and to deliver what is promised. Another key is to make it clear what is not promised either because the intention is not there or because something is beyond the institution's control.

Nevertheless, some [116] marketers live on the edge of the dark side of marketing, using dangerous and tempting notions, strategies, tactics and tools often associated with bad guy business while still thinking they are above the commercial fray. This is not isolated to aggressive private schools.

Education marketers must make the effort needed to understand the full nature of the contract and contract product promised or how the huge body of contract law relates to the contract instrument and its promises and representations. They tend to see the "contract" as that little piece of paper that the student signs (and often must sign) before courses begin and that is then forgotten. As noted, that piece of paper is not the "contract" in the sense that it is not a complete expression of the representations, rights and obligations of student and institution parties.

Strategic Enrollment Management, a common term today, must incorporate not only how to market and increase enrollment, but also measures that are focused on these legal realities. Marketers and admissions persons must understand that what they say matters in legal terms. If they want to limit liability (and they must) and have a clear idea of how to satisfy contractual obligations and, assuming they are reflected expressly or impliedly, institutions and marketers must design and present promotional materials with contract content and impact in mind.

Communications with and representations to prospective students should: be accurate, truthful, descriptive and promotional; state that they are not contractual and may not survive in the student contract unless contractual intent is clear in the materials and contract; state that the program may change before student contracts are final and also during the program; state that the final and binding obligations of the parties will be set in student contracts; state that admission is subject to admission standards being met; refer to regulations governing the institution; refer to programs offered and information generally contained in a (brief) program outline; make it clear that admission is not contractually promised even if admission standards are met; make it clear that contracts do not incorporate business policies or duties owed to regulators without express intention (the common law position).

Controversies swirl around the idea of sales and marketing professionals in the education sector getting bonuses or incentives. Clearly this is common practice in many commercial sectors, but because education is not viewed as it exists in reality, as a commercial industry with a contract product, the practice is often criticized or even prohibited. The problem is not with the incentives. It is with a lack of product knowledge that can result in persons being unable to otherwise govern and avoid possible misrepresentation and wrongful contract inducement. Incentives do not automatically result in unethical or illegal marketing and sales practices. Most commercial sectors use them. The key is whether students are induced into contracts with untrue facts and promises that are later not kept.

Even if it is not legally required (it often is), institutions should keep a record of past promotional materials. This is only practical. Websites and other promotional materials evolve day by day and must be overseen to ensure representations are in line with what is legally intended, but steps must be taken to try and limit reliance on them. Even without limitation provisions like entire agreement clauses or limitation of liability clauses, not everything said by marketers is contractual. It is often still advisable for institutions to keep a record of past marketing, promotional, advertising and recruitment materials—including a record of third party testimonials - and a record of the period when they were used. Having those records has helped some of our clients counter claims by students.

16.3 Government Branding Programs Should Be Clarified to Control Authority or Student Reliance

As part of their efforts to increase international student enrollment in their domestic systems many governments are developing "Brands" that give assurance to students that certain conditions exist and that should make prospective students comfortable about possible risks. Global branding of institutions and countries matters in a global economy: when students make enrollment decisions; when employers, professional organizations and other institutions contemplating credit transfers make decisions; when government authorities make decisions about the student and their qualifications; and when regulators in Canada and abroad assess institutions and programs.

Attempts by some governments to have regional or national quality assurance "Brands" can be, but often are not regulatory in nature in the sense that they may not impose additional regulatory requirements (although they have been known to still do it). They may directly reflect a quality assurance regulator's designation or a third party, public or private, may adopt a regulator's quality assurance designation and allow those that have earned that designation to adopt an additional label or designation (Brand). [117]

If these brands do not have specific requirements then participants, if they come from multiple systems of regulation, have not met a common requirement and that may bring its validity into question unless it has detailed systems in place to assess the various standards it accepts. Third parties (e.g. lenders or immigration authorities) or students may rely on the "Brand" or the absence of it without fully understanding the standards that underlie it. Student loan lenders have been known to assume poor quality caused defaults even if institutions had quality assurance accreditation and the additional government supported quality brand. In other cases, the Quality Brand was denied even though quality assurance requirements were met, but non-quality based lending criteria were not.

The student contract should state that no specific contractual representations about quality or otherwise are made by the institution if and when such Brands exist and are earned and are expressed in promotional literature. It should make it clear that these Brands and their implicit representations are not expressly or impliedly incorporated into the contract.

16.4 Benefits and Dangers of Third Party Recruitment and Institution Services, Related Student Services

Institutions and (usually international) students often - each on their own and not jointly - enter contracts with independent service providers that provide each with specific services. Institutions may use recruitment services. Students may use institution and program search services or related immigration services.

Agency relationships can result, even without formal agreement, with one party (the principal) being legally responsible and liable for the actions of another (the agent). Use of the term or creating a relationship that appears to be one of agency can result in others concluding that the relationship between the institution and the recruiter (or other third party relationship) is one of principal and agent and subject to the law of agency. That can result in liabilities for the institution if these other parties reasonably make this conclusion and rely on it to their detriment.

It is usually best to avoid, where an institution or student can, relationships that involve legal forms of "agency" and include provisions in student contracts and contracts the student or institution may have with these third parties that protect each party's respective interests. The application of agency law should be avoided or restricted and limitation of liability clauses should be included. These terms serve as notices to students that they should be cautious about dealing with non-institution and third party actors.

The institution-recruiter (referral) contract can and in our view should set out: that recruiters are not "agents" and not allowed to sign contracts with or accept money from students; the roles and responsibilities of the recruiter; how promotional materials are handled; what plan and strategy will be adopted by both parties; how recruitment activities are paid and budgeted for; if quotas are required; compensation and disbursement terms; terms of exclusivity, if desired (not recommended); and contract duration and renewal or termination processes.

If students enter contracts with the same firms that contract with institutions or with other firms to help them find institutions or to assist them with immigration or other (admission applications, travel, insurance, accommodation, exam prep, counselling) matters those contracts should focus on services provided and require that the service provider forward tuition money (if paid to the service provider) to the institution so it is clear what the money is being paid for.

Student contracts should include representations from institutions that they have not entered into agreements with agents or others that allow those parties to execute contracts with students or to collect student money on the institution's behalf. Institutions should ensure they are not liable to a student that chooses of their own accord to pay the third party while assuming that the third party will then pay the institution after they deduct their commission. Be cautious about regulators that do not understand agency law. In BC there is a statutory definition of agent that assumes this traditional principal agent relationship so contracts have to be precise to overcome that provision.

Institutions have faced situations where students paid third parties and then the third party (avoid agency) took off with the money. Without proper terms in student and third party contracts to limit agency law and liability generally, institutions could have had to pay the student back the money they reasonably thought they had paid to the institution via the third party. Alternatively they could possibly have demanded the education without the institution receiving the money.

Most internal admission officers, education "agents" or "referral parties" are not licensed immigration consultants (Canada) or lawyers and are not able to legally give immigration advice. Institutions should not allow them to provide students or others with immigration services because authorities could hold that the institution, without legal authority, acted through their agent to provide those immigration services. This is one more reason to avoid agency relationships in this context.

17

Acceptance of Student, Admissions, Enrollment and Student Contract

17.1 Acceptance, Admission and Enrollment Contract, Admission Standards and Program Success

This section highlights the fact that matters traditionally considered to be "academic" and beyond the purview of the courts can have strong contractual elements that should not be beyond judicial consideration. The process of accepting an application and admitting and enrolling a student is a contractual matter. Acceptance, admission and enrollment involves one party (the institution) deciding to enter into the contract because (normally) admission standards were met and other business decisions were made.

The process of being admitted to an institution and a program (not necessarily the same thing) normally involves a number of factors. Admissions can be a form of credential evaluation and credit transfer system, but there is more involved than that. Admission standards are set, as all standards are, to deal with specified risks.

Institutions must generally have admission standards for the institution and for each program that represent a threshold (See definition of standards) of qualities, characteristics and factors (age, knowledge, skills, language proficiency and abilities e.g. credential and credits) that an applicant must meet to deserve admission and the benefits that follow. Factors generally focus on and are related to the applicant's ability to succeed in the program.

Admission standards must relate to the level of program difficulty and the applicant's likely ability to be successful in the program. You cannot validly or in good faith promise to help someone achieve a learning objective if application information is such that success is unlikely.

Persons not likely to succeed should generally not be admitted because there are expressed and implied terms that focus on that success. This concept is a core element of the noted definition of education that distinguishes it from other forms of media content production and delivery. The promised product is a collection of inputs that create an environment that help the student achieve a learning objective. Actual achievement is not promised. There is an assessment element of the product offering that is there to determine whether that learning occurred. The credential is promised if the learning is validated via assessment, but the credential is evidence of academic achievement and not a property asset or promised product.

The problem comes because the ability to determine that likely success is difficult. That representation of likely success would be an inducement to the student to enter the contract. Regulations often rightfully state that persons should not be admitted because the institution wants the money from someone unlikely to succeed. The institution must also be careful not to unlawfully discriminate against the applicant because certain groups may traditionally have poor results in academic environments. Passing grades can run from 50% to 100%. The person least expected to excel at the start of the program often ends up being the best student or perhaps the most successful person in the world. Nevertheless, these judgments have to be made.

The student contract should include a representation from the institution that the admission decision was made on the basis that the student had a reasonable chance of succeeding in the program and of graduating. This protects the student and puts some onus on the institution to have systems in place to establish that this was the case.

Faculty and internal or external program advisory councils are often rightly required by regulators because they are best suited to determine what admission standards should be given program difficulty and what students must have by way of attributes to maximize their chances of success. Rarely can centralized regulators have sufficient expertise in all areas to determine what admission standards should.

As noted, the key admissions factor is generally the applicant's current academic standing or state of knowledge, as evidenced by transcripts, credentials and grants of credits from a respected source, that gives the admitting institution or party reasonable cause to believe that the student can and will be successful in the program. This current state of knowledge, skill or aptitude could have been assessed by another institution or by some form of examination system. That is always a difficult concept because pass rates are never 100%. Success generally must mean Pass.

All parties benefit from this process and judgment. Students do not generally want to pay for and spend a great deal of time in the program if they have no chance of success and no chance of earning the credential given as evidence of their accomplishment and that would help them convince others in the post program world of their accomplishment. The institution may have financial incentives to admit no matter what the qualifications are if available positions exceed applicants, but such actions would often be in violation of regulated requirements and having poor grads is bad for business.

17.2 Application Materials, Student Representations and Letters of Acceptance Can Be Incorporated Into Student Contracts, Student Declarations Irrelevant

It is not useful and it can be misleading to require or allow a student to declare in a contract (as some BC regulators have required) that they have "represented to the institution and provided evidence to prove that they meet admission requirements". Only the institution can decide if the evidence sufficiently proves that requirements were met and that comes before the contract exists.

The student is only required to provide true and accurate information that the institution can use to make the determination that the admission standards are met. The institution relies on that true and accurate information and on the representation that the information is true and accurate and not on a declaration that the student meets the requirements.

Application materials include information that the institution relies on when they make admissions decisions and the application is a representation by the student that certain facts exist and are true and accurate and that can result in an institution claiming they were induced to admit the student and enter the student contract on that basis. If student representations are later shown to be untrue or inaccurate then the institution has, depending on how serious the inaccuracy or lack of veracity, grounds for expulsion or termination of a credential. Drastic action could be difficult if the student was successful with their studies.

The student contract should state that the application is part of the student contract so that both parties understand that the information, representations and warranties included have contractual impact. The letter of acceptance is also in most cases an interim and conditional contract. The promise to admit may be conditional upon the student entering into a final written and more comprehensive contract and perhaps satisfying certain additional requirements. The letter can also be incorporated into the final contract. This is not essential, but it can be useful in certain cases.

17.3 Institution Represents That Admission Was Based on Set Standards, Freedom of Contract Principles, Non-Academic Intangibles

In the absence of expressed law or pre-student contract tort or interim contract provisions, institutions may not be required to give reasons for a decision to not admit a student. Parties to a contract have the freedom to decide who they enter into a contract with and this means an institution is not - without discrimination arguments, regulatory requirements or collateral contract arguments - bound to admit a student even if that student meets admission standards.

As noted, students can argue that payment of an application fee creates an interim contract that requires the institution to give the application full and expected consideration in light of admission standards, but this alone may not be enough for the student to argue that meeting the standards requires the institution to enrol the student if there is an available position. There may be an implicit promise or representation made by the institution that they will make admission decisions objectively and impartially with competent persons making the decision. The larger the application fee is perhaps the stronger the argument that an interim contract existed with an implied term that admission will follow if standards are objectively met.

Again, student contracts should state that the admission decision was based on the student meeting the set criteria that were in turn established to determine an applicant's likely chances of academic success. This has significance beyond the admission decision itself. The institution is stating that based on the information provided and the standards set for admission that the student should be able to succeed. They are saying that the student was not just admitted because the school needed the money (which is in many cases a prohibited action under regulations). This can create arguments for the student or the institution if a dispute does arise when a student fails to graduate.

Increasingly, institutions are also considering non-academic factors [118] when they admit persons because they realize that often it is intangible factors that determine success. This also relates to a need for broader assessments because of problems with pre-admission grade inflation. This recognition now confirms our position that these admission gateways generally must not be the final say over who gets to compete for available and scarce opportunities. Life experience tells us that it is often not the person that had the best application that ends up being at the top of the class and the top graduate is not always the person that ends up being the most successful in business and life.

There has been a problem in many parts of Canada that PSE institutions call grade inflation. Institutions at all levels are under pressure to move students through and to not limit their prospects. This can make it difficult for post-secondary institutions to make judgments about likely success in a program. This has promoted some institutions to consider a broader range of academic and non-academic factors [119] or to adopt some form of entrance exam or screening system.

Again, meeting admission standards is usually no guarantee of acceptance because the institution still has the freedom to enter a contract or not, but standards can be a form of representation from the institution that admission will be or was made on grounds based on the students likely ability to succeed in the program. This means representations about program difficulty and complexity could be of contract significance. If a student reasonably believed the program was less difficult and complex than what it turned out to be at the level of instruction and assessment (Below) and then they failed they could have a cause of action in contract.

17.4 Institution Due Diligence on Student Provided Information, Expressed Consent Is Best

The institution is legally impacted by student information. The institution makes an admission and contract decision based on it. Its regulatory duties may relate to that information and its contract decisions. As a result, the institution can argue that it has an implied right to check and do due diligence on the information. Expressed student consent is preferable, but arguably not required in all cases by the contract. Practically, collecting that information needed to verify student provided information may not be possible without that consent.

Instead of relying on this suggested implied term, the contract should allow the institution to check whether the student's representations are in fact true and include the student's consent for the collection, use and dissemination of other personal student information that relates to those student representations. The contract should not refer to "other requirements". That is too broad and likely not legally permissible. References to specified purposes might suffice, but that it still vague and open ended.

Certain BC Government recommended contracts do not allow this kind of institution due diligence even though they require institutions to declare that the standards were met. The contract provision should declare that the institution will act in full compliance with laws regarding personal information protection. These laws go beyond the consent and purpose provisions that create the need for a release or consent. There are requirements regarding: limited collection, use, disclosure and retention; accuracy; security, openness, access; and challenges to compliance. These don't all have to be mentioned.

The student contract should state that the application is part of the student contract so that both parties understand that the information, representations and warranties included have contractual impact. Applicant representations and information need not be restated in the contract. An incorporation provision is sufficient. Even without express inclusion they could be incorporated as implied terms.

Student loan lenders may require (generally without statutory authority) that institutions not enroll high risk students. The institution does not have authority to collect personal financial information that does not relate to the admission decision that has nothing to do with their likely predisposition to live up to their student loan repayment obligations. The ability to collect that information should not fall within the above due diligence argument.

17.5 Students and Institutions As Contract Parties Must have the Legal Capacity to Sign

If a student is not of the age of majority or otherwise does not have the legal capacity to contract then someone else must sign to make the contract binding. By simply requiring that a third party sign without any additional provisions you create uncertainties about the significance of the third party signature. A third party (e.g. a parent) may think their signature and consent is required to allow for admission without understanding their real legal position. As a party and a person signing for the student they would be liable for student obligations including tuition payment.

If capacity is questioned, whether the law requires it or not, a provision should state that the parent or other third party consents to the admission, is a party to the contract and responsible for stated student obligations. The student may mistakenly think that their obligations are removed if a third party signs. This is not always the case because they may reach the age of majority during the program. They should still sign the contract. Under contract privity doctrines a contract can't bind a third party so the signing third party must be a party if their signature is to mean anything and if they are to be bound to perform obligations under the contract.

If the institution is incorporated it must have the legal capacity and authority to enter the contract or the survival of the program could be threatened. Contracts should include clarifying provisions. The institution must be properly registered or accredited as applicable laws require so that they can lawfully enter into the contract and they must be in good standing with the applicable corporate registrar. If a student experienced loss because it entered a contract it is unlikely that a court would let the institution off the hook because it was not in good regulatory standing. The contract could stand for that purpose, but not to bind the student. Regulatory non-compliance may exist.

Institution signatures and admission decisions must only be made by authorized persons and not by third party recruiters, agents or immigration consultants because that admission decision is where the contract is entered into. An agent of the institution or third party could, with authorization, enter a contract and bind the institution, but in most cases it is ill advised.

18

Groups of Students, Variable Contract Provisions Within Classes and Institutions, Class Size

18.1 Institutions Contract With Individual Students Not Groups of Students

Institutions enter into enrollment contracts with individual students and not classes or groups and cohorts of students. This point can be relevant in a number of contexts including possible group legal actions that may or may not be possible depending on the specific jurisdiction or legal context involved. There is a tendency to think that contracts with class or cohort members are always identical and while that may often be the case it is not always the case because of the evolutionary, often implied and executory nature of the student contract.

18.2 Contracts May Be Uniform Within Classes Or Include Student Variation, Class Actions and Common Cause

Students within a specific program cohort and period and even different cohorts within a program over time may often have the same contract provisions apply, but this may not always be the case. There can be some uncommon provisions or different rights and obligations that arise for both parties.

Given the evolutionary, executory and often implied nature of the student contract it is possible that the relationship between the institution and student could evolve to a point where specific students have valid claims that other students do not have. For example, a student may indicate a desire to withdraw because of difficulties and to avoid future costs. The institution may then promise specific remedial work. The student could rely on that promise (not just a representation) while still relying on the general terms of the contract that apply to all students.

There is likely an implied or expressed term that the institution should do what is reasonably required to help all students succeed, but in this case there would be a supplementary provision or promise. The issue is where you draw the line generally and in the specific case. There must be a limitation to the degree to which the institution must provide additional help for a student. The word "reasonable" is commonly used by lawyers, legislative drafters and courts to allow future decision makers to draw that line in the specific context.

The attention on student success in regulations or contracts cannot bind the institution to endless and undefined obligations to each student. Regulators or students cannot reasonably argue that the program was not adequate because a few struggle or fail while others excel. They cannot all be treated the same and that variation can potentially be expressed in terms of reasonable reliance and expectation.

Other examples were cited in other sections. For example, some institutions are competing so hard for top students that they are promising everything from special mentoring and advising to invitations to special events. Grad students may be given special promises about available research facilities or corporate funding. These are all legitimate and legally significant variations in contract terms.

A student is more likely to have special needs recognized in contractual terms if those needs are recognized by both parties at the time of admission and if their intention to include a provision to address them is expressed or reasonably implied. That mutual agreement could also exist at any point from admission to graduation.

Another variation factor is the reality that services are consumed individually. All services are designed to change in some way the conditions of the consuming unit and although a product may appear to be the same when delivered to a group it is also true that each consumer consumes differently. Personal factors are relevant.

Even with recorded media, services are provided and consumed at the same time. Even when programs are targeted at a group each service is still unique as a one-time generated, rendered and consumed service and can never be exactly repeated. There is a reasonable expectation by a student that they will have their particular needs met even if that means getting services others did not get or demand. If a professor denied reasonable personal access and help that others did not need, but this particular student did need and a student failed as a result that could be considered breach of contract. Services are difficult to standardize and often must be tailored to specific client needs. Again, the hard part is drawing the line between reasonable and unreasonable demands for special services.

Student assessment services (Below) may also have to be adjusted. A common standard is generally still necessary so that grading has some relevance and credibility, but it is also possible that a student could reasonably demand changes that their conditions dictate. For example, if a single mother has a sick child and cannot make an exam then she could reasonably demand the right to re-write the exam later. A single man's excuse of having a hangover would not be as convincing. The point is that personal variation can matter practically, in policy terms and contractually.

Because students may now often be more knowledgeable coming in and become more demanding it is also possible that individuals make assumptions about content that a generation ago they would not make and that can result in a divergence of reliance and expectations that may have to be addressed. New technologies allow for greater individual emphasis and that can make common standards and assessment more difficult. The extent to which authorized institution actors accept and encourage these individual needs and expectations will be relevant.

In BC, Canada the career training regulator tried at one time to allow one student to make claims on behalf of an entire class. No procedural protections were provided to ensure common cause as class action or class proceeding legislation will do in most jurisdictions. In the face of opposition the bylaw was withdrawn. This does not mean that such actions could not be possible, but it cannot be assumed that common cause exists just because students were in the same program and class. It will depend on the allegation and whether in fact in that context the promise or representation or alleged breach involved was the same. Only then could a common remedy be ordered. Procedural protections common to general class action proceedings must, in our view, be included or procedural fairness requirements would arguably not be met.

18.3 Class Size Can Be a Contract Term and a Source of Dispute

Class size can be of contract importance if that is the parties' intention. It is common for institutions to advertise and promote that classes are small—implying or expressly stating that this is a key feature or part of the contractually promised product itself. Class size can determine the amount and quality or individual attention the student will receive. The problem is that many institutions, public and private, do this because enrollment has been poor and they try to turn a negative into a positive. Later students may complain that classes are larger than promised.

As noted, if the product offered was still successful at helping the student achieve the learning objective then class size becomes less relevant. Variation on the promised or represented class size is unlikely to result in a serious remedy being awarded if the learning objective was met. It is a factor targeted at helping achieve that objective and not something that has contractual importance itself. A student could argue that they would have done better in a small class academically or socially, but the essence of the contract is learning and not social experience. Proving that academic performance would have been better in small classes would be difficult.

The student contract should include a provision that says no specific class size is promised unless a specific and written term to that effect is included. This can still be an issue with distance learning because individuals may still reasonably expect personal attention.

19

Contracts, Risk Management, Provisions and Content, Relationship Building

19.1 Contracts, Content and Provisions, Risk Management and Relationship Building

Again, contracts are not pieces of paper or virtual documents. Documents properly assented to are evidence of a contract. Contracts are enforceable promises and contract law will determine if enforceable contracts exist, what the terms are, if breach occurred and if remedies are owed. The key point is that the student contract is usually an evolving and executory form of contract. Even if a written contract exists it may not fully express all of the parties' contract rights and duties. It may incorporate, expressly or impliedly, pre-contract representations, contract period verbal representations, implied terms, application materials and standards, interim (and conditional) letters of acceptance and other elements. A contract is volitional in nature. The parties voluntarily agree to be bound by the contract's terms.

Too many people think that if they don't sign a document or if they keep a document simple that they avoid a contract or a complex contract. They say they don't want a long contract and then turn around and say their hundreds of pages long academic calendar is a contract. A contract is not something to fear. It is a reality. If services are exchanged for a monetary price or other consideration then there is generally a contract. The volitional nature of the contract does not mean that one can choose to not have one and yet proceed to do business.

The contract is a way that the parties manage their respective risks and goals by receiving representations and promises from another in return for their own. Because the risks and potential gain can be significant they want and need to at least have the option of judicial enforcement—no matter how rare such action really is. The contract is not just about litigation avoidance and preparation. It is about relationship building, responsibility and clarity and the fulfillment of relationship goals. As noted, regulators often target the same relationship and goals as the contract, but they use different and distinct tools.

19.2 Contract Specifications and the Evolving Contract

Previous sections established the reality of the evolving, multi-faceted and executory student contract. The same principles apply to other contracts. Many sections of this work have, in response to specific issues, recommended or strongly asserted the need for specific inclusions or exclusions. These are not summarized here in detail. The following points are re-stated.

1. There should be no broad inclusion of all business policies unless contractually enforceable rights and binding duties are intended and that intention is made clear in the policy statement or contract. The business policy (asserted by authorized persons in the firm and not the contract parties) is no longer then just a policy, but a contract term. The policy alone vests no legal rights or duties. Policies can be changed by authorized persons in the firm. Contract terms are agreed to by both parties unless they agree that one party can unilaterally make the change and if that is too open ended the certainty of terms and enforceability of the contract come into question.
2. There must always be a distinction drawn between contract provisions, business policies and public rights and duties vested under statute. Violations of public duties do not automatically create private rights for protected objects of regulation. Violations of contracts do not automatically constitute violations of public duties. Regulations operate separately from the contract with separate parties, rights, duties, subjects and objects, but the targeted risks and the goal of contract performance may be the same. Minimum standards could be set, but they too must be targeted at consumer risk and not set new unrelated standards or prohibitions.
3. It is often not feasible to give students upfront all reference materials, lesson plans, outlines and instruction materials and have them incorporated by reference into the student contract and scrupulously followed without variation there is usually some

need for change provisions in the student contract. Deviations are inevitable.

a. Provisions must therefore allow the institution and its faculty to make changes without student notice or consent that they feel are appropriate given the learning outcome objective. Any content or other change must be possible or the institution cannot do what it contractually promises to do - provide a product that helps the student achieve the set learning outcome objective that itself is not promised because the student controls that outcome. Major changes may require student notices and consent. The individual facts must govern the situation.

b. It is a good idea to include in a student contract, along with these change provisions, a general summary or outline that goes beyond the catalogue description.

c. In the current environment, some change even to the learning outcome objectives may be necessary during the program. Unlike changes to the program itself that can just involve new ways of achieving the objective, changes to the learning objective itself go to the heart of what the contract and product are about. That means notice of these changes may require a greater level of notice or mutual agreement. Some institution discretion is often required, but unilateral action could give the institution too much leeway in terms of redefining the learning objective it commits to helping the student achieve.

4. Certain provisions should not be open to unilateral changes by institutions e.g. price. We take this position because it is more in tune with the contract law doctrine of certainty. Some large universities use catalogue contracts to give themselves the ability to change tuitions at any time in any amount as they see fit. Certain courts have upheld that ability even when increases were extremely high, [120] but the case in mind could be distinguished on various grounds because of how it was pleaded and decided.
5. Students should be required to voice concerns early about content and other issues so that they can be addressed quickly. They cannot wait until the end and complain that three months ago a teacher deviated from an outline or other issues existed. Silence may constitute acceptance or acquiescence. This can be

contrasted with statements from regulators that anything other than minor deviations are not permitted. Such a position is unworkable. Program changes are what ensure that the program constantly improves and adapts to external conditions.

6. Given recent case law and increased student consumer agitation and litigiousness, the parties should use a comprehensive and properly drafted contract instrument and not rely on the simple incorporation of diverse documents, brochures, calendars, catalogues and handbooks of policies and information. These practices are not worthy of sophisticated commercial enterprises that are often global in scope and handle large sums of money.
    a. Much of the content in calendars and handbooks is "information" and not focused on contractually intended promises or representations. Much of it is irrelevant to the specific program and student and contains information targeted at all programs.
    b. Institutions are not normally regulators of students and their self-proclaimed "regulations" or "policies" are only contract provisions if the facts support that inclusion and intention conclusion.
    c. Catalogs and bulletins are not well drafted contracts, but often they are relied on for that purpose. They often contain disclaimers of obligations to students and few commitments made to students. They are often vague and amended with ease at the will of the institution. [121] For example, we cite in other sections the MacDonald v. UBC case where a catalogue contract allowed the institution to increase fees at any time and they were increased over 300% after enrollment in some cases. This case is not likely a strong precedent for the principle that an institution can increase tuitions any amount at any time just because a contract expressly allows for simple "increases". Individual case facts will be important.
    d. Promotional materials err on the other side by often being too focused on inducing students to enter contracts and by not being focused enough on whether what is said really coincides with what is actually done or will be done during the program.
    e. Statements or summaries of product and program content do not have to encompass all instructional mate-

rials or even exhaustively list what is to follow over periods of months or years. Content, however, is important. Astrophysics is not the same as the history of the World War Two. Institutions cannot just rely on short little snippets that give a three line summary of what the course addresses.

f. Some reasonable summary of targeted Learning Outcome Objectives is in most cases necessary and especially given the focus of this work which is built on the common commercial principle that quality relates to a product that is merchantable and that does what it says it will do.

7. As noted, it cannot be assumed that all students within an institution or even within a program cohort will always have the same contract terms and that is because of the evolving and executory nature of the contract.

19.3 Case Study: Contract Content

The following list of potential terms is drawn from a common precedent used by our firm. It draws four corners around the contract, but also accepts and works with the reality that additional terms could be implied or included in specific circumstances. All variable information and terms are confined to Schedule B. Most clients are institutions, but a strong contract carefully balances the needs of both parties.

Main Page

- Contract Parties and Execution
- The Program, Contract Product and Tuition
- Term of Contract
- Contract Inclusions (Schedules), Exclusions (Business Policies, Public Duties), Entire Agreement

Schedule A: Terms and Conditions
Part 1: Pre-Contract Recruitment, Admissions, Tuition Fees

- Third Party Referrals and Recruitment
- Representations and Recruitment, Quality Assurance Designations or Brands

- Credit Transfer, Program Challenges, Credential Evaluation, Program Integration
- Student Application, Admission Standards, Student Success and Admissions
- Student Tuition and Program Fees

Part 2: The Program Product

- Promised Program Product, Collective (Not Individual) Factors That Create Effective Learning Environment for Student
- Program Learning Objectives (Achievement Not Promised)
- Student Academic Contributions
- Workplace Programs, Student Services, Property Assets (Not Promised Unless Expressed In Writing)
- Program and Service Changes
- Institution's Contract Performance (Help Student Achieve Learning Objective), Quality
- No Post Contract Outcomes Promised (e.g. Jobs, Business Success or Income, Immigration Permits)
- No Promise of Student Financial Aid
- Government Accreditations or Brands Are Not Additional Quality Representations

Part 3: The Student Assessment Product
and Other Student Services

- Student Assessment Systems and Graduate Credentials
- Credential Awarded If Graduation Standards Met
- No Promise of Credit Transferability Or Uniform Content, Learning Objective or Competency (Unless Expressed In Writing)
- No Promise of Professions Membership.
- Student Services

Part 4: Personal Information, Confidential
Information and Intellectual Property

- Personal Information Management, Consents, Student Photograph and Likeness

- Institution's Confidential Information
- Student Intellectual Property
- Institution Intellectual Property

Part 5: Dispute Avoidance and Resolution, Withdrawals, Dismissals, Termination

- Duty to Report Program Issues
- Dispute Resolution, Choice of Law and Venue
- Limitation of Institution and Student Liability
- Termination, Withdrawal, Dismissal, Delays, Cancellation
- Prohibited Actions (e.g. Plagiarism, Harassment, Disorderly Conduct)
- Tuition and Fee Refunds

Schedule B: Program, Program Fee and Additional Information and Provisions

- Parties' Information
- Program Outline
- Program Length and Period
- Tuition and Fees
- Other Expressed Provisions Altering Default Provisions

Execution

- Most jurisdictions have laws that allow for online, electronic and digital contracts and signatures.
- We utilize Agreement Express by Recombo to offer institutions an easy online contract option.
- Agreement Express is a leading cloud based software platform for digital signature, document, work flow and business process management.
- These systems are easy to use and highly efficient.
- With Agreement Express, signature blocks are bound to set persons, documents or document areas. It is not a digitized (image of wet ink) signature, not a click-wrap solution and not reliant on click through evidence to establish ID and contract assent.

20

Institution and Student Contract Management, Dispute Avoidance and Resolution

20.1 Contract Focus Is About Reality Management and Student Service and Not Just Disputes

It is worthwhile repeating that the focus on contracts and contract law is not is not about laying the groundwork for lawyers to take over the education system with endless litigation. It is about the opposite. It is about addressing reality and making sure that students and institutions understand the nature and essence of their relationship so that both can do what is expected of them and so that they and society can fully benefit from the interaction.

This focus arose from the observation that the parties were often not that clear about the reality of their legal relationship and that was often reflected in needless disputes, irrational claims, weak management and un-focused, unrealistic, ineffective and inefficient regulation.

If institutions, students and education regulators, funders and other stakeholders have a clear understanding of the commercial products involved, the true "outcomes" sought, the risks targeted and the contract and regulatory standards needed to mitigate risk then they can all set and achieve realistic and achievable contract and regulatory objectives and goals. Contract (students and institutions) and regulatory (institutions and government) relationships are distinct and deal with separate parties, rights, duties, subjects and objects, but they often target the same risks and work to ensure that the student receives what they were promised under the contract.

Nevertheless, private disputes can arise and effective ways of managing and resolving them must be put in place.

20.2 Public and Private Institutions, Common Markets and Common Methods of Dispute Resolution

As noted, there are few real legal distinctions between so-called public institutions and private institutions. Their separate corporate identity may arise via different legislative instruments and processes, but the status of being separate from government and non-government is the same. Non-profit versus for-profit distinctions can exist within the private sector also. Both so-called public and private institutions enter student contracts as private and independent entities (often even if tuitions are not paid) and increasingly they compete against each other in common markets where they market to and enroll from a common body of students. They are unified at the market level through the mechanism of contract law. Both are governed under the same body of common law as it relates to contracts.

As argued, education regulation should be targeted at education products and consumption risk. Regulation should operate separately from, but alongside contract law to ensure students receive what was promised to them and that products satisfy legal standards also focused on mitigating consumer risk. Regulations and contracts operate separately because parties to the regulatory relationship are the institution and public agency while the parties to the student and institution contract relationship are only those two parties. Public and private rights and duties may be similar in substance, but they are legally distinct in terms of the parties, the relationships and the mechanisms of creating and enforcing these respective rights and duties.

Students in all sectors should have the same protections and different regulations can be justified where risks differ and that affirms the principle that contract provisions drive variation. All students should have the same rights and duties, the same protection to quality assurance regulation and the same rights and duties in relation to how their products and providers are regulated and how their disputes are resolved. Again, contract variation can create risk variation and therefore justify regulatory variation. The parties setting the regulatory rules must be objective and impartial and not represent just one element of the education sector.

It is hard to argue that common domestic treatment of all providers is not warranted if they are treated largely the same for international trade purposes. In relation to the GATS (other sections), it boils down to what the phrase (required for GATS exclusion) "supplied in the exercise of government authority" really means. To many it means not in competition with other suppliers. The reality is that so-called public institutions are often not government as such and do compete with other suppliers. Even if trade agreement exclusion can be justified the exclusion would normally exist to protect domestic students (e.g. protection of subsidies). Exemptions from common dispute resolution methods or quality standards are harder to justify.

20.3 Judicial Review and the Education Sector, An Historical Anomaly

Judicial review normally means that courts review the decisions and actions of authorities that have government powers delegated to them by statute. Administrative law deals with legal limitations that exist on the actions of persons exercising delegated statutory powers that impact a person's legal and economic interests. It deals with the remedies available to those affected by transgressions of these limits. Superior courts can review some of the decisions and actions taken by these delegates to ensure the proper exercise of delegated powers, but generally cannot substitute their own judgment on the merits for the original decision.

For largely historical reasons, some persons still argue that actions by way of judicial review and not actions in contract are the appropriate forum for disputes between students and institutions that cannot be resolved internally. We and many commentators disagree. One element behind this reasoning seems to be the perception that education is a public service that somehow falls under the umbrella of public bodies that are subject to the principles of administrative law and actions of judicial review that are possible when grounds of review exist.

As said earlier, however, institutions are generally not regulators of students. They are a party to a contract and the student is also a party to that contract. So-called university "regulations" do not have the status of law unless a statute says so. Universities often argue—when it suits them - that calendars or collections of rules and policies are incorporated into student contracts. We recommend against such broad inclusion, but such inclusion must be intended by the parties. [122] They cannot be contract terms and also some form of law made by a delegated power.

In the past courts often said judicial review of [123] university decisions was possible if the complainant allowed the university to correct its own mistakes with internal tribunals before approaching the courts, if the matter remained unresolved and if grounds for judicial review existed (e.g. natural justice principles were not respected). [124]

Noah Sarna [125] points out that extending this form of judicial review to universities is stretching the principle. Universities have been held to not be government in the sense that they are not subject to review under the Canadian Charter of Rights and Freedoms. [126] Courts may choose to not review decisions of delegate tribunals for the same reasons they defer to university tribunals. They talk about parliamentary supremacy and respect the legislature's intent which is often indicated by a privative clause or [127] practical considerations of speed, informality, expense and expertise.

Sarna rightly says [128] that this is a weaker argument for deference with university tribunals than with administrative tribunals. Administrative agencies are purely public and bodies created and maintained by the state warrant greater deference than private institutions because purely public bodies require popular legitimacy and parliamentary approval. The Canadian Charter applies to administrative branches of government, but it does not apply to major provincial universities. [129] That is because most universities are essentially private in nature in the sense they are created as corporate bodies by statute and operate—at the insistence of institutions on the grounds of academic freedom - independently of government and political interference.

In addition, the Canadian Constitution awards provinces the power to make laws in relation to education, but not the sole power to provide education services under contract to students. In that sense any decision involved with settling a dispute with a student is not a delegated constitutional power even where government acts as a natural person and enters contracts with students rather than via independent corporate entities. The situation is not significantly different in most other legal jurisdictions.

In this education context, administrative law applies more to education regulators that act under statute to regulate institutions and product quality assurance. It is not suited for institutions themselves because so-called public institutions are not government and are corporately separate and distinct from government. Institutions in their public form insist on that separation because of their asserted academic freedoms.

The student may be a protected object or beneficiary of those laws governing institutions and programs and that institution-regulator relationship, but they are not a regulated party. When a student has a relationship with a public education institution it is not a citizen-tribunal relationship, but, a service provider and consumer relationship. A student's relationship with their university arises in a contractual [130] context which constitutes a private endeavor.

In many cases the legislation that public institutions operate under only gives Senates or comparable bodies broad powers to deal with academic matters. It often does not make them tribunals with independence from the arm of the institution providing the contract service. No matter what steps they take to be fair and to appoint ad hoc type committees or impartial tribunals internally it would arguably be the essence of bias or the perception of bias to have one party to a contract also pretend to be an unbiased party ruling over the contract and determining the rights and obligations of both parties. Even if the two parties jointly named a neutral mediator or arbiter to help them resolve a dispute they would do so as two contract parties. Contract actions or arbitration models, where both contracting parties have an equal say are more appropriate dispute resolution models.

Sarna and others point out that there are other reasons to hold that judicial review is not the way to settle these disputes. Unlike Acts governing many tribunals, university statutes often do not include privative clauses that try to block judicial review. An essential attribute of tribunals—expertise—is absent so deference is less justified. The tribunal must not only have specialized knowledge, but greater knowledge than civil courts regarding the matters within its jurisdiction and even if it has some expertise with education that does not mean it has expertise with contract law

Access to justice should extend to individuals usually denied meaningful redress for their grievances by the delegation of legal authority through deference to non-state normative regimes. Courts have an obligation to students to examine long-held assumptions and to respect not only the institution, but also the concerns of students. Because there was no clear law and binding contract law precedent in many cases it was easier for courts to defer and this is less true now. [131]

Finally, judicial review and administrative law would rarely result in private damages because bad faith has to be shown. When a cause of action is shown students should have access to damages when the remedy would normally be available in other commercial circumstances. Students should have the protections of contract law precedent. Tribunals or university tribunals must not make errors of law and if settling disputes they must follow the law of the land. It cannot just make up new contract law. When they make their decisions they may not follow their own precedents because they ignore them or feel they are not bound. Students often have no access to past precedent because of privacy concerns. [132] This is not the case with court judgments.

20.4 Dispute Resolution, Contract Actions

Traditional judicial deference to universities and the refusal to consider student complaints was often not just and is still often not just. Everyone deserves to have their valid legal claims and disputes heard by a competent and independent adjudicator. A constitutional argument to that effect can certainly be made in Canada, the US, the UK and other common law jurisdictions.

If the courts don't have the power to intervene in academic affairs when a true injustice (under contract, tort or other laws) has occurred then the parties are denied a right other commercial players are not denied. As observed, universities will aggressively assert their rights in contract law if a student did not pay tuition or if a contract allowed them to increase fees mid-program. Student often pay high tuitions, but even if they don't the principle remains.

Subject to what the parties may expressly agree, these laws must always be at play and the law of contract and tort and other laws must apply because law, as a unified whole, does not mean one thing for one person and something else for another and one thing for courts and something else in a tribunal. Non-court bodies empowered with dispute resolution powers generally cannot deny parties the right to the protection of the law as it generally applies. That is the rule with administrative law where an agency's failure to apply the law of the land would be a judicially reviewable intra-jurisdictional error of law.

The points above regarding the anomalous use of judicial review in the education sector bear repeating here. Again, continued deference will no doubt continue to some extent so that courts do not end up dealing with minor grade disputes, but serious actions in contract, tort or other areas of law must be and now are available to students.

20.5 Internal Institution Dispute Resolution

Whether judicial review, contract actions in court or alternative dispute resolution methods are involved there is usually some onus on the parties to take all reasonable measure to resolve the dispute between themselves first before asking others to resolve it for them. That is as it should be. Often that works and the matter is settled.

Internal dispute resolution has its place, but legal actions must be available unless the parties both agree to waive their rights and to rely on non-judicial methods. Having one party to the contract in dominant control of its disputes is fundamentally wrong. Institutions are generally not regulators of students. They are a party to a contract and the student is also a party to that contract. Both are equal parties and must have equal rights.

Internal dispute resolution methods must be impartial and if one party has the sole control to appoint an internal panel of some kind then that panel—no matter well chosen—is never truly neutral because it came into being via the actions of one party. In the past and in the age of judicial deference disputes between students and institutions were often left to internal panels. These were not necessarily really independent of the institution. The old In Loco Parentis and club models did not see the two parties as equals and the institution often dominated the process. As commentators have pointed out, [133] the agreement of students to have their internal grievances adjudicated solely by university tribunals (with questionable independence if the institution appoints them) is hardly voluntary because the institution is in an inherently stronger position than the student who must accept membership or contract status on the university's own terms—an arrangement closer to a contract of adhesion than a contract based on a consent.

20.6 Alternate Dispute Resolution

Alternative dispute resolution methods - including independent mediation and binding arbitration - are always possible. It is common in commercial contracts for the parties to agree to either. A student contract can also. The issue is too complex to address in detail here, but the use of ADR methods does not necessarily mean that the law of the land as it relates to contract, tort or other types of law does not apply. The waiver of such rights is a very serious matter especially as the degree of impact to the parties becomes more extreme. [134]

20.7 Quality Assurance Regulator Adjudication, A Poor Option to Be Avoided

Education quality assurance regulators normally enforce laws set down by or pursuant to statute. Their job is not to enforce the contract between an institution and a student. The contract parties enforce their own contract. That issue was addressed in other sections. Regulators cannot force a party to make a claim under a contract if they are not so disposed and regulators are not privy and party to the contract so they have no direct right to claim under it.

In BC, Canada, a statute gave an independent career training regulator the power to award refunds from an assurance fund if a student was, in the opinion of the board, misled by the institution about any aspect of their operations. The assumption is that this depended on a student initiated complaint because again a non-contract party could not try to claim contract breach if no contract party was alleging it.

This type of regulator based dispute resolution is often flawed for various reasons. They have no contract law expertise and - because their fundamental purpose is consumer protection—the perception of bias can reasonably exist. Education regulators, especially those that have industry elected boards, should not have the power to settle disputes. As with university tribunals, these agencies usually have no contract law expertise and contract law applies in this context because regulators must adhere to the law of the land or risk making judicially reviewable errors of law. They cannot rewrite contract law.

These agency tribunals, to be the proper and credible choice, must not only have specialized knowledge, but greater knowledge than civil courts regarding the matters within its jurisdiction and even if it has some expertise with education that does not mean it has expertise with contract law. A lack of legal knowledge in BC led to attempts to effectively abolish the principle of res judicata (a matter is conclusively and finally decided), to allow effective class actions without procedures to establish common cause, mixing public and private rights and forcing losing parties to pay government investigation costs without supporting statutory provisions. These attempts were all successfully reversed.

It can be strongly argued that these regulatory bodies are not unbiased because their very purpose for existing is to protect consumers. We have letters from the Deputy Minister in BC that says the purpose of the above noted process involving regulatory tribunal adjudication of private disputes is to protect consumers. An impartial tribunal is not there to support one of the parties. In a self-regulated environment the student can argue that the agency is fundamentally biased or that there is a perception of bias.

In BC there is a requirement that students complaining to a regulator given the power to settle certain types of disputes first exhaust internal dispute resolution processes. Arguably "internal" refers to any non-judicial method and not just informal methods between the parties. The parties can try to settle a dispute without relying on strict references to statutes or common law (e.g. contract law), but if that reliance is made then they must adhere to the law of the land. Many arbitrators must normally adhere to the law of the land when they make decisions. [135]

This BC example was also glaringly unbalanced because it only addressed private disputes in the private education sector. Again, all students and institutions should have the same protections and duties and be subject to the same dispute resolution measures because they act in a common market.

20.8 Independent Education Sector Dispute Resolution Adjudicators (UK Example)

It may be inevitable that sector specific dispute resolution bodies develop for the education sector. The earlier deferential attitude of the courts to student and institution disputes in the education sector was understandable to an extent because the courts do not want to entertain every student claim about grades, but that deference went too far and often left students unable to assert a serious claim. Serious disputes can arise and students and institutions should not be denied their day in court—or before another body that will adjudicate under the laws of the land or a mutually agreed to process. Expertise in education and law could justify such independence.

One early example is the independent adjudication model emerging in the UK as a forum to settle student and institution disputes. This UK

Office of the Independent Adjudicator is non-judicial, non-institution and non-regulatory (not associated with quality assurance regulation). This UK independent adjudication office was created by statute and deals with disputes between institutions and students. This would not rely on internal institution dispute settlement or judicial rulings. Such an agency would likely have to still apply contract law to the extent it applies to the issues raised, but this has not been confirmed. Students still have the choice to use the courts if they wish. This independent body is mandated to settle student complaints that could not be settled internally. It covers most major institutions and can potentially cover all public and private institutions.

20.9 Case Studies for Student Contract Disputes: Allegations, Media and Regulatory Frenzy, No Legal Substance; US Law Schools; The Kitchen Sink Claim

Some student complaints and claims are trivial and destined to fail from day one and others are substantial and serious complaints and claims. Many illustrate the points raised in the contract law and tort law primer materials reviewed briefly. That includes the principles of contract formation and enforceability, the substance of terms (promises, representations, conditions or other terms) and the potential breach of terms and remedies for breach. Attention must always be placed on the core elements and factors that really induced persons into the contract and that led to contract provisions that could, if breached, lead to serious remedies and even repudiation of the contract. Again, the point is to learn how to perform under a contract and to avoid disputes and not to encourage them.

Case Study 1 (Canada): Allegations, Media and Regulator Frenzy, No Legal Substance

The media or regulators often focus on emotion or the big headline and ignore contract reality. They can make even minor or legally insignificant events seem like major fraud. In one case, a media feeding frenzy began with student blog posts. Students would say things like, "I didn't get what I signed up for. I feel like I was misled." Both concepts are contractual in nature, but absolutely no attention was put on the contract or the substance of contract law.

The story referred to hardball recruitment tactics and promises of high-paying jobs on graduation. Again, this concept of "promises" is important. No one puts attention on what in fact was promised. Even if statements were made by recruiters and they often are that does not mean all representations are contractual. Courts will, even where representations are proven, hold that the complainant would not have, given their knowledge and sophistication, reasonably relied on a representation. There can be an onus on students to do their own due diligence.

In one unrelated, but on-point case, the court said: "... in assessing the likelihood of confusion, the Court ought to give the average consumer a certain amount of credit. Consumers are not completely devoid of intelligence or of normal powers of recollection; nor are they totally unaware or uniformed as to what goes on around them. The overriding consideration regarding the likelihood of confusion is "all the surrounding circumstances", that is, ... any and all facts peculiar to the case before it:" [136] Everyone knows that employment markets are tough and that institutions cannot promise students that they will get jobs. The facts and law are they key.

There were allegations related to unqualified teachers. Who says they were? Were regulations requiring certain qualifications breached? Even if they were those public duties are separate from contract duties. Regulatory violations could be evidence that an expressed or implied contract provision was not satisfied, but no automatic finding of contract breach would result. One bad instructor does not mean the contract is repudiated. No one input creates the collective product or environment that helps the student learn. The collection of inputs can still create the proper learning environment. Other students did fine and liked the course. The institution can create an environment for learning, but the student learns. The story also referred to: inadequate placement services; insufficient operating equipment; and no high-paying jobs after graduation. Were these contractual promises? Most jurisdictions forbid making promises about future jobs. Again, reasonable persons arguably won't or should not rely on promises they know the promisor cannot deliver on.

Claims were made about inaccurate and misleading information about class sizes, enrolment costs and student loans. No details were provided and no complaints were filed. If the size difference is significant and actual inducement to contract is established this can be a valid claim, but a student likely still has to prove that the change hampered their ability to achieve the learning outcome objective. If that was not the case there is no real loss and no real remedy warranted. One wants small classes because they think it will enhance learning. Violations can be technical in nature and not cause serious risk or loss and penalties should reflect that.

The Canadian regulator involved became concerned by media reports, but there were no specific allegations of infractions of law and few student complaints. The regulator cannot enforce the contract. Only the contract parties can initiate those actions. The case illustrated how regulators often forget that they enforce laws. They do not have limitless consumer protection or public interest protection powers. They must act under the law and use the tools given by statute. The tools they have for consumer protection are the laws they enforce or in some cases make and enforce. Public interest powers normally extend again to using those existing powers in the public interest.

Case Study 2: USA Law Schools

In early 2012, [137] more than twenty law schools faced litigation or class actions over allegedly deceptive job-placement rates. The law schools say the schools must be careful about what is said to applicants, but they also say disclaimers should not have to be five pages long and students should not have to take an oath that they won't sue if they don't get a job. They say law schools don't control the economy. That is confusing two issues. Institutions cannot be held liable if students cannot find jobs (aside from misguided student loan policy). These law students are focused on the misrepresentations, but it is the lack of jobs and income that create the loss. If stats were misleading and jobs were found and money was good then they might not have a loss to remedy.

The issue then seems to be that students were allegedly misled into enrolling because of misrepresentations about job and income prospects and therefore exposed themselves to debt and perhaps lost opportunity and the loss of time invested. Was it reasonable for the students to rely on that information and did they rely on it to their detriment? Most people are aware that markets for lawyers are tough. Was the information wrong and known to be wrong or was it correct when given and then became outdated?

In most cases, the students are not claiming that they did not get a good education. The students will have to show that of all the reasons why they chose law as a profession and that specific school that the reason they decided to attend was the representation about prospects. That could be tough. A class action is tough because students have various reasons for enrolling and common cause could be hard to establish.

It is important to note that an institution has a separate contract with each student and generally does not contract with a group of students. Class members purchase and consume a common product so class actions could arise, but the evolving nature of the product is such that contracts and individual circumstances can vary. At one point, the province of BC in Canada tried to facilitate class actions without requiring that common cause be proven as it must be with all class actions. The bylaw was withdrawn in the face of opposition. Courts intimate they could entertain class actions. [138] There was no indication in any media reports that US education regulators were taking any action against the schools involved despite widespread media coverage.

Case Study 3: The Kitchen Sink Claim

This case is a good example of how legal illiteracy can get out of hand. Students had paid substantial tuitions for a technically oriented course. A cohort of about fifteen students virtually all became gainfully employed in the field of study after graduation including the claimant. Initially there were some legitimate issues raised by the class and the eventual claimant and the school resolved most of them to the satisfaction of the class - except for the claimant. Upon graduation and getting a job in the field of study one student laid a claim to get their entire tuition back.

It was easily argued that there was substantial performance and that no real loss occurred and the case was dismissed, but not before the claimant had mixed up private law and public law to an extreme degree. The student literally copied the entire set of public regulations that applied to the institution and systematically pointed out where they felt the institution was not in compliance. In most cases the institution was in fact in compliance, but the point is that such compliance was largely irrelevant to the contract claim. As noted, public law violations do not generally give rise to private rights. Initially, the regulator given power to adjudicate the complaint (a practice opposed on legal grounds) did not see the distinction and was prepared to consider the public law points raised. They were convinced that they could not do so and the claim was dismissed.

Part 4

Education Regulation In An Era of Disruptive Innovation, Quality Assurance Delimited

21

Education Product Performance and Quality Assurance Foundations

21.1 Contract and Regulatory Quality Assurance, Common Aims But Legally Distinct Parties, Methods, Rights and Duties

Quality assurance is a concept that relates to the separate worlds of contracts and contract law and the world of regulation. In commercial terms, products are expected to be merchantable, that is, they should do what they promised to do and be what they were promised to be. Contract laws ensure that: the parties have an enforceable contract; the parties perform under the contract; and the parties have legal recourse if non-performance occurs.

As noted, the student enrollment contract and what is promised by way of product generally triggers regulation. Regulation of a legal entity and its products or services generally arises because of the nature of the enterprise and its products and the consumption risks posed by the product to the consumer. Regulation utilizes prohibitions, standards, standards compliance and permissions granted upon compliance as means to mitigate that risk.

Both contract parties and regulatory parties are therefore focused on products, consumers, consumption risks, standards, compliance, rights, duties and permissions. Contract and regulatory systems are separate and distinct in legal terms with separate parties, subjects, objects, rights, duties and tools. Contract parties enforce their own contract and regulators use the tools and powers granted to them by statute.

Stephen Covey, in Chapter 5 of his book "The 3rd Alternative", attacked the industrial age mindset that saw the school as a factory and the student as a product produced for the economy. He quoted from a 1927 article in the American Education Digest: "A dispassionate study of the product of the educational system forces the conclusion that the product is falling far short of what modern business is demanding."

Sadly, this mindset still often distracts managers and regulators from the reality that a student more normally consumes a contract product for a price. The person only becomes a product after that when they offer services in workplace, professional and business markets.

21.2 Consistent Legal Theories of Quality Required, Product Focus Needed As Exists With Other Commercial Sectors, Order Sought By Law Is Order in Student and Institution Relationship

A major problem with education regulation in some jurisdictions and across jurisdictions is the lack of a consistent, uniform and legally sound approach to quality assurance. This is not the same as the need (as some argue) for uniform standards between jurisdictions. You do not want uniformly bad standards based on unsound legal theories about quality.

The issue of uniform standards is addressed in sections on assessment, innovative regulation and briefly below. The bottom line there is that uniformity should only involve certain types of standards and any need for content, learning objective, competency and credential uniformity should be left to private parties outside the realm of quality assurance regulation because quality does not require or dictate uniformity. Diversity is reality and good.

Approaches to quality assurance can be made consistent if they focus on the essential commercial and contract nature of the buyer and seller relationship and on the products contractually promised. Products may be extremely diverse and serve very diverse markets and forces of demand, but that inherent commercial, product and contractual promise reality does not change.

Put another way, quality assurance regulation for the education sector should focus, as regulators for other commercial sectors do, on understanding the product bought and sold under contract and on ensuring that it is merchantable, that is, that it does what it promised and was supposed to do and in this case it is supposed to help a student achieve a learning outcome objective. The focus should be on product, product quality and product consumption risk. Law aims to establish and maintain order and equilibrium in relationships and with the student and institution relationship it is the student contract and its product that defines the relationship and its risk or state of order.

Education regulation is not about protecting both parties from all of the vicissitudes and risks of life. Regulation targeted at this relationship should be confined to this and not used as a tool to achieve unrelated social or economic objectives. Consumers are consumers because they consume "under contract" a product.

Regulators can, if they have the delegated power, mandate behaviors that may increase the chances of contract performance, but their job is not to enforce the contract. Again, only the parties can enforce their contracts. Regulators cannot force a party to take action under a contract or take their place as plaintiff. Regulators enforce laws. They cannot normally declare that a party was in contract breach and if they had that delegated power that would be the power to adjudicate a dispute or Lis Inter Parties. It would go beyond the normal regulatory power where an agency enforces and acts pursuant to powers granted by statute and where public duties exist.

21.3 Quality Assurance Efforts Must Focus on Merchantable Products (Outcome 1) That Help Students Achieve Learning Objectives (Outcome 2), Subject Matter Content, Levels of Complexity and Expertise

These points were first made when Outcome 2 (Achievement of Learning Objectives) was first introduced.

The learning objective idea encompasses subject matter content and levels of difficulty. Obviously a learning objective is different for a physics course and a biology course. In every area of knowledge you also have multiple levels of difficulty, sophistication or expertise. Quality programs can exist at each level and quality standards can be adapted for each level. Comparisons can be made between disciplines. Courses on bartending may not be as inherently difficult as a program on astrophysics, but both programs can be of quality. In all cases, admissions and assessment systems reflect the product and learning outcome objectives as they relate to content subject matter and levels of difficulty, sophistication and expertise.

This is important because of the approach taken to quality assurance. Quality should be confined to the commercial concept of determining whether a product was what it was supposed to be and did what it was supposed to do. In other words, a quality product is a merchantable product. It is of merchantable quality.

The term "merchantable" is used in the way it is normally used in commercial environments. A merchantable (quality) product is one that is reasonably fit for the ordinary purposes for which it was produced and sold. Education firms should be and are, like other sellers or producers, required by law to make products of merchantable quality. The ordinary purpose for an education product is to help a student learn and to achieve a set learning objective. [139] What the student may then do with that in terms of jobs or business is a subsequent matter that the product producer has no control over. No one would tell Ford that its trucks were not merchantable and of quality because a buyer failed in the construction business they bought the truck for.

This allows, as is advised, for quality assurance to capture or encompass any level of difficulty or expertise. If a person or authority needs to do more than just determine if a product is of quality and able to help a student achieve a learning objective then they should look beyond quality. For example, a product could be quality assured, but perhaps - because it does not lead to the level of knowledge and expertise required - still not be one that a lender wants to lend for, that an immigration authority wants to admit a student for, that a profession does not want to use for admission purposes or that another institution does not want to give credit for.

21.4 Products and Quality, Unsound and Inconsistent Use of Terms Like Outcomes or Student Success

As noted, quality in relation to the education product relates to the ability and capacity of the education product (that collection of product factors) to help (as contractually promised) the student achieve the learning outcome objective. A quality education product is one that is merchantable and that does what the seller said it would do. In line with services theory, it helps the consumer change their own knowledge and skill conditions.

Regulators are relying on and falling in love with words and concepts like "Outcomes" and "Student Success", but then they often use those terms in an infinite number of ways—many of which are divorced from learning, legal and commercial realities. A student contract, the contract product that is bought and sold and the regulation that runs separately, but parallel to that must focus on whether that product worked in the way it was supposed to and on the risks associated with consumption.

Concepts of education quality must focus on whether learning occurred and not on outcomes that might arise or what might be done with the knowledge gained far into the future. Student success should focus only on academic and program success and not future workplace or business success. More emphasis should be placed on assessment systems (Separate Sections). This is the only practical approach as opposed to trying to determine what the quality of a program or institution was because of how the knowledge gained was used or not used later or able to help ex-students achieve certain objectives in environments uncontrolled by students or institutions.

As noted, contract and regulatory standards must be doable and achievable to be legally valid, acceptable or appropriate in relation to the principles of regulatory best practices and often in relation to principles of law. Standards that are impossible to achieve are not standards, but new and impossible to overcome absolute prohibitions. For example, it is common in our experience for BC regulators at least to refer to academic success in a program and career success in the same breath even though education and post education workplace and business systems are distinct in terms of real cause and effect, objectives and legal and commercial relationships.

In Canada, in early 2012 there was an interesting spectacle. Public sector faculty members gathered for a two day conference focused on several questions: What do we mean when we talk about student success? Are students, faculty, administrators and government talking about the same thing when they talk about student success? How can we ensure that our students are getting the education they need to achieve their goals, succeed in the workforce and be the citizens and leaders of tomorrow? Are today's students ready to succeed? What do students really want? Are we set up for student success?

At the same time we were fighting for clients faced with undefined student loan designation requirements that designated institutions must "ensure" student success. Such terms, open to vastly divergent interpretations, have no place in regulation unless those interpreting them are given interpretive guidance. This is again discussed in relation to the distinction between the notion of "employability" and the concept of requiring institutions to meet set employment rates for grads even though they clearly cannot control that. Measures of standards are distinct from legal standards. Standards that require impossible (for the regulated party) feats are not standards, but new absolute prohibitions that are not allowed without clear statutory guidance (rarely the case).

The reality is that no institution can ensure even academic success (because the student controls that outcome) let alone post student contract success in the workplace or a business marketplace. At the most it can only help a student learn in a program targeted at a workplace or business need. Again, standards are set to address specific risks that are mitigated when standards are met. Impossible requirements are not standards, but new prohibitions that generally cannot be set by those with delegated powers.

21.5 Quality Cannot Be Seen As Changing As Economies Change

As discussed in other sections, education quality must focus on the education product that is the object of quality. That product is designed to help the student consumer achieve a set learning objective. Quality must focus on standards that the regulated parties can achieve and on standards that reflect risks associated with the consumption of the education product as opposed to risks associated with economic cycles and events and decisions beyond the regulated institution's control.

Education quality cannot logically be seen to go up and down as employment rates go up and down. It is unwise and legally unsound in many cases to propose a definition or concept of quality that would see an institution judged as providing poor quality education one year because employment and business prospects are poor and then, with the identical program, judged to be of good quality when those prospects improve.

21.6 Product Focus of Quality Is On Collective and Not Individual Inputs, The ISO Example

Quality also cannot focus on specific product factor inputs alone because collectively all of the inputs might still be successful at helping the student achieve the learning outcome, validate the achievement with assessments and benefit from other services provided under contract. Regulating inputs is perfectly feasible and proper provided the collective impact of the inputs is the key measure to determine the overall quality of the program. As discussed in other sections, a bad teacher or a series of computer crashes do not automatically constitute sufficient loss, contract breach or breach sufficient to warrant a serious remedy.

The International Standards Organization (Below) and others properly focus on student consumer expectations and that requires a focus on contractual promises and representations and that in turn points toward an education product that helps the student learn. Reasonable students do not expect every professor to be wonderful and every other input to be perfect. The key is whether, on balance, the program was able to help the student achieve the desired learning objective and state of knowledge. In the contract terms referred to in other sections, the key is whether there was substantial compliance with the core promises that induced the contract.

The ISO [140] education standard works with other ISO management standards and focuses on: whether the institution is able to facilitate the learning results required or desired; the fact that only the student can achieve learning objectives (the correct standard); how learning is validated; and ensuring that proper assessment is done credibly. The institution can only contractually promise to have a learning environment that is capable of helping the student achieve the learning objective. It cannot and does not promise the achievement because only the student can learn.

The ISO says quality management systems, quality policy and quality objectives and activities are aimed at meeting customer demands (as manifested by contract terms) and efforts to continually improve performance and particularly "product and program performance". The ISO says quality management identifies and documents the needs and expectations of learners and these expectations can't be separated from the contract and the parties' contractual intentions.

It says curricula must include outcomes and performance indicators, but its "outcomes" concept is learning and not job focused. It defines institutional requirements for quality systems as actions required for continued improvement of quality and quality management systems that are learning not workplace focused. Outcomes based education is, according to most experts, about assessing whether students are meeting measurable learning objectives and not about post contract outcomes. Unfortunately, some regulators do not seem to grasp this fundamental reality.

21.7 Products and Product Providers, Education Quality Is About What Service Providers Do, Objects of Quality v. Subjects of Regulation

As noted, the object of quality must be the consumed product. Statutory references to "quality standards for accredited institutions" or "registered institutions" are common, [141] but that does not make the institution as a corporate entity the object of quality. Institutions might be the subject of regulation because regulators want to target an entity that can be subject to law and made to change behaviours that put consumers at risk, but they are not the object of quality. Student consumers do not consume the institution. They consume what the institution and corporation offer to provide and provide under contract. If the institution never provided a product there would be no student risk and no need for regulation.

The quality standards are there to modify institution behavior so that it is more likely that the product is as contractually promised and that it will be merchantable and functional and do what it is designed to do. They are designed to force institutions to act in ways that make them worthy of the permission to operate and to engage in otherwise prohibited actions. That is done by assessing the risks of consumption and by setting standards that relate to those risks. Regulators could focus on how the institution chooses to decorate its offices, but that would not relate to student consumer risk.

21.8 Object of Quality and Product Focus Allows Adjustment to Education, Assessment and Other Services

Again, to be clear, quality must refer to whether the promised education product (Outcome 1), as a collection of inputs or product factors, was sufficient to help the student achieve the contractually unpromised (student controls) Second Outcome or state of knowledge and learning outcome objective. Assessment results are the measure. If 90% of students pass and 10% do not then that is a good indication of education product quality if the assessment system is properly in tune with the program offered and its learning objective.

If students have quality issues or complaints they must bring them up immediately so they can be dealt with. They cannot wait until the end and expect action. This goes to the need to mitigate loss.

Similarly, assessment products can be considered of quality if they were effective measures of learning and academic achievement and met expectations in terms of objectivity, impartiality and credibility (See Assessment). Other services must also generally be judged according to whether contract expectations were met. Minimum standards could be legislated, but they too must relate to real consumer risk and not general social or economic policy objectives that have nothing to do with the purposes of the governing education quality assurance statute.

21.9 Quality Does Not Require Uniformity, Where Uniformity May Be Appropriate and How To Do It

Uniformity issues were discussed in greater detail in other sections (Assessment Products). Briefly put, products do not have to be the same in order to be of high quality. If there are contract promises regarding common learning objectives, content, competencies, assessment, credentials and related credit transfer or credential recognition then that promise must be kept.

That could fall under "quality" guidelines because a quality product does what it promised to do but, this must be separated from the core concept of quality in education which must focus on whether the product helped the student learn and achieve a set learning objective. The separate equality factor is best worked out by the contract parties and by the efforts of institutions, industry bodies and other stakeholders and not by central quality assurance regulations.

21.10 Media Reviews Are Not Reliable Legal Measures of Quality

They may have some value as consumer information, but media reviews of institutions are not reliable legal measures of quality because they fail to focus on the fundamentals of actually helping the student achieve learning objectives. They lack the precision needed in a legal environment.

The annual Macleans survey of universities in Canada or the US News and World Report in the USA look at various categories of institutions. Macleans classifies institutions as: medical doctoral; comprehensive; research; graduate; undergraduate; or professional. It looks at factors like: number of student awards per 1000 students; student-faculty ratios; faculty awards; faculty time spent on research v. classes; research money as a percentage of the budget; student support; scholarships and bursaries; student services as a percentage of budget; library acquisitions/holdings per student and total holdings; reputation. They also rely on views of quality and innovation from hundreds of university officials, high school principals, guidance counsellors, CEOs, recruiters and organization heads. They look at, but do not factor in supports for entrepreneurship, study abroad programs and community outreach.

As noted, the focus must be on whether contractual promises to provide a learning environment conducive to learning were kept. Institutions do not and cannot promise that a learning outcome objective will be met. The student must do the learning. These media review factors are relevant to student choice, but ultimately they are not reliable measures of what occurs or can occur in terms of actual learning. Learning can occur quite well without virtually any of these factors existing. Many students could care less about research money. They may benefit indirectly, but it is not what they purchase and expect. Student supports are relevant to learning, but there must be some specificity. Scholarships and bursaries are great, but they relate to how a student pays for the product and not whether the product works and does what it is supposed to do.

22

Education Product Quality Assurance Risk and Workplace and Business Risk Distinguished

22.1 How BC Government Evolved Bad Regulatory Concepts About Outcomes Because of Undefined Outcomes

This is an example of how a BC bureaucracy started off with a modestly reasonable concept of "employability" and ended up with accreditation requirements focused on impractical ideas about industry average rates of employment or industry averages related to other outcome measures.

A task force report said institutions should be accountable for the extent to which students achieve outcomes "promised" and implied in their programs and advertising. They could not bring themselves to talk in contract terms even though that is the legal reality they refer to. They said regulation should focus on the "results of an institution's work with a student" and not on how things are done. They should have just said regulations (separate from contracts) should focus on modifying behaviors that make contract performance more likely.

Regulators enforce laws and not contracts. The parties enforce their own contracts. Regulators may or may not have limited powers of dispute resolution (See other sections), but where they do the decision to use that dispute resolution option would be up the contract party.

The "results of an institution's work with a student" referred to in the above task force report cannot reasonably extend to post student contract workplace and business results because those results do not result primarily or substantially from that student and institution relationship. Workplace and business results involve highly complex cause and effect relationships. Systems, as noted, have their own objectives and cause and effect relationships. Those relationships define the system. They are not the "results of an institution's work with a student". This comes back to the earlier point about smart and best practices management and regulation that require that management and regulatory goals be focused on realistic and achievable goals (results).

A government news release then announced that results based accreditation would hold private institutions accountable for the extent to which students achieve "stated program outcomes". They did not initially state what the stated outcomes needed to be about and said schools may choose the outcomes measure and then would have to publicly report on that as a condition of its accreditation so students can make better informed choices. They did not state who the institution was supposed to be "stating" this to and for what purpose. If it is to the student it has contract implications and institutions are normally forbidden from making workplace or business result promises or representations.

These ideas appear to be an attempt to make the institution "accountable" for outcomes that the student "achieves". They refer to what is stated to students to be the outcomes of the relationship. The fact they refer to the institution choosing the outcome means they were not talking about an agreed to outcome. The fact they wanted the student to have information to help them make choices leads toward the existence of contract or pre-contract representations of fact that can induce a person into a contract.

This is again an example of how either legal illiteracy or willful blindness can result in bad policy and bad law. The fact they referred to institutions being held accountable for the student not achieving program outcomes again requires that the outcome be something within the institution's control. Holding the institution accountable for a student failing would be ridiculous because the product itself might have been perfectly capable of helping the student achieve the learning objective is the student had worked. Again, just using the term "outcome" without further clarification is unworkable and legally unsound.

A later letter from the Minister to the agency did not require the "averages" bylaw, but said bylaws may refer to student employability. There was no reference to specific employment results. The term "employability" refers to the ability of a student to find employment and not to the student or a percentage of their class finding a job. Somehow they ended up with a bylaw stating that an institution's accreditation could only be maintained if 70% of grads became employed. After opposition that bylaw was withdrawn and the industry average idea was substituted. It was not about reporting. A standard regarding industry averages had to be met for accreditation to be maintained.

Using industry averages for outcome measures for accreditation and quality purposes is beyond the pale because averages themselves implicitly involve parts of the sample being above and below the average. Someone would always be below and according to a strict reading of the BC law—albeit unenforced—they could lose their accreditation. If the average was low then even poor results could be acceptable. If an average was high some high performers would still be below the average and ruled out.

22.2 Education Quality, Irrelevant Stated Job Outcomes and Contractual Impacts

A requirement that institutions collect and provide job placement information is questionable on its own because it is largely not relevant to education quality and student consumer protection. Again, student consumers are at risk as consumers when they consume a contractually promised education product and legal standards must relate to that risk. Education quality regulation is not about protecting ex-students from unemployment or bad business risks that arise far beyond the contract and product consumption period.

A consistent and sound theory or definition of quality must exist and a program cannot be of quality one day and not the next because employment rates fluctuate.

As outlined, the B.C. Canada regulator of private career training institutions came out with confusing and internally contradictory pronouncements that institutions must live up to their "stated outcomes". This eventually evolved into a bylaw that required institutions to maintain outcomes (stated outcomes must still be published) that exceed industry averages in relation to a "series of outcome-based measures" that include a range of stated outcomes (and unstated incomes) with stated outcomes including job placement outcomes. That sounds awkward but that is how the law was worded. The idea of an institution's stated outcomes being their choice evaporated. This provision has not been enforced and is almost certainly ultra vires the statute, but regulatory language still revolves around this idea of stated outcomes.

It was not clear who this was supposed to be stated to and the regulator did not seem to think that even mattered. Voluntary or not or the institution's option or not, any statement about employment results or incomes "stated" to "students" would violate regulations in BC and would have contractual impact if students are induced into a contract on those grounds. In most cases courts have ruled and are likely to rule that institutions do not make promises about jobs. In BC there is a bylaw that no such promises can be made yet they encourage and arguably require institutions to make "statements" about past employment results that may induce contracts and that could increase the likelihood of students being misled, student litigation or even success with that action.

In the section on marketing it is suggested that materials and contracts distinguish between market or workplace "information" and pre-contractual or contractual representations. No statements should be made or information provided if that comes close to inducing students to believe that attendance is likely to result in specific workplace results unless this sort of qualifying statement accompanies it.

US law schools have been advised by some experts to provide detailed job placement data because recent graduates have sued their law schools, claiming the schools engaged in false advertising by providing deceptive job placement stats. [142] The problem is that prospective students may not make the distinction between information and contractually significant representations. The information is hard to verify and often unreliable.

Student contracts and promotional materials must include provisions stating: that where data on employment or business results is provided it does not constitute any form of contractual promise or representation; that students should not and do not rely on any data provided when they decide to enroll. It can always be argued that reasonable persons would not rely on representations about jobs because they know that no one really controls those results, but the more sound risk management approach is to address the issue upfront contractually with clear promises, representations and provisions stating what is not promised and represented (See Contracts Above).

22.3 Education Quality, Consistent Definitions, Not Related to Vagaries of Economic Development and Workplace or Business Risk, Past Results Are Not A Predictor of Quality Standards Now Met

As stated and explored in more depth in other sections, education quality assurance regulation must be consistent and uniform across public and private sectors, institution and program types and preferably jurisdictions. They must also be separated from the risks associated with job markets, student loans or border controls. Definitions and concepts of quality should be consistent and not variable so regulatory certainty exists, all students are equally protected to the greatest extent possible and all institutions are treated equitably, fairly and in an unbiased way.

Education quality must focus on the education product that is the object of quality. That product is designed to help the student consumer achieve a set learning objective. Quality must focus on standards that the regulated parties can achieve and on standards that reflect risks associated with the consumption of the education product as opposed to risks associated with economic cycles and events and decisions beyond the regulated institution's control.

Education quality cannot logically be seen to go up and down as employment rates go up and down. Such criteria can be a minor measure of education quality, but never the standard itself that is required for permission to operate. Again, it is unwise and legally unsound in most cases to propose a definition or concept of quality that would see an institution judged as providing poor quality education one year because employment and business prospects are poor and then, with the identical program, judged to be of good quality when those prospects improve.

Education can no longer be viewed in a linear way and in terms of predictable and controllable strict cause and effect relationships, that is, go to a good school, learn, pass the tests, get the credential, get the job and live happily ever after. That is no longer legal, social or economic reality, but the mindset often lingers and it is distorting public policy, law and management in the workplace and in the education sector. As noted in other sections, if border control, student loan related taxpayer risks or other risks require additional standards beyond quality assurance then that is fine, but too often these other agencies are expecting the quality assurance regulator to do it all for them.

Even if employment results for a past group did reliably reflect the quality of education (which we reject) provided for a past group that may not be an accurate reflection of what is in place now and regulators are supposed to be determining whether current students are at risk from a program now. As with financial statements, the time required to gather, analyze and report information can be years and the past may be completely irrelevant to current circumstances. Again, employment and business results are not contractually promised and are not reasonable education regulation targets.

22.4 Quality Standards Distorted by Drawing Cause and Effect Links Between Education, Work and Business, Hard Choices Require Clear, Consistent, Objective Focused and Fair Criteria, Supply Can Precede Demand

As important as formal education often is to finding work and business success it is also a distortion of reality to try (as some regulators are doing) and draw strict cause and effect relationships between education and work and business opportunities. Some regulators and lenders are drawing false conclusions about the quality or social and economic value of specific education programs based on workplace and business results.

One cannot say there are zero linkages, but education is never more than one of a multitude of factors that influence workplace and business results. It is never possible—and the BC government has studies to this effect [143]—to predict exactly how many jobs or business opportunities there are going to be in general or in specific areas of work or geographical regions. They cannot even predict the kinds of jobs that might exist in the future. Even if they could predict it and only train that number that would needlessly stop others from being in the position to compete for those positions. It would put the power of individual futures into the hands of admissions officers and those that decide to fund or not fund a program.

It should be remembered that innovative and insightful education providers have created new industries. For example, it was often education innovators that saw that new technologies could allow computer animation to become a mainstream industry in many places outside the traditional southern California base. Supply can precede demand. Steve Jobs predicted a market for products that consumers had not yet thought of. After all, what use did the average guy have for a computer? Ted Turner thought people would watch an all-news channel, but industry veterans said no way. Anything that stifles education providers now could stifle future innovation.

Hard choices often have to be made where public dollars are limited, but decisions need to be based on reality and clear, uniform, unbiased, consistent, objectives focused and fair criteria and not on faulty concepts of quality and false conclusions about scarcity and cause and effect relationships between education, work and business. If funders only want to fund products that directly lead to jobs in that field of study then the law should be clear and applied across the board. That is not realistic, but some "quality plus" criteria are required. If they cannot fund all quality programs and institutions (the accreditation focus) in accordance with the realistic concept of quality proposed they cannot distort quality concepts by saying products are not of quality if jobs did not directly result.

22.5 Quality Assurance and Employment and Business Opportunity Quality (Jobs v. Good Jobs)

The folly of linking employment results to education quality becomes even more apparent when you face the issue of employment or workplace opportunity "quality". Everyone knows there are PhD holders selling coffee at Starbucks not because they were poorly educated and from low quality programs, but because the opportunities for them to capitalize on their training were not there or because of personal factors. Measuring flat employment results cannot be a measure of education quality for all of the reasons mentioned, but also because of this factor.

Even many of those that are using these unreliable cause and effect relationships to make regulatory and policy decisions are saying that they do not care if the job is even in the field of study. They say they just want to know if the person is working. It is hard to understand how a computer science grad driving a cab is a measure of the quality of the computer science program yet this kind of twisted logic is popping up in BC and some other jurisdictions.

If regulators think they can regulate and control employment in terms of the number of jobs then one assumes they will next try to do the same with the quality of employment and hold all public and private institutions responsible for the quality of the job [144] and not just for whether a "paying" job is found. That is not a reflection of the quality of the program. As noted in other sections, many regulators say they don't care about whether a student gets a job in their field of study or not, but it is illogical to state that employment of a philosophy grad as a cab driver is an indication of the quality of education that the person received as an under graduate or post-grad student.

22.6 Education Quality Acts Are Not Workplace Statutes and Should Not Control Provider and Program Supply (Law and Medicine Examples), Legal Standards Versus Measures of Standards Performance

In virtually all jurisdictions, the words "job" "work" "outcomes" or "business results" do not appear in education quality assurance statutes (See exception below). This is the case in BC, but still they have tried to build an accreditation system around terms that do not appear in the statute and that are statutorily undefined.

An "accreditation" system can be called anything of course because names are irrelevant, but whatever it is called, it must comply and be in tune with what the statute is all about (its purpose) and that is generally always about protecting students from risks associated with the consumption of an education product and not what might happen in the distant future in relation to what is possible done with that education.

At the most, what happens with jobs and work can only be a measure of what may have happened earlier and it cannot be the legal standard that must be complied with in order to be granted permission to engage in the otherwise prohibited act. It is not something an institution can ever control and impossible to achieve standards are absolute prohibitions not standards. Past employment matters may be a measure of something, but a measure of whether a standard was achieved is not the same thing as the standard itself. A job is even a poor measure because of the multitude of factors that come into play when workplace or business results evolve over time.

They cannot be the quality standard because they do not relate to the object of quality (the program product) delivered and consumed during the contract period. Placement information is not necessary to determine if the quality standard—a program that helps the student meet a learning objective and desired state of knowledge - is being met. The issue is addressed in detail in sections on education products and product quality.

Quality assurance statutes should not be used to control workplace results. If a government does not want to fund specific programs or lend money to students in specific programs then that is their choice—depending, of course, on what their governing law says. If they make that choice they cannot or must not block other non-funded programs from proceeding to offer an in demand program that meets quality assurance standards by establishing that it helps students achieve set learning objectives.

Buyers and sellers of education products should make informed decisions, but if a person wants to study law, medicine, engineering, acting, architecture, computer science, fine arts or any discipline they should make that decision and if opportunities in the world of work and business do not work to their advantage and others take available jobs and business opportunities then so be it. At least they had a shot. Even if only fifty percent of a class did that was fifty per cent that otherwise would have gone down a path chosen for them by others. To block the program because only fifty percent became employed on the false grounds that this resulted from a poor quality program denies the fact that the product delivered what it was designed for and that fifty percent found success.

In Canada several universities in Ontario indicated interest in having law schools and the Ontario government said they would fund no new law schools. Interested universities had asked about the standards they had to meet in Ontario. The standards were lacking at first, but now law school standards are set nationally by the Federation of Law Societies of Canada. The Ontario government chose to not fund new law schools, but there is no reason why a private unfunded school should not be allowed to operate if they can meet the content and quality standards. Each year there are thousands of Canadians that go to study law, medicine and other disciplines overseas because they are turned away in Canada. That money goes elsewhere. With law, some stay in Canada and study law online with long standing universities in the UK. They can then enter Canada as foreign lawyers and go through Federation's foreign lawyer program and eventually be called to the bar in Canada.

Similarly, students are being blocked from attending medical school and then they are seeing foreign trained doctors coming into Canada (which we support) and having their credentials accepted. Canada then effectively outsources that training. Canadians studying medicine overseas have a hard time finding residencies and work in Canada. Shortages of family doctors have eased in recent years, but in Canada there are still many people turned away from Canadian medical schools and forced to study overseas. Many commentators say it is wrong to rely on foreign trained doctors to deliver healthcare.[145]

The Canadian Medical Association has put forward the ideas of private medical schools, increased medical school enrollments or the entry of US medical schools into the Canadian market to deal with doctor shortage and cost issues. Even in the absence of shortages people should be able to study what they want and then let markets decide who succeeds in this world of work and business.

22.7 Terms "Training Required for Employment" or "Employability" Don't Relate To Hard Employment and Business Results, Canada and US Examples, Employability Can Be a Standard But Not Hard Employment

Certain regulators tend to turn their attention away from their governing statutes. In BC, the only reference to work or jobs was in the definition of career training that referred to 'training or instruction in the skill and knowledge required for employment in an occupation defined in the regulation". Quality career training then would be that which helped a student meet those requirements - that helped them achieve a learning outcome objective. The learning objective could relate to a workplace or business need, but not all education is about jobs and work.

This definition was arbitrarily distorted to argue that training was not quality career training unless a set percentage of a cohort actually achieved employment, self-employment or business success. The mistake was focusing on workplace and business outcomes as opposed to preparation. Again, a legal standard must be achievable by the person that is subject to the standard. Something that is impossible to control and for them to achieve by their actions are not standards but absolute prohibitions. The standard must relate to real risk.

Agencies in the US and Canada have also used the term "employability" which also relates to preparation and the ability to be employed if work presents itself. In the US the Higher Education Act term "preparing for gainful employment" was also not followed when subordinate regulations were passed requiring specific employment results. A legal challenge is active. The main argument is that actual employment can never be assured and never a reasonable legal standard during the worst recession since the 1930s. There is a distinction between being "prepared" and being able to find a contractual partner (service consumer) that will pay you as an employee, independent contract or service provider for doing the work that you were trained and prepared for.

If a person does not get a job that does not mean they were not prepared to do so or that they did not receive training that was "required" for work. Other factors like personal choices, global economic decisions, company decisions, may have impacted whether a job or business opportunity existed or not. Law school grads receive the same education year by year. Articling jobs vary, but quality is not seen as going down in years of fewer jobs. Their level of preparation for the "requirements" of work does not change. This issue is discussed in other sections focused on future quality assurance measures.

Designating institutions for student loan purposes often focuses on quality assurance elements, service elements (help with administration0 and risk management (avoidance of default). This risk management element in turn often considers "student success" which in turn is based on the assumption that successful students are more likely to repay loans. Government student loan lenders in BC are asking institutions to focus on student success and on avenues to retain students to the completion of their program and to ensure students improve their employability so they are more likely to repay loans.

That sounds fine, but in practice they are going beyond principles in governing statutes focused on employability to focus on hard employment results. Officials have said they will consider actual employment results when determining if an institution is designated so students will get loans (even in the absence of serious defaults). If governing laws were changed things could be different and lending could perhaps be so restricted, but even then the concept is highly questionable for several legal (depending on applicable law) or policy reasons.

For example, there is no way that centralized parties can look at employment results at any one point in time and determine what training is required in the future. The data they use will always be one to two years old at least and the training being decided on at that time and allowed through institution and program designation and loan eligibility will not come on stream for years in the future.

Secondly, there is no strict cause and effect relationship between employment and education quality and lending criteria should be focused on quality. Finally, some students study for joy and self-fulfillment and not just for short term employment. Often it is people that get a broad education that do best provided they also have real workplace skills. One can be employable and prepared for work and still not find work.

Student success must focus on academic success and not later workplace or business success. In this way success can relate to quality in a real way. If an education program is shown to be capable of helping the student to achieve a set learning outcome objective then it is successful and of quality and the student is successful if they achieve that. What comes later is not in the control of either the student or the institution. You cannot practically be considered a failure or a success when the objective is something you have zero control over.

Employability can relate to this if the learning outcome objective is focused on a specific set of workplace skills or on some package of professional knowledge, but that is not always the case. If narrow employability standards are the key then there are scores of academic programs that should not be designated for loan purposes. Lenders may have hard decisions to make in this age of limited funds, but the criteria behind decisions should be clear.

As mentioned, under the federal US Higher Education Act's Title IV [146] rules there is a phrase that requires institutions to "Prepare students for gainful employment" in a recognized occupation or profession if they want their students to get loans. The US Association of Private Sector Colleges and Universities (APSCU) has taken the federal Department of Education to court by way of judicial review to challenge regulation under the HEA and its regulations. [147] The action also alleges grounds under the Administrative Procedure Act (like judicial review in Canada) and the US Constitution, but the key in this context is how the regulations in question relate to the statute.

The APSCU contends that the regulations are contrary to Title IV of the HEA, arbitrary and capricious and in violation of the APA and the Constitution. Their focus is on what they see as a wrongful use of the decades old HEA term "prepare students for gainful employment" in a recognized occupation or profession. It says the department has concluded that students are only "prepared" if tests related to student debt-to-earnings ratios and loan repayment rates are satisfied. They do not seem to have threatened to do what BC has threatened to do, that is, to use actual employment results. APSCU says Harvard Medical School would not satisfy the tests.

The APSCU says the tests are beyond the Department's HEA authority. In the HEA, Congress set forth the Title IV eligibility requirements for institutions, programs, and students and they address maximum student debt levels and loan default rates. The APSCU says in the HEA Congress did not grant the Department authority to use regulations to override statutory requirements. It says under the HEA programs must only prepare students for employment that is gainful and not actually secure employment at certain salary levels. A similar term appears in the law in BC where career training was in part defined as training in the skills and knowledge required for employment in defined occupations. The same argument exists that you just have to have the knowledge required for work.

ASPCU says the regulations impermissibly evaluate the quality of a school's enrollees, the wealth of those students, those students' labor market decisions and other similar factors, like economic trends, that are either beyond the school's ability to control or unrelated to the quality of the school's programs. As noted in other sections, you can also argue that a legal "standard" must be something that is achievable and not impossible. APSCU argues that the regulations impose disincentives on private schools that seek to educate low-income, minority, and other traditionally underserved student populations because it is those populations who are the most at risk for failing the Department's arbitrary tests. It says the result is that instead of furthering the purpose of increasing the availability of higher education, the regulations compel schools to limit opportunities for traditionally underserved groups.

The APSCU says the regulations are arbitrary and capricious and in violation of the APA because they punish schools for outcomes that are already a matter of historical fact and beyond their control. They observe that they are punished for employment and income outcomes arising out of the largest economic downturn since the Great Depression.

Like Canada, the HEA specifies that postsecondary institutions may not participate in Title IV programs if their students' default rates exceed set limits. Those cohort rates measure the percentage of an institution's students' loans that have defaulted within two years of the loans entering repayment. The regulations require institutions to describe how they determined program need and to submit information from employers and others about program viability and current market demand before being allowed to create new programs. Here again lies the important argument about the need to let buyers and sellers make these decisions because the gap between reporting past results and projected needs could be half a decade apart and in a rapidly changing economy that just won't work.

The repayment test also arbitrarily fails to count students as being in "repayment" even though they have been excused from making payments or are making the payments they owe. Students who take advantage of congressionally authorized deferment or forbearance are counted against schools in the repayment rates; and only a limited number of students in income-based repayment and income-contingent repayment plans can be considered in "repayment." This has the effect of holding schools responsible for the choices made by students to avail themselves of temporary debt relief programs created by Congress—which is particularly illogical during economic downturns like the current recession that are entirely out of schools' control. The Department did not explain how student debt relates to whether students are prepared for gainful employment. The department did not put forth an analysis purporting to explain how students with unaffordable debt accrued that debt and they failed at repayment.

In both countries, it is the lender that makes the lending decision. The institution offers a program in a market and the lender chooses to finance the transaction that involves a program that satisfies practical quality assurance standards. If loans are not available for "quality assured" programs then other clear criteria should exist. Loan defaults do not establish poor quality.

In summary, terms like "Training Required for Employment" or "Employability" do not relate to actual employment and business results. These terms can relate to quality assurance if a product is designed to help a person to achieve a learning objective that is related closely to being prepared for specific types of work. To have contract impact the learning objective and the work involved would have to be certain enough to satisfy the certainty requirements of contract law.

22.8 Temporary Poor Markets, Bad Supply Decisions, Cancelled Programs, Increased Entry Requirements To Discourage Demand Limit Access For No Reason

In response to current market conditions governments or institutions can make bad long term decisions by cutting back on programs that are in demand, but that have poor employment results. There are many examples of where governments and institutions read the market wrong and then over supply or under supply results. [148] If a subject falls out of fashion for a couple of years that does not mean it should be abandoned. Again, the outlay of public funds changes the issue. Choices must be made. If other suppliers want to serve that need they should be able to.

Central planning is not a solution and is often the problem. Supply cannot just be turned on and off especially with large organizations. Programs that are flexible and less focused on extreme specialization are a solution. [149]

In 2012 with poor job prospects for teachers in Canada colleges have announced that they may increase the length of the course to tamp down demand even though there is no evidence additional training is required. Poor jobs results does not mean quality was poor. Many of those grads may be better teachers than those working now. The same is true if institutions choose to increase entry requirement or to make programs longer in an effort to discourage demand when the changes have nothing to really do with workplace or business competency needs. If government chooses to control supply then they cannot block non-funded options that meet quality standards and quality standards should not be distorted to include irrelevant workplace result factors.

23

Student Finance, Institution Designations, Avoidance of Reality, Distorted Visions of Quality

23.1 Need for Student Finance Reform and Quality Plus Designation Criteria Given Changing Institutions, Students and Products

Issues related to student finance, student loans and institution designations for loan programs could easily be the subject of ten or more books on their own. This section can only identify some of these issues and comment briefly on how they relate to the issues discussed in this work on education freedom, commerce and law.

If students do not have the cash needed to pay required tuition and if student aid is not sufficient their access to education is limited. On the other hand, existing loan programs are not really structured to address the kind of diversity of demand that exists and the risks that go with it. Most student loan and institution designation (for loan) programs arose when students, student demands, products and providers were less numerous and diverse. New finance systems are necessary now so there is less reliance on financially constrained government lenders and so the diverse needs of institutions, programs and students are met. They are required to ensure that education innovation is not stifled.

There is a tendency within most systems of public administration and in this case with loan systems (See Innovative Regulation Sections) to reflex back to the support of traditional institutions and programs. There are fewer of them and they are less complex and easier to grasp. Student loan and finance systems should ensure that quality education is supported and not just government funded education or education that a few isolated public servants consider to be of economic and social value. For example, student loan lending and designation programs in BC, Canada are making arbitrary decisions to exclude private and purely distance learning programs—not because they are of lower quality or not in demand, but because they are "private".

In many jurisdictions (variations exist, but themes are common), institutions are designated if they meet quality standards (usually governed by independent quality assurance regulators), perform certain administrative services to facilitate loan processes and they meet some loan repayment risk criteria. The first two are not normally the problem.

The criteria for government support may have to be "quality plus" standards because the criteria should not distort the simple, but common sense concept of quality recommended here and that coincides with quality standards in other commercial sectors. If funds are short then criteria should limit lending on substantive policy grounds and not just public private splits and then decisions should be evidence based.

23.2 Cancelling An Institution's Designation Does Not Save Taxpayer Money Unless Education Is Not Pursued or Loan Payment Occurs At Other Institutions

Cancelling an institution's designation for loan programs (so students are eligible for loans) only saves the taxpayer money if the student does not pursue an education program at all or if they attend another institution and do not default. Defaulting at another institution may not trigger a designation problem because of lower existing default rates (or other cited factors) at the second and substitute institution, but the taxpayer is out the same amount of money—assuming the amount borrowed does not vary.

If the student does not attend another school it could be because of a personal decision, restricted enrollments in programs of choice, inability to meet admissions standards or many other reasons. This taxpayer saving - in cases where the student wants to pursue their education and has their options and freedom limited - is not compatible with the expressed purpose for most public sector student loan programs which is to expand education opportunity. It cannot be assumed that students from de-designated institutions would then go to other specific institutions or types of institutions. [150] The reality is often that students that are of greater risk of default do in fact gather in specific institutions because of limited options elsewhere.

Taxpayer money could also be saved—which is one program purpose next to expanded opportunity - if the student decides to repay the loan when they attend another institution. If the designation is not given or not renewed because it is assumed that enrollment at a second substitute institution and payment of the loan are the likely results of the decision to not grant a designation then that implicitly involves a decision by the designation grantor that is based on some causative factor existing with the first institution that does not exist with the second and substitute institution. The assumption is often made that factors only existing at the first institution are the cause even though there is no expressed contention of that fact or evidence to support the contention.

A BC government agency publicly connected defaults to the lack of job ready training even though the evidence strongly supported the opposite conclusion. Real causes related to economic opportunities, personal finance and demographics. They take an arbitrary default rate (e.g. 30%) and claim it is unacceptable and related to poor job preparation while ignoring that the same program mysteriously prepared the other 70%. Terminating institution designations for loan programs because a minority defaults denies the majority access to that program.

23.4 Student Obligations To Repay Loans Are Not Conditional, Vague Terms Like "Acceptable" Risk Do Not Award Open Ended Discretion

The student's obligation to repay their student loan is not conditional upon any judgment made about program quality or any other factor. In any event, allegations about poor quality are usually unfounded because the institution in question is normally in good standing with quality assurance regulators. Students and institutions are party to and bound and protected by the student contract and the same is true of students and lenders under the loan contract that gives rise to default risk. The student is responsible for the default and no one else.

Obligations that institutions have to quality assurance regulators and their designating authorities are public duties distinct from private duties and must be performed under law. Some student loan lenders and designating authorities are holding institutions responsible for loan defaults even though they are in compliance with student contracts and education quality assurance laws. Designating authorities are often left grounding decisions to not designate institutions on vague and undefined terms such as "acceptable" risk or student "success" (See other sections). Their attempts to link these concepts to quality have been disjointed and irrational in most cases.

Vague terms like "acceptable" risk should be avoided unless they are subject to clear interpretative guidelines and only if there are practical ways to assess the real economic and social return of loan programs. Designating authorities, if they use a concept like "acceptable" risk must show why a certain quantum of risk is acceptable in one context and not in another. Strict adherence to a cohort default percentage rate or other fixed factor can potentially violate principles of law that require all relevant factors to be considered. Arguably it cannot just be a subjective sense of what acceptable means if the statute or its subordinate laws emphasize specific factors including socio-economic factors. Discretion is not absolute power and must always be exercised in accordance with the expressed or implied purpose of the statute involved.

23.5 Student Debt and the Real Costs of Education

It may often be the case, but it is not automatically the case that the benefits of a degree or diploma financed by a student loan will lead to incomes capable of paying off the loan in a reasonable time.

Issues of student debt cannot be addressed unless the actual costs of education are analysed from a business perspective, that is, from a strict analysis of product factor input costs and how they can potentially be reduced. That is difficult if managers do not view their organization as commercial and contractual in nature and focused on product, product inputs, input cost and price. The solution to student debt is often seen as more money being poured into the top of the hopper, but when that occurs the money often just goes to cover higher input costs with tuitions continuing to rise - tuitions that need to be financed.

Assessment and credential systems were discussed in other sections as being designed for a world where degrees or diplomas were awarded to a person who then (often mythically) worked in the field of study credentialed and lived happily ever after. In the same way, current student finance systems are designed for that system and not for a world featuring career and job mobility and the constant need for life-long learning, retraining and professional development. Huge student loans for under graduate work can make it impossible to then pursue the practical training they need to get the real job in the real world.

Ideological arguments do not solve problems, but it must observed that education subsidies and easy loan money can often distort markets and result in short term buying decisions that would not be made in normal commercial circumstances if true costs were reflected. Decisions may not result in achievement of the goals sought through the program and the financing of it.

Students often incur debt because they know the market recognizes certain program brands. In many cases the same state of knowledge could have been attained through other means, but the same market recognition might not have been there (See Assessment). They may also "buy" an education product because it is priced below its real cost of production and then finance the purchase and use borrowed money to pay for living expenses in the learning period that may be longer than really necessary.

23.6 Risks Regarding Loan Defaults and Education Access Are Distinct From Quality Assurance Risks

Students are often eligible for loans only if the institution of enrollment is designated by the lender or some related authority and that generally requires that it meet quality assurance, administrative service and risk (default) management criteria. [151] Government loan programs balance the desire to increase access to education with the need to protect taxpayers from undue risk of loan default and risk.

Student loan and institution designation systems integrate quality assurance elements. Even where institutions are in good standing with quality assurance regulators these lending and designation authorities may say decisions to not grant designations were justified on the grounds that the institution failed to maintain acceptable levels of risk, minimize defaults and ensure student success. [152] These concepts relate to quality assurance because the only way the institution can really do any of that is to deliver a quality product that helps students achieve a set learning objective. They cannot significantly influence post student contract decisions made by workplace proprietors or goods and services consumers. Student success must also focus on academic success.

Lenders want to lend to and grant permits to the students of "quality assured' institutions, but their criteria must relate to factors that go beyond quality assurance because product quality concepts cannot encompass the kinds of criteria needed to address every kind of lending risk. Each regulator of public administration sector addresses specific risks and they must be isolated and addressed with links only made where true common features exist and where the distinct system risks are addressed first. Concepts of quality can otherwise become distorted. Similar standards distortions can occur with study and work permits where standards must go beyond quality assurance.

23.7 Challenges to US and Canadian Designation Programs Are Symptoms of Outdated Law, Innovation Needed

Legal challenges are being made to public student loan program designation decisions in Canada [153] and the United States. [154] In the US that involves Title IV of the Higher Education Act and its regulations. The essence of that action is set out in other sections on keeping education quality assurance and workplace issues (like employability) separate.

In Canada, there is the Canada Student Loans Program governed by the Canada Student Financial Assistance Act and the Pan Canadian Designation Framework which address institution designations. [155] In BC there is no provincial statute which confers the power to designate institutions. The province operates as an agent of the federal government with respect to designating institutions for Canada loans and it carries on with those systems for the purposes of BC student loans. The federal and provincial framework agreement exists to help govern institution designations and it provides direction to provincial designations. Provincial policies are not laws and are only enforceable to the extent they are consistent with federal law and the framework.

Aside from the legal problems that are being addressed by way of judicial review, the bottom line from a public policy and legal perspective is that having a province dole out hundreds of millions of dollars in loans via a designation and loan system that has no provincial legislation to guide it is unacceptable and dysfunctional.

These legal actions (judicial reviews) revolve primarily around administrative law issues, but the real issues arise from loan and designation programs that were designed for a different time. Attempts to limit loaned funds and to control defaults are leading to statutory interpretations, policy and standards distortions (See other sections) and actions that may likely be held to be ultra vires the statutes involved. In the BC case the laws are not only outdated—they are largely non-existent and there is no real legislative direction. With increasingly diverse product demand and potential providers there will have to be major changes made. Reality can only be avoided in the short term.

Even if these legal (judicial review) actions result in the challenged decisions and actions being upheld that will not mean that all is well with the status quo. The reality will not change. Demand is not just for degrees and diplomas and traditional onsite education offered term by term, but for lifestyle, lifelong learning and professional development adaptive products delivered on demand. Traditional providers can and are (see other sections) providing new and innovative education products as are new providers that take on multiple forms. New ways of assessing and validating states of knowledge gained within and outside institutional environments are rapidly developing. Student finance systems must adjust to these new realities and not just keep doling out money for traditional programs at traditional institutions. Decisions as to who to loan money to and as to which institutions or new parties to designate for loan program purposes must be based on clear, consistent and evidence based public policies and laws that are applied fairly and impartially. This will all require major law reforms and shifts in attitudes and culture in many public and private organizations.

These two judicial review actions are not reviewed in detail here although the US case is summarized briefly in the section on separating workplace and business risk from education quality assurance risk. Briefly put, US law refers to employability and training that prepares a student for gainful employment as a factor to consider when institutions are designated. BC career training quality assurance law refers to training "required" for work in specified vocations and those laws are effectively incorporated into institution designation (for loans) programs via the requirement that designated institutions must be accredited. This arguably blocks attempts to make hard employment numbers or income levels the focus of designations because there is a big difference between being prepared for work and meeting the requirements for work and actually being employed or having your own successful business (and earning a set level of income). The latter requires decisions and actions by countless third parties in the future.

23.8 Designation Factors and Criteria, Social and Economic Considerations

In most cases, designation decisions must place sufficient weight on all (Canada) of the primary purposes of the relevant statute and those purposes generally include access to education and taxpayer risk. When criteria are set (especially when they must be set) they usually must be followed because of reasonable expectations or other arguments (See Administrative Law). Regulators or designators cannot pick and choose the criteria they like in order to get the result or make the decision they are inclined to make. The Canadian framework expressly states that all stated criteria must be applied.

The Canadian (Federal Provincial) designation framework permits the designating authorities to consider the "role the institution plays in fulfilling regional, socio-economic or cultural provincial policy priorities". Unlike the other criteria listed, the framework does not explicitly require, but permits the designating agency to consider socio-economic factors. Government could be held to have acted unreasonably in rendering a decision if it completely ignored the socio-economic factors when they present themselves and instead focused entirely on default rates.

Some government officials in BC argued that they cannot take socio-economic considerations into account for designation and loan decisions, but this was never the case. Aside from the above reference, the reality is that public loan systems are built on socio-economic factors that arguably must be considered as relevant when facts present possible socio-economic reasons for the default. If consideration of such factors was not needed agencies could just act like or rely on the banks and other commercial lenders.

23.9 Lending Risk Management the Responsibility of Lenders Not Designated Institutions

In an attempt to limit its risk exposure, the BC Canada lending and institution designation authority began to require that many institutions not enroll students that the school felt were default risks. This was a problem for many reasons. They have no right to collect the kinds of personal information needed to do that kind of risk management work. They can only collect personal information that relates to the specific service they provide and they are not a lender. They do not need that information to make admissions decisions and they are not acting as a government agent on the lender's behalf. They have no risk criteria provided by the government designation authority and that authority has the statutory responsibility to protect taxpayers and not the institution.

The authority cannot delegate what they don't have. If they have the power to limit loans on a risk managed basis then they have the first responsibility to exercise that power and they can't delegate powers unless the statute allows it. In many cases the statute does not allow such risk management at the loan level because they refer to students being eligible for loans if they demonstrate need and if the institution is designated.

As noted, institutions are often designated if they meet quality standards, perform certain administrative services and meet some loan repayment risk criteria. Risk management at the institution level is straight forward at the product quality level because separate agencies govern quality assurance, but loan risk management governance at the institution level is difficult because the reasons for default are diverse and individually focused.

Denying enrollment is difficult if it is based on criteria not related to likely academic success, but on personal factors that could involve race, immigration status or economic status. Any decision based on race would be contrary to human rights law. Denying enrollment and therefore education because of perceived loan default risk based on inability to pay may run counter to the legally stated purpose of these programs which is to expand access to those that are economically disadvantaged. The institution only strives to provide a quality product that the lender then decides to finance. The institutions were effectively asked to limit access to education with methods the lender refused to use.

The fundamental purpose of public student loan systems is usually to increase access to education and they may also monitor the institution's management of risk, but the institution is not a lender and has no power or capacity to assess real default risk or to change student behavior. It can only do what its business is—provide a quality product. If lenders only want to lend to students that are more likely to repay the loan then they should just be a normal commercial lender and assess that risk and make the lending decision on that basis. Instead they impose no real risk management upfront and then assume that the cause was institution based with no evidence to support that view.

In administrative law terms, risk must be assessed reasonably and the government lender and institution designator has no authority to assess risk based on irrelevant factors or in such a manner so as to render that assessment unreasonable. They must take all risk assessment criteria into account, along with factors outside the control of institutions. They cannot "fetter their discretion" by focusing only or even primarily on default rates. Otherwise, they would not be acting within the jurisdiction granted.

References to inherent financial risks of an institution deny the fact that institutions create no risk. The student poses the risk. Risk arises because the institution offers a program in a market and persons enroll. Lenders then lend to that student and program cohort with knowledge of their past student loans, finances and other program and economic factors that institutions do not have. If quality assurance requirements (See separate sections) are met then the reason for the lost designation must relate to default risks which arise from factors beyond the institution's control. The lender and designator is then in the position where it is really deciding that specific demographic groups, certain individuals and certain program types are not going to be eligible, but they don't want to be seen as the one's doing that. They want to be the party of "Yes" and not the party of "No". Some try to hive it off to institutions and enrollment decisions even though institutions have no practical or legal capacity for it.

With student loans and related defaults, private lenders may only judge a portfolio of loans on the basis of hard numbers. Public loan programs must consider a broader range of factors because they have a public purpose - to improve access to higher education for those that may not qualify for loans from a pure commercial lender. These programs contemplate loss and risk and socio-economic benefits that are beyond those experienced in normal lending environments. Unlike commercial lenders, public student loan lenders do no real risk management upfront and collections work at the backend is often limited. In fact, such risk management and due diligence is not even possible because the law or policy may state that the student is eligible if they demonstrate need according to a set formula and enrollment in a designated institution.

With student loans, fairness arguably dictates that designating authorities consider: institution, program and overall portfolios; real default rates for various portfolios of loans; overall portfolio performance in terms of risk and in terms of return via interest and economic contribution. Even commercial lenders have a predictable level of default and they often know quite precisely where and why defaults are likely occur from sector to sector and borrower to borrower. Public student loan lenders should at least do that lending analysis and then they at least make the lending decision knowing what the likely risk is. Instead they often just assume that the fault was with the institution.

23.10 Certain Administrative Law Principles Ignored

Designation decisions (and likely lending decisions also) are subject to the principles of administrative law (See that section). The following points illustrate only a few possible issues that could be raised.

If designating authorities say they are considering a range of factors like withdrawals, employment rates, incomes, socio economic considerations, future incomes, institution to institution comparisons and other factors then they must normally show how those factors were considered and weighed in the decision. To not do that would arguably constitute a failure to disclose the true reasons for the decision and that would mean the subject person was given no notice of and had no way to respond to allegations as the rules of fairness require.

Institutions subject to designation decisions can and must demand that they be given reasons for the decisions so that they can properly respond to the allegations made or properly appeal further. It has been common in BC for lenders making designation or appeal decisions to provide the same form letters to a variety of parties without addressing individual points of appeal. Statutory decision makers must, and this is evidence they did not, consider the facts of each school's individual case. They must explain how the various factors were considered and weighed and provide some reasoning for that consideration and weighting.

Institutions faced with lost designations because of allegations of high defaults have the right to demand that the allegation be empirically proven with reliable evidence. Definitions of default must be clear. Allegations cannot be proven unless there is full disclosure of specific student default information. Aggregate default rates are composed of individual defaults. Information on specific defaulting students is also needed so default reduction programs are more effective and the institution can take all practical steps to reduce defaults. This disclosure issue was the subject of US litigation (held for the institutions and disclosure required), but has not been judicially considered in Canada. [156] In most cases (e.g. BC), government lenders and designating authorities are not constrained legally, as they often claim (as the BC agency did), from disclosing individual default information either because consents exist or because exceptions to non-disclosure rules allow disclosure for the purposes of collecting government debts. In BC, the information was disclosed to debt collectors, but not to institutions that were in a position to minimize defaults and aid in collections.

Access to specific student default information is also required to ensure that data is not corrupted. In BC, issues existed with regard to the integrity of the samples because of unclear practices and methods about how once defaulting, but later students in good standing were removed from default samples. There was evidence they were not removed and that would corrupt default samples. Proof of removal from samples has not been provided. In addition, old programs that were no longer offered and that skewed samples were not removed and that meant the decision was based on past risk and not risks associated with current or future lending and designation decisions. Risk is distorted if a student with already high student loan amounts applies for new loans and the last school attended may bear the burden for all past schools. Risk should be seen as a burden that the institution brings to the designating party. Institutions do not know what past default rates for applicants are and cannot determine how that previous debt load may incline a student toward default.

24

Study and Contract Period Or Post Grad Work Permits, Not Promised Products and Quality Elements, Global Branding, Confusion of Agency Mandates

24.1 Permits Related to Immigration and Border Control Permits Are Never Under Institution Control and Never Promised Products or Elements of Quality

An ongoing issue in most countries that encourage international students to physically come to and study inside the country is whether those students should be allowed to not only study, but to work during the program and to stay and work after graduation. Many governments are encouraging them to stay to help meet labor shortages in key areas. Some of the schemes set to regulate the process have been poorly thought out (in Canada).

The ability to enter into, stay in, study in or work in a country is never something that an institution has any control over and never something that it can or should promise to a student. It is never a product quality element because quality relates to whether a product does what it is supposed to do.

Student enrollment contracts should make all of this clear. This should be the case even if study permits or work permits are already granted or even if an institution is somehow designated by government authorities so students are eligible to work during their studies or upon graduation. Immigration and border control agencies can always assert great discretion and have their own guidelines for when permits can be granted and removed.

24.2 Work Permits for Foreign Students Graduating from Domestic Institutions, Education Quality Assurance Laws Are Separate From and Not Effective Immigration and Border Controls

Allowing a person into the country to study with a reasonable prospect they will return home is one thing. To allow them to work is something else because of concerns about taking jobs away from citizens or other economic development, security and border control issues. There are dangers that study permits become a back door to generally applicable immigration law and a way for persons inside and outside the country to manipulate or ignore the rules.

Education quality risks are separate from economic development, immigration and border control risks. Authorities can't expect education quality regulators to be the primary screens that address immigration and border control risk. Immigration officials say they don't consider the quality of the school when they make a decision. It says the focus is on the student's ability to finance their stay in Canada and on facts that assure CIC the student will return home. That really cannot be the case for national economic development officials because if they want Canada to be a destination of choice for international students then quality concerns are important. In reality, immigration officials do consider quality matters in regard to study permits because they will refer to accreditation status which is quality focused. Work permit issues commonly trigger quality assurance issues.

Immigration and economic development officials have no expertise in and jurisdiction over education so they rely on quality assurance regulators, but sometimes that reliance goes too far. The need for "quality plus" screens and standards to address border control, immigration and economic development standards increases with work permits as opposed to study permits not only because the stay is longer, but because the risks are different.

24.3 Failed Canadian Attempt to Link Immigration and Economic Development to Education Quality

Many governments have struggled with how to govern these work permits as they relate to private institutions. In Canada, as in many federal countries, sub-national jurisdictions (provinces) regulate education, professions and most workplace and employment matters while the national and federal government regulates immigration, border control, national economic development, inter-provincial commerce and international trade.

Student contracts are still central to these processes because enrollment triggers eligibility for study permits and grads wanting work permits emerge from those contracts. Traditionally, only the grads of public institutions or private degree granting institutions were stated in policy as being allowed to apply for work permits although anyone could technically apply. Immigration authorities always have discretion. It was open to privates operating under the same rules as publics, but conveniently there were no common standards so privates were fully excluded unless authorized to confer degrees.

Pressure to include private institutions created a quandary for federal authorities that grant work permits. They knew that many private institutions were good institutions that had graduates that were equal to or superior (in some cases) to those from public institutions and that could contribute to the country in areas where shortages of highly trained persons existed.

Nevertheless, these authorities feared opening up the gates to all private sector grads - even at a policy level where discretion could override policy for border protection purposes - because of the number of institutions, questions around their regulation (despite accreditation processes) and products and the tendency for there to inevitably be occasional institutional failures and related political problems. Opening things up to the number of private sector grads is not really a valid concern because their numbers are small in comparison to the public sector where not all grads are suited for integration into the economy given current conditions either and yet remain eligible for work permits simply by virtue of their public (government funded or as otherwise defined) institution grad status.

This resulted in poorly thought out attempts to screen and reduce the number of private institutions that would be eligible for a proposed pilot project. They chose one province and used a provincial (BC) marketing designation called the Education Quality Assurance designation as the qualifying criteria. If the institution had this EQA brand on a set date then its students could apply for the work permit. EQA was said to impose no new standards on these institutions and only relied on established provincial quality assurance standards. The problem was they never told anyone that there was a cut-off date and that only institutions with EQA by a certain date would be in the pilot project. It is not clear if certain schools were told and others not.

This caused havoc and great unfairness in dynamic and competitive markets. In some sectors, newcomers with little international experience and questionable quality (few grads going on to university) were in the program because without knowing they just happened to get the application in early while institutions with decades of international experience and established quality (with grads attending major universities) were blocked out. The desirability of the work option caused students to bleed to the less established institution with little international experience. Some students exposed themselves to greater risk in their search for the work permit.

Now the options are to: again keep all privates out despite their obvious quality and their highly trained grads; make the pilot project permanent and enshrine the market injustice; or expand the project to include institutions that meet set criteria. The latter is likely the only logical choice, but no one wants to do the screening work. At this writing, we are retained to try and resolve the matter for institutions hard hit by the policy.

The bottom line is that the criteria for work permits can never realistically just rely on education quality assurance because, as noted, that must realistically focus on whether the institution is able to help (as contractually promised) the student achieve a set learning outcome objective. Again, legally sound and consistent definitions and concepts of quality must be used and quality cannot be seen as going up and down with the vagaries of workplace and commercial markets with false links being made between jobs, business results and quality. Immigration, border control and economic development policy may legitimately vary over time as economic and social conditions change.

Put another way, lenders and work permit grantors naturally want to lend to and grant permits to the students of "quality assured' institutions, but their criteria must relate to other factors also (Quality Assurance Plus) because product quality concepts cannot encompass the kinds of criteria needed to address every kind of lending, immigration, border control or other risk. This has become an issue in BC and other jurisdictions and the concept of quality becomes distorted. It must stay focused on what is necessary to protect student consumer rights and expectations.

It was announced in April 2012 that this private sector work permit pilot project would not be renewed. Reasons likely revolved around complaints from those not in the program. This solved the problem of the un-level playing field in the private sector, but it did not solve the larger problem of private vocational sector exclusion which cannot be justified on policy grounds. Concerns about alleged marketing excesses were easily solvable with greater understanding of contract realities and specific and well drafted contract representations that make it clear no legal rights exist contractually or by law. Provisions can make it clear that students should not rely on any information provided about work permits. It can be made clear to students that institutions have no control over what immigration authorities do.

Concerns over total exclusion and the problem of total inclusion of private institutions left the only real option—the development of realistic criteria. The entire immigration system is built around such criteria. The current system that is built around public institutions and private degree programs is unsustainable. Many private institutions provide equal or better learning outcome results and they must not be excluded. Public and private sectors are now unified in one market and they and their students should have equal rights and duties.

24.4 Confusing the Mandates of Different Systems of Regulation, Regulating Without Authority, Marketing Brands Example

It is important to distinguish various public bodies involved with different and separate regulatory regimes. They may emerge from a common Crown or Constitution, but they each have their own statute that gives them life and legal power and authority. They each have their own separate objectives and targeted risks.

The BC example used above in relation to work permits also illustrated this point. There was a provincial initiative to give public and private institutions a common quality assurance designation (EQA). The designation was given to private institutions that were accredited by education quality assurance regulators. No standards beyond those quality assurance standards were required because no new laws or ability to make laws were in place, but there were vague references to having to be in "good standing" with the Ministry.

It is unclear what legal authority they act under when they determine "good standing", but that has not stopped them from making decisions that have economic and competition impacts. They make decisions that impact persons so they must be acting under some law and are subject to all of the principles of administrative law when they make those decisions. With few exceptions, actions which infringe the liberty of the subject require the authority of a statute. Every official act must be justified by law. If an official acts outside statutory authority they enjoy no more powers than a private individual.

In one case they decided that the EQA could not be awarded because the institution in question had been denied designation by student loan lenders. The institution was in good standing with the education quality assurance agency. The loan designation was lost because of high default rates. Designations for loans are granted if quality assurance status exists (via the agency that continued to grant that status), if loan administration services were provided and if the institution maintained an acceptable level of risk and took steps to minimize defaults.

The lender had no legal authority to regulate in the area of quality assurance and to make decisions regarding anything except grants of loans and institution designations for the purpose of providing access to education and to protect taxpayers. The student loan system also has no provincial statutory foundation and relies on a federal statute and a federal-provincial agreement mandated to increase education access while protecting taxpayers. Nothing in these instruments gives the BC government new powers to award a benefit to one institution and not another for international education marketing purposes or foreign student protection purposes.

The non-profit that administers the program and grants the EQA designation to institutions approved by the Ministry has no requirements that require "good standing" and no authority to establish new standards. If BCCIE and the Ministry had only used the accreditation standard granted pursuant to statute then nothing more by way of legal authority would be necessary. An "accredited" agency would also be labelled an "EQA Designated" agency. Because they went beyond that, it can be argued that decisions are being made without legal authority. This assertion has not been advanced by way of judicial review.

24.5 Keeping Immigration, Professional Organization and Quality Assurance Standards Separate, Required Contract Provisions

If a country has other criteria for admission to the country based on valid border control, economic development, immigration or social issues then that is fine, but it should not be disguised and shelved off to a professional group that is then forced to distort its primary mission which is to protect consumers of members' services by applying objective membership criteria based on what is needed to address that consumer risk. In the same way, the decision should not be shelved off to education quality assurance regulators that are forced to distort the concept of program quality which should be focused on risks to students arising from consumption of the education product.

Foreign credentials should be evaluated with equivalency alone in mind. Immigrants or Canadians trained in private or public schools in other countries should be able to exercise their professional skills in Canada if doing so does not compromise current consumer protection standards.

The student contract should state that no specific contractual representations or promises are made with respect to quality or otherwise when such Brands exist and are earned and expressed in promotional literature. It should make it clear that these Brands and their implicit representations are not expressly or impliedly incorporated into the contract. Immigration authorities have control over who studies or works in a specific country. Student contracts do not and must not contain provisions regarding promises from the institution concerning study permits, work permits or other immigration matters. These are matters between the student and the government involved.

It does not matter if you are talking about immigration or professional groups the reality is that the institution cannot at any time control what those parties do in terms of standards set to regulate access to their respective benefits. The student contract must make it clear that no promises or representations are made to students about future benefits these authorities may grant. That should be the default and if specific circumstances exist where such a representation or promise can be given then it can be included.

25

Professional Organizations, Credential Evaluation, Access to Professions, Professional Services Consumer Protection Distinguished from Education Quality Assurance

25.1 Professions Regulators Deal With Risks to Those That Consume Member Services, Credential Evaluation, Anti-Competitive Measures Prohibited

Professions regulators have multiple functions, but generally they are targeted at protecting persons that consume the services of its professional members from risks associated with that consumption. Advocacy for the profession normally is and must be separate. Administrative law applies to these professions regulators if they are given powers through legislative channels and they generally are. They may have legislative, adjudicative or administrative powers.

Membership standards will normally relate primarily to education standards (necessitating the evaluation of credentials from multiple sources) for initial admission although experience may be a factor. Ongoing compliance with professional standards (often including additional professional development education) is also required.

These targeted risks are separate from the risks associated with student contracts where students are protected by contract provisions and by separate quality regulation targeting the contract relationship from the risks associated with consumption of education services.

When they consider the admission of new members, these regulators apply specified standards and this can involve domestic or increasingly internationally trained graduates. These organizations must validate learning and states of knowledge from disparate sources. They can accept foreign credentials outright after internal analysis or retain third party credential evaluation services. They can also require that an applicant take additional programs of study and write additional examinations.

This process must be done objectively and impartially. These professional groups are supposed to act in the public interest and in the interest of their members' consumers and not in ways that protect the interests of their members. Ultimately, third party credential evaluators only provide information and the professional group makes the final decision.

The purpose of professional regulation is to protect those that consume the services of professional organization members. It is not supposed to be for the purpose of protecting members from competition, that is, from the admission of new members that meet set standards. In most cases these groups are professions regulators and not advocates. Protection of existing members from new competition is not a valid screening criteria and misuse of such screens can be and has been in some cases ruled as anti-competitive practice.

Even where admissions criteria are objectively met there are those that raise arguments about crowded markets and the need to protect the integrity of existing services from excessive market disruption. Arguably the principle of education freedom should prevail and that is that qualified persons should be admitted and then the market will decide who succeeds. Limited availability of programs or seats in education programs can have the same result.

25.2 Professional Organizations Can Aid Education Development, Graduation Does Not Guarantee Admission to Profession, Required Student Contract Provisions

Professional organizations are involved in the post grad period and may also work with the education institution to influence the development, application or monitoring of the institution's program admission standards, curricula and content and student assessment, graduation and credential systems. Institutions of higher learning cannot promise a student membership in a separate professional or vocational body even with this upfront involvement.

Even if an institution and a professional group had an agreement with regard to curricula development, assessment and other factors it is unlikely that admission to the group would be promised by that contract and even if it did the student would not be party to the institution and professional group contract. As with articulation, third party rules would have to be used to vest enforcement rights in the student.

If materials say a program is recognized as a valid program for training by a professional or vocational body or government agency the institution should record a statement recognizing the program signed by that body. Student contracts should make it clear that the institution makes no promises, representations or warranties regarding the institution having any form of agreement or arrangement with the professional group that would result in the student having any kind of membership rights—unless of course the agreement exists and that would be rare given that professional groups (like credit accepting institutions) prefer to retain their powers or discretion to deny entry.

If education quality assurance regulations require that institutions have certain courses approved by a professional organization that could only relate to concerns about institutions falsely claiming that passing specific courses or the credential may relate to a profession's admission criteria. Education regulators otherwise would have no reason to require such approvals. It can only relate to an institution making claims about links to professions.

There is a danger that declarations about professional body approval of the course will lead to unfounded conclusions that the profession is somehow bound to then accept that credit transfer. The professional body has no agreement with the student and even if it had an agreement with the sending institution that would not give the student a legal right to the transfer. Even if a professional organization approved a course that alone does not guarantee admission to the profession or vocation. If the Institution offers a program and successful completion of that program is one qualification required for admission to a professional organization then the student contract should state that factually without trying to infer anything more. It should be clear that the Institution makes no promises, representations or warranties about that admission and membership.

It does not matter if you are talking about immigration and border control authorities, economic development officials or professional groups the reality is that the institution cannot at any time control what those parties do in terms of standards set to regulate access to their respective benefits. The student contract must make it clear that no promises or representations are made to students about future benefits these authorities may grant even if they played a role in setting curricula or impacting and even approving other program features. That should be the default and if specific circumstances exist where such a representation or promise can be given then it can be included in the control.

25.3 Professional Organizations, Institutions and Limited Seats for Programs and Membership

Despite the fact that professional organizations are supposed to be focused on their members' consumers and not member protection, professions and institutions that train persons for professions have been known to act together to limit the number of seats available in institution programs that may possibly lead to future professional admission and to limit the number of professional memberships. This is an unjustified restriction on the aspirations of others that are denied the opportunity to compete for opportunities in the profession and the workplace.

Even something as simple as an articling requirement could be an unreasonable limit or gateway. If articling positions are not available this can block a person from admission. It can be argued that such a requirement is not essential to legal service consumer protection because many jurisdictions have no such requirement and consumer protection is not compromised.

Persons should not have to study for four or seven years only to have current economic conditions stop them from pursuing their aspirations. The only and deciding factor should be the free market. New entrants may in fact be better for consumers. In the legal world there is a need for a complete shake up because of the severe problem with access to justice for individuals and small business. Service innovations will only be inspired by new entrants and not entrenched interests. Diverse products should be available to ensure that aspirants can pursue their goals.

Regulators, professional organizations and education institutions do not have the capacity to determine future demand for professionals so education sector market demand and supply should prevail and professional service markets should be left to determine who succeeds or not.

Again, whether limited positions result from shortages of public funds or attempts to restrict membership for the protection of existing members, this is why alternative providers of education must exist to meet this demand. The market will decide who succeeds in the profession. This mindset that the education system is supposed to train a set number of persons to meet an anticipated number of positions must be replaced with a system focused on learner demand and freedom. Buyers and sellers will naturally with market information make decisions that are more likely to reasonably connect workplace demand with the number of trained persons.

25.4 Keeping Immigration and Economic Development Separate From Professions Controls or Education Quality Assurance

Again, immigration authorities and not professional groups should determine if a foreign trained professional is admitted to the country. The same admissions criteria applying to domestic students should apply to foreign trained students. Criteria for admission to the country set and applied by border control, immigration and economic development agencies must exist, but they should not be disguised and shelved off to the professional group that is then forced to distort its primary mission which is to protect consumers of members' services and not to protect the border or enhance economic development.

The decision should also not be shelved off to education quality assurance regulators that are forced to distort the concept of program quality which should only be focused on risks to students arising from consumption of the education product. That quality should focus only on whether the program was capable of helping the student achieve the set learning objective.

Foreign credentials should be evaluated with equivalency alone in mind. Immigrants or Canadians trained in private or public schools in other countries should be able to exercise their professional skills in Canada if doing so does not compromise current consumer protection standards. Many Canadians support allowing immigrants to use professional skills gained in foreign private schools and still oppose similar private schools in Canada.

25.5 Access to Professions Laws Mean Little if Education Opportunities Do Not Exist

Some Canadian provinces have passed statutes that require access to professions to be demonstrably transparent, objective, impartial and fair. [157] Similar steps are afoot in the some US states. Governments can also enhance that objective by allowing for more available programs (See Program Availability). Public (government funded or as otherwise defined) law school positions are limited. The private sector is less constrained, but cost issues remain along with education regulators and student loan lenders that may (without authority often or unjustifiably in our view) restrict new programs that can meet demand for professional training.

If governments believe in access then they should expand capacity and allow education providers and consumers to meet up and marry supply and demand without the unjustified intervention of education or professions regulators and central planners. Regulation should not needlessly limit seats in programs, block new education programs, inflate admission standards or deny admission to qualified persons. Standards should target risks associated with the consumption of member services and not risks to existing members that fear competition from new entrants.

25.6 Pre-Approval of Foreign Credentials

As discussed in other sections, the recognition of foreign credentials—in this case by professional organizations - is a process that focuses on post credential periods and this means persons can invest years of time studying in programs without knowing whether their credential will be accepted or not. Immediate changes by professional organizations and others that accept credentials should be made so that the acceptance can be given before the student commits to a large investment of time and money.

Rights to membership in professional organizations are arguably more likely to exist than rights of credit transfer. The word "eligible" is always open to some interpretation, but generally if criteria for membership are set then the professional group must grant admission. Where this is not the case it should be the case.

For example, foreign trained law students (some who study at a distance from Canada), including some Canadians, can apply to the Federation of Law Societies when they graduate and if they successfully pass several exams set by the FLSC they can apply to provincial law societies for membership just as if they had graduated form a Canadian law school. There is no reason why judgments could not be made in advance. Students should be able to get a legally binding statement from the profession involved that their foreign credential will be accepted.

26

Payment Security Risk and Quality Assurance, Protecting the Bargain, Financial Viability and Program Delivery

26.1 Student Tuition Payments and Quality Assurance, Payments for Collective Not Individual Factors, Unearned Income

The issue of payment security and regulatory standards that target the associated risks fall under quality assurance systems. Quality relates to the program product. Outcome 1, as that promised collection of inputs that creates a learning environment that helps the student learn and achieve learning objectives, is an object of quality. In classical commercial terms, a product is merchantable if it works as promised to help achieve the learning outcome. Tuitions paid for that product are separate from the product and object of quality, but the student does not receive the quality product paid for if it is not merchantable.

As stated repeatedly, education regulation should focus on student risk. Obviously one of the key risks is that a student pays money and does not receive delivery of the product or receives a product that is not of the quality expected. The quality issue is addressed separately.

The issues surrounding who pays what to whom and for what is too often overlooked. The "for what" relates to the discussion about products, but each of these issues can only be considered in the context of the nature of the student contract which is an evolving or executory contract.

Payments are usually or often made before services are provided. This is unlike certain other service and executory contracts like employment contracts where persons agree to contract terms at one point and then perform over time with payments being made after services are provided. There are laws in most jurisdictions to protect workers and service providers that are not paid for services provided. Professional services provision is different and there it is common for payment to be made first with payments often being held in trust.

The quality assurance elements discussed in other sections relate to ensuring that the promised product (Outcome 1) is of such quality that the student is sufficiently helped to achieve the set learning objective (the un-promised Outcome 2) and that the promised assessment system credibly validates that learning. Payments are made for the product that results from all product factor inputs acting collectively. Students do not pay so much for faculty, so much for classroom space and so much for equipment. The contract "consideration" for payment is that collection of factors. That is what the student pays for.

Many of the problems that arise in the private education sector involve students paying funds and then not receiving training because of institution failure. Even when failure does not exist it is always an issue when income is received and payments are made, but services are not provided until later. Classic "unearned income" problems persist.

The income is unearned in the sense that tuition is paid for the entire program, but tuition portions are not normally attributed to specific production factor inputs, lessons or modules in terms of time or the importance of the material. Calculations are just normally done by straight division.

The problems of unearned income can be addressed: if money is paid incrementally after services are provided; if money is paid prior to service, but held in trust and released after services are provided; or if contract remedies, assurance funds or bonding systems work to provide refunds to students that pay for products not delivered. All of these options are available to regulators or the contract parties and individual options may be suited to specific circumstances. The relative bargaining power of the contract parties is a factor as is the focus of the regulator. Post-service payments or trust fund options would be overkill and unwarranted in many circumstances.

26.2 Tuition Refunds and the Law of Remedies, Innovative Payment Systems Required, Assurance Funds and Bonds

Most regulators have some kind of provision that institutions must return tuitions paid if withdrawals or dismissals occur at specific times. Usually there is a point where refunds are no longer owed. This is reasonable. If funds are only paid for small increments of service at a time then many of these refund issues disappear.

It is worthwhile considering what courts would rule. The answer is not clear. A full examination of the law of remedies would be required. Essentially the question would be whether a student would always be able to receive a refund for that portion of the tuition that was as yet unearned on a straight time division calculation and that would be unlike the way many tuition refund systems work where at some point no tuition refund is considered payable even though some portion of the program remains undelivered.

Institutions argue that they often turn students away and take a risk of students not continuing. If a student does withdraw or is dismissed then they would argue that they must be allowed to retain the tuition at some point because they could no longer fill the spot. This is an acceptable argument, but in reality the point at which you can no longer recruit someone into a set time period program comes pretty early and well before the normal cut off for the lost right to a refund.

It becomes increasingly difficult to deny refunds when large sums of money are involved. This is especially the case if the student is forced to withdraw for personal reasons related to health or family welfare, but even if academic reasons exist such as failing grades the student can argue that they should not have to surrender large sums of money paid for an entire program much of which was not received. They could try to shift the blame to the institution and claim they should not have been admitted, but if admission standards were met then the institution can claim that it can only do so much.

The better approach would likely be a straight contract approach, but again many contracts in the sector are poorly drafted and do not address these matters. Institution and student contract provisions should, where possible, parallel what would likely happen in the jurisdiction if a court were to rule. That may not vary that much from jurisdiction to jurisdiction because contract laws are remarkably similar from place to place. Where clients direct or negotiations result in provisions that are not conclusive then the parties can negotiate it out at the time and a foundation of the discussion will again be or can be focused on what the likely legal result would be. The key is to have a lawyer assess local circumstances.

If training is ongoing and individualized with constant enrollment and progress is continually assessed then strong arguments can be made for payments that closely track the progress of students. This would in fact do away with a lot of regulation and the need to protect students. If quality was considered poor by the student, but the ability to pursue legal action was not possible or unlikely to succeed given existing contract terms then the student would only be out any amount paid and have the loss of not being able to attach the training received to date to the final credential. Proper recognition of knowledge gained and the ability to transfer credits gained during that period would diminish that loss. Credit transfer systems can help, but the same problems exist with matching up the programs in terms of content and sequencing.

Innovative payment systems could drastically reduce regulation and problems of student loss. Institutions may oppose such ideas, but they would have to calculate over time how much they lose as a result of the change and tuitions could be adjusted to make up that loss. It can certainly be argued that the disintermediation that is expected (see other sections) will generate the need for equally innovative systems of payment and financial protection. If regulatory burdens were lowered as a result then that is a gain for the institution.

It is important to again establish that tuitions are paid for that product or collective set of inputs and not for any specific input or for the final credential. If they paid for the final credential and refunds were allowed not just for remaining portions of the program, but the entire amount because the program was not finished then the student could attend the entire program, get a free education and just be out the credential.

In most jurisdictions, regulations have established either assurance funds or bonding systems that institutions must participate in or carry so that upon financial failure or closure of the institution the student can be compensated in whole or in part when funds are paid for undelivered product. Students are often only compensated for what they did not receive in terms of education even though the final planned credential could not be issued. A final credential cannot be issued unless the program was for all intents and purposes complete.

In many cases (as in BC), students will be given the option to attend another similar institution so that they can complete their planned education, but this can often be a challenge given program variance from institution to institution in terms of content and sequencing. Student contracts generally do not have to address this because it is not a contract matter. In relation to the points raised in other sections about distinctions between public and private duties, in the event of failure or closure the student would by virtue of enrollment in an institution participating in a fund or a bonding program have a valid legal claim vest in them. Normally third party beneficiaries (objects) of regulation or contract do not have private rights vest in them. In BC the assurance fund is also used to compensate students that successfully prove they were misled, but they must establish a valid cause of action in contract.

26.3 Comparisons With Traded Hard Goods Payment and Delivery Protections, Payment Innovations

With the global trade of hard goods very sophisticated systems have developed over centuries for ensuring that sellers get paid and that buyers receive delivery. There are advanced payments, payments with-held until delivery, letters of credit systems and documentary collection systems. Factoring and forfaiting systems or assignment of debt systems are also a part of that.

The service economy in its modern global manifestation has not yet evolved a similar kind of sophistication with regard to payment and delivery protection and this is especially true with education. As noted in the section on recruitment, both students and institutions should be cautious when using third party recruiters or service providers, avoid using them as financial intermediaries and include provisions in each applicable contract to limit liability.

There is room for innovative problem solving in this area with education service payments and unearned income. The administrative cost of handling complex payments are reduced by electronic systems. Innovative banking programs are a possibility. Trust accounts facilitated by lawyers are an extreme example, but they could work and legal profession regulators would likely permit it if contracts were well drafted and applied when payment or refund systems were used.

The point here is not to present final solutions, but to point out that the amount of regulation could be reduced if this one large and significant problem and risk was properly addressed. Bonds and assurance funds are targeted at situations where losses have already occurred. More prevention focused solutions are required. Again, the problem is largely due to regulators not treating education as a commercial enterprise and programs as commercial and contracted for products.

26.4 Payment Regulation Must Not Relate to Price, Power to Regulate Financial Viability Relates to Student Payment and Product Delivery Protection and Is Not the Power to Micro Manage Corporate Finance

With private and unsubsidized institutions the regulation of payment issues generally does not and must not extend to the fixing of prices and fees charged. The bargain is the parties' bargain. The result otherwise is price controls without regulated cost controls and investment return guarantees.

In BC, the career training regulator has the power to set fees that it charges regulated institutions, but it cannot set any kind of fees charged by institutions to students. That has not stopped the regulator from setting application and administration fee maximums. They have not extended their imagined power to tuitions. There are other jurisdictions where governments have given regulators the power to regulate tuition, but for the reasons stated above these powers have not been exercised. The law should not exist.

It is common for private education sector regulators to have the power to govern the "financial viability" of institutions. This is often fine because it may be necessary to pro-actively avoid business failures that impact students and to protect student payment security. The power must be confined to student payment protection and the contract promised provision and delivery of promised products. It is not the power to micro manage corporate finance. The term "viability" must only be considered in relation to the ability of the institution to deliver the promised product to current students under contract. In other words, it is primarily a cash flow issue and income statement issue as opposed to a balance sheet issue.

This concept of financial viability should not beyond the issue of immediate cash flow management. Regulators should not impose themselves into the price bargain or how money is managed and allocated to inputs because no specific promises are made in that regard. It is not for them to say an institution is not financially viable because their asset base is not great enough or because financial ratios are poor. Control of student funds that are yet unearned is important, but refund provisions must allow institutions to keep funds paid after a certain point and this is usually the case.

Finally, regulators regularly require the filing of financial statements, but the reality is that these statements are often of little real use in regulatory and consumer protection terms. By the time the corporation prepares them and files them and by the time the regulator considers them the students that were involved during the examined period are long gone. The time delay can be years and not months. Again, innovation is needed at the regulator and institution level.

27

Education Program Quality and Workplace Experience Elements

27.1 Two Common Forms of Workplace Experience, Quality Expectations of Students Versus the Expectations of Workplace Proprietors or Consumers of Professional Services, Contract Terms

It is becoming more common for education programs to incorporate workplace experience elements. This can be highly valuable for students, but the legal technicalities can be complex and a potential source of problems involving misrepresentations, misunderstandings and insufficient contract provisions and regulations. These workplace experience program elements take various forms.

The institution itself might be integrated with a market centred business and offer goods and services to the general public in addition to students. This is common with massage, hair styling, automobile mechanic, bi-cycle mechanic or esthetics schools where students practice or apply their skills to serve consumers of those types of services. Student contracts and contracts between the institution business and those massage or other clients must make it clear that product expectations must be adjusted and that the student has no liability in relation to the service. Because they are not employees of the institution, students would not (or may not if laws vary by jurisdiction) be protected by vicarious liability laws and other laws that shield employees from the actions of clients that do business with a firm.

A second example would involve practicums, co-op programs, internships, work placements or similar programs. The student contract should state that these programs are by default not part of the promised program, but rather an experience provided to help the student with practical application. Credit would not be given. If that default is not intended in specific circumstances then very specific provisions should be included with respect to time and credit. If this type of program is part of the Program then the contract could state that the student is solely responsible for arranging it because otherwise, if positions do not exist, the institution could be held in breach.

In most cases there is no direct contract between the student and workplace proprietor. If that is the intended arrangement then the contract should be clear in terms of how that contract relates to the student contract. There must always be a contract between the institution and workplace proprietor and that is not a simple workplace service contract. The purpose is to contribute to an education product and how that relates to the work to be performed must be clear.

In these workplace environments it should be clear contractually who the parties are and what they promise to do. The student contract can only relate to the student and institution parties. It should clearly set out all details of how the workplace experience will work in terms of service, payment, protections and liability. If the student is to have a direct contract with a service client, employer or workplace proprietor then those terms should be clear. Common service contract terms will apply, but there will be great variation on the facts. If these workplace programs exist there should be a contract between the institution and the service client or workplace proprietor (individual or corporation) also setting out how the arrangement will work whether or not the student has a direct contract. It is often best if students do not directly contract with the institution's customers or the workplace proprietor.

In all cases the quality expectations of consumers or workplace proprietors that may receive the attention and services of students should be modified by the respective service contra. More importantly, for education quality assurance purposes, the contract must set a default position that no promises or representations are made to the student about the quality of this workplace experience. If specific factors allow the default position to be modified then that can be managed case by case. In most cases, the experience should not be made a condition precedent to the contract and should not be grounds for any repudiation of the contract or any claim of loss.

In both cases (client service model and workplace experience or work study model) the involvement of students changes everything. If an institution runs a business within itself that serves customers (massage, automotive services, hair styling) and it has its students serve those clients as part of their training then the normal business and client contract of service must be modified to reflect the parties' rights and duties. If a separate legal entity associated with the institution is involved then its role and the role of the institution must be clear. Each case is different and the contract must reflect the facts of each case. Normally a contract does not exist between the client and the student, but if that is desired the contract must be carefully drafted to reflect what the parties want. The institution may or may not be a party to this second contract involving the student and client.

The same issues arise with the workplace experience or work study model. This is not a normal workplace (employment or independent service contract) contract. The institution and workplace proprietor are not promising to provide workplace services for the other although that may be an element. It is really a supply contract—much like a faculty contract—that the institution uses to enhance the education product (Outcome 1). The involvement of the student changes the legal reality and the contract must reflect the specific facts, purposes and desired party rights and duties. Again, there would often be no contract between the student and the workplace proprietor, but if that is desired then it must be carefully drafted—again to express what the parties want. The institution may or may not be a party to this contract involving the student and the workplace proprietor. If a separate legal entity associated with the institution is involved then its role and the role of the institution must be made clear.

There is a great need for work study programs. Students want them. Most employers (91% says one study[158]) say they want to hire people with internship experience, but few offer them. More sophisticated legal models need to evolve. There is no escaping contract law, tort law (creates duties of care even if contracts do not exist), employment standards laws, vicarious liability laws, employment insurance laws, workers compensation laws and many other areas of law.

27.2 Joint Assessments Possible But the Institution Is Responsible

Regulations often require that there be some kind of joint assessment in these circumstances, but only the institution can be ultimately responsible for assessment because it is part of the promised product and product expectation. In our experience, public and private institutions in these cases have inadequate contracts and related protections for the student, the institution, the service client and the workplace proprietor. Regulators should be requiring this and reviewing those contracts with competent legal counsel.

28

Attendance, Contracts, Regulation and Business Policy

28.1 Attendance Is Generally Not a Contractual or Regulatory Requirement, Student Success

The issue of attendance is of continued relevance notwithstanding revolutionary changes in post-secondary education, education technologies, student consumer attitudes, learning methods and contract relationships.

Student attendance in class is, without express terms in a contract, either not a contract promise at all from the student or not generally a condition of contract that, if breached, could result in repudiation of the contract.

A student contract could expressly set an attendance requirement, but it would have to be specific in order to be enforceable. If a contract or an incorporated outline or policy on attendance said a specified degree of poor attendance could result in a grade penalty that is likely the only penalty that could be given. Generally, it is best to not broadly incorporate all business policies or calendar items into a contract.

If an institution is required by law to do what they can to maximize student success (which we confine to helping them achieve the learning outcome objective that the student controls) then one could argue that they should require attendance if that is shown to improve student performance. This is hard to do because many students are academically successful even though they rarely come to class.

It would be hard for an institution to repudiate the contract and expel Patch Adams, Steve Jobs, Elon Musk (E-Bay, PayPal, Tesla Motors, Space X Founder), Albert Einstein and other persons [159] that either never attended institutions at all or were enrolled, but preferred to study on their own. As discussed in other sections, it is becoming even more common for students to pick and choose which elements of a product they want to consume. Many would rather just get someone else's notes than go to class themselves.

The legal reality is this. If a requirement for attendance is set, but the student does not attend very often and still is successful academically then no one is hurt and no one has experienced a loss. If the student does not attend and does poorly the institution has not done anything wrong legally and contractually because the student's loss is of their own making. A student could not validly claim that there was something wrong with the product when they chose not to consume it. We have successfully argued this point in student and institution disputes.

28.2 Non-Attendance Is a Consumer Decision to Not Consume Part of the Product, Dismissal Often Not Warranted

The commercial and legal reality of attendance in most cases is that a consumer has made a conscious choice to not attend class and not to consume that element of the offered product. Choosing to not consume the provided product is not a breach of contract by the student unless there is a clear provision that it is required. Non-attendance would become more of a factor if the student claimed that the reason for not attending had something to do with a deficient product. That would have to be dealt with through regular dispute resolution channels.

Again, poor attendance, as a decision to not consume what are perhaps important elements of the product reduces the viability of a claim that the student may try to put forward later that the quality of the program was not sufficient to achieve the learning objective. Again, it would be hard to expel a student and end a contract for breach of an explicit provision of a contract if the student was strong academically. Poor attendance can also be viewed as not attempting to mitigate loss if legitimate complaints were made. Consumer protection is not about protecting consumers from their own decisions.

Most institution managers are not going to want to be portrayed as or compared to the Dean of Medicine in the movie Patch Adams that was prepared to expel Patch because of his poor attendance (and other bad behaviours) even though he was a top student and the patients (and most of the profs) loved him. Ultimately, it is about satisfying contract promises and achieving a learning outcome.

Absent clear law or contract provisions, dismissal for poor attendance is not usually required and it could be dangerous. Dismissal policies could refer to poor attendance being grounds for dismissal, but caution is advised because the student could still argue that given his academic performance and other factors that dismissal is not appropriate. Legal counsel should be consulted before any dismissal because of the contract implications.

Poor attendance is not a fault of the institution and is not a contract breach by the institution. Arguments and issues regarding attendance can equally apply to lateness and punctuality or even withdrawals. This is a problem with some student loan programs where withdrawals are considered in designation cases as an indicator of likely default. Again a student has decided not to consume an offered product and one cannot assume from that the fault was with the product. Often the real reasons for withdrawal are demographic and financial.

We have used these types of defenses more than once. In one case a student tried to claim a full tuition refund of $30,000.00 plus even though they graduated and found work (which may be evidence of quality, but not a legal standard) and even though the rest of the class was pleased with the program. The student lost.

28.3 Reporting Attendance and Its Relevance to Loan, Immigration and Related But Separate Regulatory Regimes

Reporting attendance results is a different matter. Immigration or student loan authorities often want to ensure that students are attending their program although their policies or legal rules generally focus on "enrollment". Education regulators often require an attendance policy, but they do not mandate specific content.

Education regulators may require attendance reports to ensure that the student's commitments to those other public authorities are being met. Education regulators seem to act here as a kind of agent for immigration or loan authorities, but they must be cautious about intermingling completely separate systems of regulation or risk management. Immigration and student loan authorities deal with different risk sets in comparison to education regulators.

Violation by a student of a duty a student has to immigration or student loan authorities to be enrolled in a specific program and institution (attendance is not normally the key factor) is not violation of a duty a student owed to the education regulator because the education regulator does not regulate student behavior. Education regulators have jurisdiction over institutions and that power is targeted at protecting students from risks associated with the institution's actions or omissions. They are not there to protect the student from themselves. If a student chooses to not attend and consume a product the institution has not done anything wrong.

In other words, violation by a student of a duty they owe (to be enrolled or rarely to attend class) to loan or immigration authorities does not and cannot constitute a violation by the institution of a duty they owe to an education regulator that normally only requires that some kind of attendance policy exist. They can't be expected to force feed the student. The institution generally does not have a direct relationship to immigration authorities and duties owed to public loan lenders through designation processes are targeted at protecting taxpayers. If a duty to report is owed there then it is not related to education regulation and cannot be used for the purposes of quality assurance regulation.

Attendance or reporting on attendance does not often relate to the quality of education products. Again, non-attendance itself is a decision to not consume a part of the promised product and to attend or not has nothing to do with the quality of the product. Assumptions made that students don't attend because of poor quality are often misguided and not based on evidence. The overall results are the key indicator.

This is another example of the need for each regulator or public system to clearly distinguish what they are tasked to do from what other agencies of government are tasked to do in terms of risks, regulated parties and non-regulated, but protected objects or beneficiaries of regulation.

The duty to report may be the student's duty or a duty assigned to an institution, but any duty assigned to an institution would have to validly come under a statute to which the institution is subject and the duty would have to fall within the purpose of that statute. Education quality assurance statutes are about protecting students from institution action or omission as they relate to the education product they consume whereas attendance is about a student deciding to not consume. Inter-agency agreements or arrangements can exist, but they do not create duties for institutions unless the quality assurance statute or other statutes contemplates those duties.

In most cases, attendance and the reporting of it is a duty the student owes to those authorities. Again, however, if the student is engaged and doing well academically it can be persuasively argued that non-attendance is not relevant to issues of student consumer protection, immigration requirements or student loan requirements.

29

Quality Is Not About Price, Affordability and Debt But the Debate Points Are Similar

29.1 Insights Into Cost, Affordability and Debt Can Emerge from Discussions About Commerce, Contracts, Products and Disruptive Innovation, The Bargain Is The Bargain

It may seem obvious that quality assurance is not about price, affordability, student debts or social investments, but the point seems to be lost on some regulators, students and media outlets. Failure to fully appreciate the point is again likely due in part to the cited reluctance by many to view education as a commercial sector. Some prefer to view it as a public service that must be delivered at an affordable price. Generations of high public subsidies have created expectations that distort policy discussions and legal claims about product quality.

It is often the case that even students that were happy with their education are more likely to complain and initiate legal actions because they feel they paid more than they should have. The concept of a contract bargain escapes them because that is not how they view education. They just think they paid too much because friends took comparable or different courses in subsidized programs and institutions and paid less.

This issue of quality cannot be separated from broad business, economic and social debates about how to deliver education in ways that are affordable. Even if claims about quality are legally unsound and unenforceable because contract performance existed in an environment it can still be a business relationship problem if students felt prices were too high. It is in everyone's interest to have a concept of quality that is commonly held and a realistic understanding and appreciation of the commercial and contractual nature of the relationship.

It is also in everyone's interest to have an intelligent debate about the cost of education and how it can be reduced. That full debate is beyond our purposes, but the points raised in this work on education freedom inevitably relate to cost. If quality assurance focuses more on products and product factor inputs and how they help a student achieve a learning objective then the debate is the same as it is for cost which ultimately is about how product input factors are assembled and intermediated in different ways that result in set individual and collective costs.

The common assumption or expectation that governments will and can fund increasingly diverse education providers and products is now clearly not realistic for two key reasons - costs continue to go up and public finances in many jurisdictions are more constrained than at any time in recent memory.

At the same time, there is this growing debate about disruptive innovation and about how education can potentially change in a positive way. This is not just about technology. It is about changing lifestyles and the need for education providers and products to adjust to new technological and social realities—one of which is this reality of higher costs and constrained public funding and the increased ability and capacity of diverse public and providers, domestic and foreign, to meet needs. The potential is there for highly positive change that could not only meet needs, but also make education affordable and accessible for all. That won't happen if the parties cannot break out of old In Loco Parentis and "Club" mindsets. The must keep their eye on the ball and the ball is the reality of commerce, law and contract.

What will not work is trying to build the future system around the past because that way these built in costs will never be fully addressed. Too many people still think the solution is just to pour money into the top of the hopper without paying attention to how it is spent and to how innovation can ensure that people do not pay for what they can do themselves or what they can get for less elsewhere if there is innovation in terms of how factor inputs are assembled, offered and provided to students.

This allows the two issues of quality assurance and affordability to be seen together—not because quality depends on price - but because solutions to respectively problems may coincide or coalesce around a focus on product, price, commerce, law and contracts (and contract law). If a product is produced and delivered and the cost is beyond the reach of many consumers then a product that can accomplish the same objective and meet the same consumer need at an affordable price must be found. That means the future education product may and likely will look very different than that which you had in the past.

It is clear that many students complain not because they did not receive the product promised, but because they feel they paid too much for what they received. The media or regulators often do not seem to comprehend that the law is that courts will enforce the bargain made and students cannot expect regulators or courts to save them from what may turn out to be a bad bargain from their perspective if incomes are not what they hoped for or jobs don't exist in the field and even more education is needed. There is no getting around having to focus on what was promised and what was delivered and that is the essence of quality assurance also.

Distorted expectations are a core issue. Students will often say privates cost too much, but that is because their reference point is a subsidized public sector. Now they think that public sector programs are getting too expensive because of their historical reference. It is not rare for them to complain and even to take legal actions based on these perceptions, but on those grounds alone they will fail because courts uphold bargains. The price is a function of cost and business return and absent a hardnosed business approach the debate and analysis never really get off the ground. Rather than focus on product, factor inputs, price and innovation the solution is always to ask government for more money. In the private sector that is not an option.

The costs for most inputs in the public and private sectors or between institutions within each of those sectors are often not that different. Some may have lower real estate and facilities costs (e.g. government provided assets), but they may have higher faculty costs. Most factor inputs have to be purchased in the same markets and the only variation will be that large institutions may have bulk purchase options that smaller institutions do not have.

Large institutions have multiple programs and faculties that have shared costs. Because governments often provide the factor inputs it can be difficult to cost them out. The willingness to consider per program fees by isolating expenses on a program basis and here by taking on a share of overall costs is often just not there. The same would be true of revenues where a clear explanation of program specific expenses and revenue (tuition and other sources) would be helpful. This is done at some institutions, but many others are still not able to produce proper income statements on a program basis so that program specific prices could be set.

29.2 Looking Beyond Government to Achieve Education Ideals

This work has emphasized that education ideals can only be achieved with a broad spectrum of public and private providers and programs and an emphasis on commercial, contract and product realities. Even if so-called public institutions were not fiscally constrained any student and public or private provider should be free to engage in education transactions without needless regulatory restrictions that go beyond real consumer risk.

Daniel Woolf, vice-chancellor of Queen's University in Kingston, Ontario is a progressive leader, but in a recent article [160] he arguably displayed common tendencies that illustrate how perspectives are slow to change. His article said: "The reality is that universities — like many public institutions — are in trouble…[The] Canadian public has placed a higher premium on health care and kindergarten to Grade 12 education than it has on post-secondary education, which still smacks of elitism to some. They are thus reluctant to put up with tax increases sufficiently large to guarantee that the quality of what their children receive once inside the ivory tower maintains a reasonable consistency and high level".

He continued: "Students … have found their contribution to their own education by way of tuition and fees has been steadily rising as a proportion of overall cost and they are extremely resistant, especially in the face of uncertain job prospects, to pay more, especially for a bachelor's degree in a non-professional program…. the system built in the 1960s for a much smaller participation rate and a much more modest engagement in research is not sustainable…We cannot continue to absorb ever-increasing numbers of students, maintain or increase educational quality (which he says no one has yet agreed on a way to measure) and participate in a national innovation agenda, all on funding that continues to lag behind the actual cost of doing business".

He referred to data showing that students are resistant to the three-year degree programs as opposed to four year programs because they fear it would devalue their qualification. The only solution he offered was to provide more funding for second degrees that would more likely lead to professional work. A number of comments are notable.

- The uncompromising characterization of universities as "public" can limit one's ability to consider new options and innovations. The term implies "government" and that most often creates the image of money and beneficence from above. Accepting the reality that they are in fact independent (non-government) legal entities that operate in commercial environments and markets forces new ideas into the mix.
- More tax increases often will not solve anything. The money just gets eaten up with existing aggregations of inputs. Changing products with changes to the manner of input intermediation is more important than tax increases. Opportunities for entrepreneurship exist on campus, but they are rarely seized.
- He correctly points out that students are resistant to pay more for undergraduate programs because of questionable job prospects, but student expectation are based on false reality. If job prospects are weak and they do not want to pay more then why should the taxpayer pay more? The sale then has to focus on some non-economic value added argument.
- He points out that student numbers and research demands have both increased and he implies that these are both cost problems. In many cases it is not even clear at institutions how student revenues and research funding is apportioned and applied in relation to program viability because of the common (not universal) lack of program specific income statements.
- He says no one has agreed how to measure quality. That is true and that is why we present the ideas we do in this work on education freedom and commerce. It is not that hard if you accept commercial reality and focus on the product and what it is designed to do (Outcomes 1 and 2). If such a high executive questions what quality means in the public sector one is left wondering how it is that private education sector regulators think that they understand what it means. They don't in many cases and that is why we present this simple commercial model.
- He refers to funding lagging behind the cost of doing business and again that is because he only thinks funding should come from government. If programs are not going to be in market demand if reality and cost based fees were charged then that should tell people something about their real perceived market value and about the need to perhaps deliver the same product

benefits in innovative ways without just relying on government funding.

- The reference to students not wanting to experiment with shorter programs for fear of credential value loss again relates to the observation that the credential is on one hand considered to be of questionable economic value given jobs prospects and yet somehow something of value to protect. Again, the sale must be based on some other value added factor. Education is not just about jobs, but then the question is why the taxpayer should pay. This goes to the social contract argument and what it is that the taxpayer is willing to subsidize.
- The funding for more professional and post grad degrees does not solve anything in monetary terms because the same or more time would be spent in school. Such programs can in fact be more expensive to provide. Time would just be spent in programs that hopefully produce better economic prospects. If in fact there is evidence of great economic prospects then the ability of students to finance their own education should be greater. Another problem here is that limited seats in professional programs would still limit access. Some would be publicly subsidized and others would have to be full freight while their parents or they themselves pay the taxes to subsidize the student that is fortunately enough to be offered one of the limited seats.

29.3 Don't Make the Student Pay for What they Can Do Themselves or With Others Inside or Outside the Institution, True Value Added for Each Product Factor Input

Just pouring more tax money or borrowed money into the top of the public institution hopper does not mean that students will pay less and have to borrow less because the money may get spent in unaccountable or unanalyzed ways. Someone has to plug the leaks in the boat. If public funds are restricted then the money has to come from somewhere else. If public sector institutions cannot provide a product that is in demand because of cost constraints then alternatives must be in place. One model is not enough.

There must be new approaches to analyzing and addressing issues of education finance as it relates to institutions, students and student loan lenders. There must be greater understanding and disclosure of where student tuition, taxpayer, research, corporate project and donor money is spent. Students should not have to pay for anything that they could achieve themselves or with others inside or outside the institution without direct outlays of funds. The true "added value" of each specific product factor input must be clear on the facts. Ultimately if campuses are seen as places where learning is inferior to other models or worse as places where learning is restricted and stifled or more expensive than necessary the role of the campus experience will be undermined. [161]

29.4 Case Study: South Africa, Free Education Models, Creative Product Assembly and Intermediation

No one is suggesting that this particular example is replicable in any other specific circumstance, but it does illustrate what can be done in extreme circumstances where the government is not able to come to the rescue. An acquaintance of ours, Dr. Taddy Blecher of Johannesburg, South Africa,[162] is credited with being a major force in that country's free education and free university movement. He has founded multiple institutions and universities that have trained thousands of South Africans that could not otherwise attend mainstream institutions because of financial constraints. The quality of the education has generally been excellent and students have gone on to work and excel in many professions.

Costs are kept down in several ways. Corporate sponsors provide financial support for student scholarships. All students have a work-study job in the university and donate their time to run the campus and keep overheads low. Students run the admissions office, work in the library and act as janitors and audiovisual technicians. Technology enables lecturers to reach students in more than one classroom through state of the art video equipment. Instead of carrying a large overhead for faculty salaries, corporations provide many of the lecturers. Students receive lectures from industry professionals, rather than simply learning textbook theories. Many other suppliers also contribute their products and services. Government approved curricula fulfill accreditation requirements for degrees. In some cases, parallel businesses are being set up (e.g. call centres) to employ students and produce revenue that can be used to help fund school operations.

Again, this type of approach may have limited application, but it does have application and students can take the initiative in many cases. In Canada and the US it could have application to First Nations education or inner city education or anywhere you have affordability and access issues. In the developing world the applications are clear.

What often remains unresolved is the exact legal nature of the bi-lateral or multi-party relationships involved. Legal reality must be sorted out or the house of cards will eventually fold either because of disputes or because the lack of clarity and multiplicity of interpretations stifles or incapacitates management. Student contracts and related service contracts must be sufficient to capture what can be complex legal relationships and expectations. The application of laws (common law and statute) regarding employment, professional service, education services, sales of goods, agency, joint venture collaborations and partnerships, gifts and corporate organizations must be clear. In most cases it will be various types of contract instruments and the applicable law of contract that take centre stage.

29.5 Case Study: Quebec Student Disputes 2012 Illustrate a Failure to Grasp Commercial and Contract Realities

In the spring of 2012 there were huge student demonstrations in the province of Quebec in Canada. The dispute focused on what many considered to be minor tuition increases. In an attempt to settle the dispute, the government did not back down on increases, but it allowed student groups a say over how universities spend money. An interim council was to be made up of university executives, student representatives, union people, business sector representatives and government representatives. [163]

The enforceability in legal terms of the political compromise is questionable. It is fine for a council to present ideas, but ultimately the institutions (legal entities) involved have to make decisions and cover expenses with revenues from somewhere. University executives say their institutions are underfunded (by government) and student groups say there is too much waste.

Talk is cheap, but the realities of costs and revenues cannot be talked away. Institutions are separate from government and governments have a responsibility to taxpayers and citizens. They are not just there do to the bidding of institutions and students. It is not clear if student groups truly represent all students. They do not agree amongst themselves. Some groups demand free education and others do not. One group wants universities to stop advertising by institutions, zero new construction and taxes on banks. Stopping advertising when competitors are gearing up global advertising efforts would be disastrous.

In all of this, the parties seem to have lost sight of reality or they never had it to lose. As argued, the student and institution relationship is commercial and contractual in nature in most cases where tuitions are paid and often when they are not. Consumers do not have the legal capacity to demand that a product be sold to them at a set price. The institutions are also not masters of their universe. Governments or private entities that subsidize the legal entity's operations and capital costs under separate contracts with institutions have a right and responsibility to say no and to assert their own agenda. The product factor input providers that institutions bring together to create education, assessment and other service products also have contractual relationships with the institutions. That is where costs come from. Those parties in turn have real cost and revenue realities to deal with.

These old ways of thinking about institution and student relationships (In Loco Parentis and the Club ideas) and a failure to work within legal and commercial realities can cause problems and an inability to solve problems.

The term "strike" used by the students is out of place. Strikes are normally carried out by providers of services that assert collective rights or demands under Labor Relations Laws. They have bargaining power because they have legal rights to withdraw services if a collective agreement is not in place and employers are limited in their ability to hire replacement workers. Students, on the other hand, are consumers that pay for services under contracts (that may exist even if tuitions are not paid as noted in other sections). Consumers assert control by decisions to enter contracts or not and by contract enforcement.

Certain student comments appear to reflect remnants of old In Loco Parentis concepts. Léo Bureau-Blouin, president of one of the student federations, when referring to Premier Jean Charest's plans to introduce legislation forcing the opening of classrooms, said: "A good father does not call the police into his home to solve a problem with his children. A good father addresses his children and talks to them to settle a crisis".

It may have been more effective to argue that the institutions could not increase tuitions for current students given contract law constraints (e.g. certainty doctrines). Unfortunately, calendar contracts may allow universities to increase fees at any time and certain courts have upheld their ability to do so even when the increases were extremely high.[164] Students are often not aware of this. Future students could refuse to pay higher tuition, but finding lower tuition could be hard. Another legal issue is whether a student signs a four year contract for a four-year degree program (our view) or a year by year contract. The latter is unworkable in most cases and not in tune with the expectations of most students. These points are discussed again in relation to issues about contract changes during the contract term and about contract periods.

Students could "strike" in the sense they could boycott and not consume an offered product, but current students have already entered contracts. If the contract obligations of the institution to provide the product during a set period at a set price are satisfied then the students could find themselves having made payments without a legal right to demand future performance. The government is a funder and not the independent institution that provides the service. Students can demand that their contract partner sell products at a cheaper price, but that party has freedom of contract rights to enter such a bargain or not.

Ultimately, as noted in other sections, problems associated with the education product, the price of that product or how that price is paid and financed are best addressed with innovation and with the parties practically addressing their respective interests in the context of the real legal and commercial relationships that exist.

29.6 Profit in Education Is Not Bad and Can Serve Public Interests, The Reality of Education Finance and the Need to Encompass Diverse Business Models

There is no rational reason why for profit models cannot work in the education sector as they do in other commercial sectors where they also serve the public interest. With education, the regulatory focus must be on major risks surrounding payment security and program quality. If societies can regulate the manufacture and use of airplanes that fly people across the sky (and soon in space) at high speed then they can regulate education.

If the same learning objective is met and the cost to taxpayers is less, a social and economic objective is met without it costing the taxpayer anything or perhaps as much. If profits or zero or restricted return (via Social Business options[165]) goals are met for a private firm, it allows for greater capacity in the system to serve a growing and increasingly diverse demand for education services. The program, operating and capital cost investments came from private investors rather than taxpayers. If they make a profit in return for taking those risks then good for them.

Profit (or social benefit) attracts investment in programs and rewards those that take risks. People get the education they seek even though: it may not be available in the public sector (as defined); it may be available at a lower quality in the public sector; or public programs may only be available to a select few people.

With Social Business options, investors invest because of a hoped for social return as opposed to a direct financial return. Social Business firms can choose to not pay dividends or restrict returns to set levels while still utilizing the management and financing strengths of a for profit business model.

Public (definitions vary) institutions can often make profits on individual programs or on all programs collectively and they just plough any surplus back into the operation. They cannot send money back to shareholders because they don't exist. The profit exists and distribution is different. If the principle behind criticism of private profit is that a student should only pay for program cost and not subsidize others or contribute to profit and private investor return then government funded institutions and programs should return funds to students when program revenues exceed program cost. Other objections to profit should be critiqued in the same way.

Whether a public or private institution is involved there are investments that have to be made. Any calculation about a student paying for more than they receive relies on a calculation of revenue and cost and a focus on sources of revenue and cost. Students pay a set fee and that revenue for the institution is used to help pay for operating, capital and investment costs. Public universities access taxpayer money, donor money and borrowed money and pay interest. A private institution should then not be penalized for borrowing money and paying interest or for paying private money to private investors when capital gains occur or dividend are paid. There is no real difference.

In other words, both public and private institutions use debt financing and both must generate sufficient revenue from operations to pay interest on borrowed funds. This is not significantly different than paying equity investors a return on their investment.

Profit-focused enterprises are not in conflict with social responsibilities and can be of social benefit. In BC the terms of reference for a major government study asked the question in relation to private schools: How do you reconcile making a profit with the social responsibility associated with education? [166] The reality is that firms in all sectors from farming to transportation and beyond make profits and are of social benefit. This question illustrated a culture within the education sector—a culture that must change.

The bottom line is that the education sector needs everybody to step up. Government cannot do it all and in many cases its structure is just not suited to business enterprise and that is why these so-called public institutions are really just a form of private enterprise in the sense they are separate legal entities and deliberately kept separate from government. Each corporate form or public organization form has strengths—government, Crown corporations (or their equivalent), non-profit corporations, for-profit corporations, cooperatives—and weaknesses. Even for-profit corporations can—if necessary—be adjusted and become Social Businesses with limits on return while retaining the benefits of a corporate form that is well suited to financing and operating an enterprise.

In this context it is also appropriate to mention again that innovations with the corporate form are continuing. Many jurisdictions are engaged in law reforms to accommodate social business and social entrepreneurship. The strengths of all corporate forms—cooperatives and not-for-profit or for-profit corporations—must be harnessed and the weaknesses of each need to be acknowledged. The blind hatred or profit and the blind reverence for non-profits just won't cut it in the future.

29.7 New Key Metrics: Costs Per Training Outcome for Each Contributing Payor, Delivering the Best Product At The Least Price

There is always a cost to students, governments, taxpayers and others of pursuing and achieving learning outcomes. Those costs and who bears them can and some would say must be a factor in calculating social and economic value. Any cost per training outcome in any education sector must consider a wide range of factors.

Amounts paid by governments and taxpayers may be in the form of direct operating and capital costs or student loan defaults. These can—where it is useful to do so - roughly be apportioned to each student. Institutions commonly complain that their cost per student funding is being reduced. In a public context both the taxpayer and student pay. Debtors and suppliers rarely go unpaid. Loan defaults are a factor. All costs can also be apportioned to and amortized over the entire institution or a program cohort and factored against collective benefits.

In a private context with no public subsidies only the student pays unless investors (debt or equity) invest and fail to recover their investment or suppliers provide services and are not compensated. Losses from student loan defaults are not direct subsidies, but they too can be factored in (See Other Sections). In the private unsubsidized program and institution context, the student pays and the public will only pay indirectly through loan defaults. Again, all costs can be apportioned to and amortized over the entire institution or a program cohort and factored against collective benefits.

Expenditures in the form of public subsidies and loan defaults are only a real loss or a problem if you do not consider the social benefit and the return on investment in a holistic way. In ways that are blatantly unfair, self-serving, biased and narrow, analysts will often consider these benefits and returns on investment with publicly funded institutions, but not with privates where loan defaults may come into the equation and where privates clearly provide many of the same learning outcomes and post-grad benefits for individuals and the socio-economy.

Calculation of eventual benefit in terms of future income, increased taxable income and contribution to the broader socio-economy are difficult. Nevertheless, if a person achieves a learning outcome and earns greater income and pays higher taxes as a result then that contribution is a viable factor to consider within the overall social and economic context. A recent January 2012 report from the Canadian Centre for Policy Alternatives argues that students more than repay the costs of their tuition subsidies with higher taxes in the future. If this observation is to have policy significance with public institutions then to be fair and effective it should be used for private institutions as well. Analytical tools and methods should aspire to improve the entire education system and not just to enhance narrow political interests.

It is not uncommon for huge public investments to be made in public programs where the cost per training outcome becomes unrealistically high and out of proportion in relation to what it is in the private sector. For example, if forty million dollars is put into a program that only graduates thirty students per year (there are real life examples) then the amortized cost for training each student is extraordinarily high. If research and not just teaching is involved then the analysis changes, but in many cases these funded programs have minimal research elements.

The same is true for some private investments in public institutions. Huge corporate donations to one program may drastically increase the cost of training those graduates and it is often not the most efficient use of private donations. If scholarship funds were set up with that money it could be used to fund the studies of many more students from multiple public and private institutions. As in the real world, investments are most effective and efficient when they are tied into some form of system that allows returns to be demonstrated and quantified.

The objective for all must be to deliver the best product (in terms of meeting desired learning objectives) at the most reasonable cost and price to students and taxpayers and other investors or paying parties. A cost per training outcome metric must track what each party contributed and what they collectively contributed on a per graduate basis. The detailed calculation of eventual benefit in terms of future income, increased taxable income and contribution to the broader socio-economy is more difficult.

30

Innovative Regulation, New Objects of Accreditation, Diverse Providers and Impartial Regulators

30.1 Disruptive Innovation in Education, The Difficulty of Adjusting Regulation and the Tendency to Fall Back On and Use Old Models

Education is going through and will continue to go through for some time the same kinds of disruptive innovations that other industries and particular media content industries have faced. Traditional methods of regulation and management often just won't work with new systems. Here the focus is on some of the ways that regulation may have to change to respond to innovation in education systems.

This idea was first explored in depth in the 1980s when new information and telecommunication technologies were sweeping the globe and changing every industry in sight. [167] Ithiel de Sola Pool, the founder of MIT's political science department and the one who coined the term "convergence" wrote in his book Technologies of Freedom [168] at that time [169] that it was common for regulators to want to regulate new technologies in the same way they had regulated the old technologies.

Pool pointed out that print developed largely without regulations because it was too hard to regulate. The church controlled print and knowledge for a long time. This refers to the European context of course and we are not exploring the great knowledge traditions of the Middle East, India and China that go far back in history.

The scarcity of knowledge began to dissipate when the printing press came along and more people began to read. This resulted in huge social change because the church no longer controlled who learned what. Only totalitarian regimes were able to successfully restrict print and eventually technologies that went way beyond the printing press were important elements of the breakdown of many totalitarian regimes including the Soviet Union and more recently certain Arab spring regimes.

To make the connection between technology and regulation Pool looked at various technologies. Telegraphs often initially ran along rail lines so they were regulated along with railways. Telephone and broadcast regulation unfolded differently with the former focused on carriage and the latter more on content and carriage. The legal principle of common carriage helped protect universal access to the post office and monopoly electronic carriers. Broadcast regulation developed for public interest purposes.

Convergence called much of this into question. Common sense thinkers like Pool asked whether cable and telecom carried content should be subject to the same content regulation as broadcasting even though scarce and rationed electromagnetic spectra were not involved. Cable could be more of a common carrier and thus beyond regulations as to who can access it. Multiple carriers and expanded bandwidth (that unfolded after Pool died in 1984) have made the modern internet and all of its repercussions, including expanded educational services, possible.

Unlike telephone and telegraph regulations, governments were aware that broadcast regulations would infringe traditional US first amendment or Canadian Charter of Rights principles, but they could see no way to avoid a regulated system because of those technical restrictions. Not just anybody could be a broadcaster in those days. The system was not of common carriage. Many governments tried to and did regulate content and carriers self-censored to some extent. Many newspapers tried to limit early classified ad systems placed online by telephone companies. Monopoly rights and public access rights clashed. It was unclear if cable and telecom carried content would be subject to a regulated broadcast or unregulated press model.

These debates continue even today. The multi-channel system has now evolved and product points on the Internet are almost unlimited. It seems unlikely now that online news or any other content—even when the same broadcast audio visual content carried by regulated broadcast media is often carried on the Net—will ever be regulated in terms of its content. Some would still like to try.

With the education sector, institutions and other service providers and regulators are going to be faced with similar issues. They cannot regulate and manage a twenty first century education system that is onsite and online (Often 24/7) and global in scope in the same way they regulated and managed institutions in the past. For example, the discussions on assessment and uniformity point out that trying to regulate around the "degree" or other credential is—while still perhaps necessary to some extent—problematic because of the diversity of programs and providers, the diversity of students and the need for new credential systems that capture the reality of ongoing and lifelong learning.

30.2 Public and Private Institutions, Common Markets and Common Methods of Regulation

These same points were made in relation to dispute resolution, but they bear repeating. There are few real legal distinctions between so-called public institutions and private institutions. Their separate corporate identity may arise via different legislative instruments and processes, but the status of being non-government is the same. Non-profit versus for-profit distinctions can exist within the private sector also. Both enter contracts with students (often even if tuitions are not paid) and increasingly they compete against each other in common markets where they market to and enroll from a common body of students. They are unified at the market level through the mechanism of contract law. Both are governed under the same body of common law as it relates to contracts.

As argued, education regulation should be targeted at education products and consumption risk. Regulation should operate separately from, but alongside contract law to ensure students receive what was promised to them and that products satisfy legal standards also focused on mitigating consumer risk. Regulations and contracts operate separately because parties to the regulatory relationship are the institution and public agency while the parties to the student and institution contract relationship are only those two parties. Public and private rights and duties may be similar in substance, but they are legally distinct in terms of the parties, the relationships and the mechanisms of creating and enforcing these respective rights and duties.

Students in all sectors should have the same protections and different regulations can be justified where risks differ and that affirms the principle that contract provisions drive variation. All students should have the same rights and duties, the same protection to quality assurance regulation and the same rights and duties in relation to how their products and providers are regulated and how their disputes are resolved. Again, contract variation can create risk variation and therefore justify regulatory variation.

As already stated, it is hard to argue that common domestic treatment of all providers is not warranted if they are treated largely the same for international trade purposes. In relation to the GATS (other sections), it boils down to what the phrase (required for GATS exclusion) "supplied in the exercise of government authority" really means. To many it means not in competition with other suppliers. The reality is that so-called public institutions are often not government as such and do compete with other suppliers. Even if trade agreement exclusion can be justified the exclusion would normally exist to protect domestic students (e.g. protection of subsidies). Exemptions from common dispute resolution methods or quality standards are harder to justify.

30.3 New Forms of Accreditation for Institution Elements—Product Delivery, Mentorship, Assessment, Authoritative and Credible Credentials Granting, Credential Evaluation, Credit Transfer

Institutions are commonly accredited or in some other way given permission to engage in otherwise prohibited activities because it has met required standards that mitigate risks associated with the prohibited actions.

If institutions can be accredited and given permission to engage in certain bundles of tasks, actions and functions in quality assured ways—product delivery, mentorship, assessment systems and credential declarations as evidence of academic achievement - then these individual elements could be and perhaps should be subject to accreditation in their own right so that they can be credibly and authoritatively offered by more people and third parties beyond traditional institutions in diverse circumstances. This would allow many of the disruptive innovations to proceed and to be realistically managed and regulated—if in fact regulation is warranted.

These systems of accreditation do not have to be mandatory for operations although in some cases they could be. They could be built around prohibitions and standards that are risk based and then permissions or licenses can be granted when standards are met. This is the common regulatory model. In other cases, they could be voluntary and built around permission to use a designation if certain standards were met.

30.4 Regulation of More Diverse Education Providers Must Focus on Product Quality and Access Risk

Education regulation, whether focused on public (government funded or as otherwise defined) or private sector institutions, has focused on student consumer protection initiatives that govern institutions to the extent they provide services to students. This is important work, but students are also hurt if they can't access the education they want and need and if their freedom of choice is needlessly restricted. It is not just the institutions that create risk for learners, but public policy that limits options and freedom needlessly and that is based not on consumer protection, but the protection of vested interests or the related risk of being too wedded to outdated concepts and the unwillingness to innovate.

If public funds are limited then other means of building the capacity to meet demand must be free to act with reasonable regulation targeted at serious risk. This is why new providers, large and small, local and foreign, must be encouraged to participate in the market. The three elements of the education product—education products, assessment products and service products—must be allowed to be offered collectively and individually through classic disintermediation or just simply product unbundling that has so productively benefitted other sectors. Benefits flow to consumers that want and receive greater choice and lower prices and producers that want and receive more avenues for their expression, creativity and services.

Regulation must focus on the simple concepts of quality assurance presented with the focus on product and product performance. The contract promised education product (Outcome 1) must be sufficient to help the student achieve the un-promised learning outcome objective (Outcome 2—un-promised because the student controls it). The assessment product must be sufficient to credibly validate the learning achievement. It does not have to be much more complicated than that aside, of course, for the protection of student payments.

As noted, issues regarding uniform content, learning objectives and competencies—usually pursued so that credits are more universally recognized and transferable - should be separated from quality assurance and left to private contracting parties because quality is not about sameness and uniformity. Quality should also be separated from outcomes (Outcome 5) that come in the future with the use of the knowledge and skills gained. These are all valid objectives and considerations, but they should not be allowed to distort basic concepts of commercial quality. Immigration authorities, professional organizations and others cannot escape the need for their own sets of criteria that address the risks targeted by their respective regulatory regimes.

30.5 Decentralized and Expert Enforcement To Meet Demands of Dispersed and Diverse Education Providers and Products

Give the current and growing trend to more education, assessment and related service providers and the global nature of education there is also a growing need to have regulatory systems that have the decentralized capacity and expertise to regulate in that environment. Existing regulators are already stretched too thin. Dedicated public servants are being asked to do or trying to do too much.

Regulatory functions can potentially be split by sector or by function. This already occurs to some extent where you have professional groups and institutions working together. Centralized supervisory functions may still be required, but not all functions need to be in-house. Many education regulators already rely on industry panels or advisory councils for institutions and that idea can be extended.

New education regulators should encourage and facilitate voluntary compliance and decentralize oversight, enforcement and compliance processes where possible. New technologies and management systems allow for it and existing enforcement resources cannot handle what has come and is coming. There is and will be a tendency to want to limit the number of providers because of that difficulty and that will be a serious obstacle to creating the kind of education freedom and capacity needed.

Decentralization is needed because governments can't afford to have large forces of inspectors and investigators on staff at all times that are institution, program and industry sector savvy at all times. Community, business and corporate resources can assist. A decentralized range of professionals can contribute to a functioning regulatory system. They include specially trained inspectors, accountants, lawyers and private registrar systems like those used in standards setting systems like the International Standards Organization.

This is not a revolutionary idea. Independent (of government civil service) inspectors operating under public legislation are common in many sectors including home inspection, food monitoring, aircraft and pilot regulation and many other sectors. Education regulators already rely on audit panels and on institution-based advisory councils. They cannot be expected to have the needed expertise and regulatory capacity in-house.

Decentralized systems more easily allow institutions that have had compliance issues to be subjected to additional requirements without the business being disrupted. Those with few problems could be left alone and only monitored in an ongoing way to the extent required. Serious issues like can often not be handled properly with a few centralized public servants.

These dispersed systems are even more important when rapid change in the industry and the institution is so dominant. Relying on financial statements from a previous year is an outdated system. By the time the statements are done, filed and analyzed for hundreds of institutions the period of time in question is back in time a year or more and the institutions are in a completely different place corporately and in completely different business cycles. Conclusions reached and disciplinary steps taken may be completely inappropriate in current circumstances.

30.6 Regulators Must Be Impartial and Not Tied to Vested Interests That Are Slow to Innovate, Self-Regulation Generally Not Advised

Scores of commentators are predicting major disruptive innovation in the education sector just as it occurred with other content industries like music recording, film production, broadcast media, the Internet, newspaper publishing and book publishing. It is happening, but it is slower in education for various reasons. One of the reasons may be public sector domination over services and public policy processes.

We ask a simple question: If government providers had dominated newspaper and book publishing, recording, film production and radio and television in terms of production and regulation would those industries have changed as much as they have? Arguments can be made either way. There are those that would prefer to still have us in the three TV channel, one-daily newspaper universe, but I think the majority of persons like the diversity they have as consumers and the opportunity for expression and service that they have as producers and creators.

Because public sector education providers have dominated it is only natural that ministries of education and advanced education are dominated by persons that were trained in and that worked as managers in the public sector. They should be congratulated for building a system that has served Canada well, but often their thinking is rooted in old models of what institutions are and completely unaware often when it comes to the commercial and contractual realities of education and the upcoming disruptive innovation. Often they are dismissive or downright hostile toward private providers in ways that are often completely unjustified based on actual facts and events.

Education must be regulated as a commercial sector with an emphasis on product and that regulation must be unbiased and open to all of the changes that are to come. Self-interested parties should not be allowed to slow innovation down. It cannot be assumed that they have the expertise needed. They may have had expertise with past systems, but that may not extend to emerging systems. Again, expressions of regulatory best practices often stipulate that regulation be driven by evidence and expertise.

As has been the case in most sectors, disruptive and positive innovation in education will in many cases come from outside the system. In any sector, current market leaders often do not have the peripheral vision to see change and even when they do see it they can't respond to it because they are locked in structurally. That provides an opportunity for upstarts to work their way up from bottom end niches. [170] There is a valid concern that this process will be slowed down with education because of the dominance of vested interests.

Self-regulation is in most cases also not well suited to the education sector. Self-regulation is best confined to professional service sectors where practitioners have an agency or fiduciary relationship with their clients and already in a position where they must put their clients' interests ahead of their own. In purely commercial and competitive sectors like education (this does not mean collaboration cannot occur) self-regulation presents serious issues. If independent agencies exist those boards are better populated by persons that are separate from those that represent traditional vested interests and separate from the regulated industry. Both these groups deserve to be represented on these boards or on advisory councils, but they should not dominate.

30.7 Higher Education Commissions and Broad Input to Education Law and Policy

The hard realities are that: education is vitally important as an industry itself and to all sectors; education is vitally important to personal development and economic security; there is a growing diversity of institutions, programs and desired learning outcomes; and education must reflect and serve global markets and workplaces.

These realities dictate that major changes must be made to how education and especially higher education law and policy are developed and administered. Professional public servants in Ministries of Advanced Education or their equivalent in other jurisdictions are influenced largely by traditional publicly funded institutions and major faculty associations and unions. That is understandable because they have been dominant providers that governments have depended on for advice and public service and because many fine public servants often come from their ranks.

These institutions and groups, however, have narrow vested and selfish interests that they often want to protect. Despite their assertions they are not just acting in the public interest. They must not have the power to dominate policy development and law reform or to assert their interests over those of other diverse parties that exist now and that are emerging as innovative players in the education sector. It can also no longer be assumed that they have expertise for a new era of education that features the kind of technological, social and business transformations that are now emerging. Again, expressions of regulatory best practices often stipulate that regulation be driven by evidence and expertise.

They cannot be allowed to dictate systems that impact so many in such vital ways. It is not enough that bureaucratic systems dominated by these narrow interests have brief "consultations" once in a blue moon with other existing and emerging players to satisfy calls for consultations and that are often ignored.

Education policy and law must be developed by a broad base of social, education, business and economic stakeholders and administered by impartial and independent professionals. Traditional interests must share power and influence with community groups, industry groups, business associations, legal professions groups, relevant technology companies, professional groups, students, a full range of education product providers and emerging service groups like credential evaluators and third party assessment systems. No group should dominate. There should be common approaches (not the same as uniform content and learning objectives) where parties operate in common markets and variations allowed when different risks warrant it.

This must be formalized in law. Higher Education Statutes should create Higher Education Commissions that will formally embrace participants from all of these stakeholder groups. These statutes and commissions do not have to integrate, override or embrace all existing education sector and related (e.g. student finance, credit transfer) statutes and systems, but they must have significant and sufficient power and capacity to ensure that core education system objectives are met. These objectives are outlined and summarized in various other sections, but they include:

- Fair and equitable credit transfer systems (bi-lateral, multi-lateral, public or private and possibly accredited) must exist and focus on real states of knowledge no matter where a credit was earned or validated.
- Uniform, but simple domestic and international quality assurance systems that: apply the same standards with the same systems notwithstanding the corporate structure, ownership or funding source of the provider; ensure program products are able to help students achieve set learning outcome objectives; leave objectives regarding uniformity for institutions, programs, learning outcomes, assessment and credentials to be developed by agreements involving institutions, students, industry and professional groups or workplace and business groups.
- Systems that support and respect contract relationships involving diverse education providers and students.
- Financial aid systems that focus on quality assured education products and other criteria that apply equally to all education providers.
- New accreditation systems that look beyond institutions and programs to include third party assessment firms, credit transfer systems, credential evaluation firms and other service pro-

viders. These accreditations would arise on the principle that if government can accredit institutions it can accredit those that provide the individual functions that institutions have traditionally intermediated and exercised.

- Diversified and decentralized enforcement systems.
- Common dispute resolution systems if non-judicial forums are adopted - forums that must (the common law position) still be bound by the common law of contract or tort.

Conclusion

31

Conclusion

There are many books about disruptive innovation in education. There are few books about the likely and needed commercial and legal underpinnings for these emerging systems. This book is an attempt to contribute to that much needed debate.

To repeat what was said in the introduction, the practical pursuit of high education ideals requires that those in pursuit have their feet on the ground. The legal foundation for many emerging public and private post-secondary education systems in this time of disruptive innovation can be found with legal traditions that have governed commercial enterprises and transactions for centuries. Strong relationships and effective regulation will be built on that foundation. These laws have greater application to education now as institutions aggressively engage competitive domestic and global markets, more students and more diverse students.

Some of the points raised in this book that are most relevant to this conclusion are set out below.

1. Governments have no exclusive power to provide education and private education is not based on delegated or extensions of government power.
2. Governments themselves rarely provide education directly as the legal entity that is party to a student contract.
3. Private (non-government) corporate entities created under general corporation statutes (for-profit or not-for-profit), institution specific legislative charters or universities and colleges statutes provide most education services. They now serve and are unified in common markets where they seek to enter, often with the same prospective students, contracts governed by the same common law of contract.
4. With education or related systems, governments facilitate the provision of education services, regulate some providers and

programs, lend money to students, control borders and engage in economic development. These roles involve separate governing laws, parties and authorities, objectives, rights and duties. These roles can have operational linkages, but they must stay legally separate to avoid, in each area, distortions of purpose, violations of mandates, ineffectiveness and inefficiency.

5. Students must understand what the relationship with an education provider really is so they can effectively assert and protect their rights and live up to their duties. They are no longer In Loco Parentis - under the care and parental control of institutions—or seen as being in clubs or partnerships with institutions.
6. Courts in many jurisdictions have affirmed that students and institutions are engaged in contract relationships, when tuitions are paid and often when they are not, and that reality must be reflected more in management and regulation. Courts will hear and rule on student claims if they properly articulate causes of action under contract law or other laws despite the fact that they arise in academic forums.
7. When contract parties understand their rights and duties it helps avoid and does not encourage disputes.
8. Personal control over one's own learning is vital because economic security depends on it. If a person is not satisfied with what certain institutions provide then the system must allow for the diversity of providers and products. Students—so they can pursue opportunities of choice in the world beyond education - must be able to access the education products they want and not only those that others choose for them or restrict them to without justification.
9. Governments and a few institutions must not solely determine which programs are needed and provided, how many positions will be offered and, with admissions, who gets the prize. Those not making the cut need diverse providers and products that allow them to compete for available opportunities.
10. In an age of lifelong learning, students cannot expect governments to provide them with free or highly subsidized education from cradle to grave in every conceivable discipline. The demand for diverse products from increasing numbers of students is too great for traditional government funded models to handle. The disparity between current programs and skills

demanded—the jobs without people and people without jobs phenomenon—illustrates the need for product diversity.

11. There should be less talk about education rights and more focus on real life legal and commercial environments where persons will not soon or ever have a right to education (let alone free education) from cradle to grave in the sense of a legal right to claim a legal remedy at court under law if they are denied the ability to take specific programs.
12. Students do have a right to freely contract in free markets and an efficient market with diverse and innovative providers and affordable products is increasingly viable given technological, economic and social change. Scarcity is less of a problem because there are more knowledgeable people and experts can use technology to reach more people.
13. Students must demand that this right and these efficient markets not be needlessly restricted by regulations that go beyond what is needed to protect them from prevailing risk. They must be protected from the risk of poor access and not just quality risk.
14. Students are now increasingly accessing, online and worldwide with greater institution and student mobility, new providers and products. This includes new forms of credible and authoritative (institution and third party) assessment systems and credentials.
15. New accreditation systems should look beyond institutions to target those that provide unbundled services and functions so that regulation is more in tune with emerging service providers and products.
16. Regulatory bodies should not be dominated by the narrow views of those with vested interests in the status quo. New impartial entities with broad representation from all providers, the community, government, the corporate sector and business organization should dominate law reform and public administration.
17. Regulators operate separately from contract, but regulation is often triggered by contract features and product consumption risk. Regulators may enforce laws to protect against that risk, but they do not enforce contracts. Only contract parties can do that. Institutions do not promise in student contracts that students will get jobs or have business success so unemployment and business failures are not contract risks.

18. In legal environments words are important and there must be a high degree of legal certainty. There must be greater and more consistent definition for what specific terms commonly used in regulation really mean. There must be sufficient legal certainty to allow for enforceable contracts and regulations targeted at contract product consumption risk. This book has provided detailed and practical provisions for defining what true outcomes and education products really are and for what quality and success really mean in a commercial setting.
19. Education quality assurance should operate like similar systems in other commercial sectors with the focus on merchantable quality products - products that are reasonably fit for the ordinary purposes for which they were produced and sold. With education that means products that help a student achieve a learning objective (change their knowledge conditions), credibly assess and validate the learning achievement and authoritatively declare the achievement to the world. That is what the parties intend contractually and that is all they control. Management and regulation should have purposes and goals that are achievable.
20. Quality does not go up and down when job results or business results change. Quality is also not about uniformity of content, learning objectives and competencies. Diverse products targeted at similar types of work can all be of quality. Uniformity can be a quality factor if it is promised in contracts. Poorly planned and inappropriate uniformity initiatives stifle innovation.
21. Looking beyond education and assessment products, institutions should carefully choose which support and other services they want to be contractual. If they induce students to enrol because of services like daycares, job placement services or business development services then there must be clear expression of what is really promised and they can't just cancel the services at will unless the contract gives them that unilateral right.

Appendices

32

Diagrams and Diagram Explanatory Notes

32.1 Introduction to Diagrams and Diagram Explanatory Notes

A series of diagrams helps to graphically illustrate key points in the main text and the introduction and executive summary. There are two main diagrams and each has several parts.

32.2 Diagram 1 Explanatory Notes

1. Diagram 1 roughly deals with education systems, the main players and the often poorly understood outcomes and products that are central to the private law world of contracts and the public law world of regulation that responds to contracts and products that have set features. Both govern the student and institution relationship.
2. Diagram 1A illustrates how a traditional institution aggregates and intermediates—pulls together—a group of product factor inputs to create an education service product, a learning environment, that is capable of helping a student achieve a set learning outcome objective. This can include all of the factors listed above and in the main body of the text. A particular bundle of factors will be assembled for each course or program area.
3. The arrows pointing down from Diagram 1A to Diagram 1B indicate that these collective and not individual inputs are used to create three contract promised products or outcomes.
4. The education product (Outcome 1) is constituted by the inputs that collectively help the student achieve the learning objective (Outcome 2). Outcome 2 is not promised by the institution to the student or by the student to the institution for the reasons expressed in the main text. The main reason is that the student is in control of the outcome and the institution cannot

promise contractually that it will be achieved. Course failure is not contract breach. If failure occurs because of problems with the education product or the assessment product then breach could exist, but it would not be because of the failure.

5. The assessment product or Outcome 3 is contractually promised. It must sufficiently test the student who must establish that they achieved the learning objective. If the assessment is too difficult that could have contract importance. If it is too easy then the student may be happy on one level, but not well served on the other because weak assessment institution wide weakens the credential.
6. Outcome 4 involves non-education and non-assessment related service products that the institution may also promise. For example, it may directly promise to provide career planning services or business development services or represented their existence as facts that could induce a student to attend.
7. The final set of outcomes (Outcome 5), are not contractually promised because most institutions are barred by law from making that kind of promise or representation to induce a contract. They are not promised because practically they cannot control the outcomes. Complex cause and effect relationships and third party actions and decisions determine—based on third party criteria - if jobs exist and are offered, businesses are begun and fail or succeed, credits are accepted for transfer, work permits are granted or professions grant admission based. Again, contracts and regulations must set standards that are achievable and not requirements that are effectively absolute prohibitions.
8. Again, to repeat, contract parties or regulators must only set standards of performance that are achievable by the parties and that relate to contract and product consumption risk. Impossible to achieve standards are not real standards, but absolute prohibitions. The purpose of contracts and regulation are to address specific risks and contract and product risks are separate from the risks associated with this type of post contract objective.
9. Only the three contract promised Outcomes or Products have arrows coming out of them because they relate to Diagram 1C which illustrates how pre-contract marketing and recruitment representations about products and admissions decisions lead the parties to the student contract. The arrow emerging from

the student contract box in 1C goes to 1D which illustrates more fully that primary student and institution contract relationship that is central to education in its private law and public law environments.

10. Diagram 1D is the centre of the universe. The two central players are the Student who should always come first given the real purpose of education and the Institution which assembles and intermediates the three products—education, assessment and other service products - provided under contract. The arrow flowing from right to left from the institution into the Product Box and to the student illustrates the three pronged contract product consideration offered by the institution to the student at the left.
11. In 1D, the middle line between the student and institution just illustrates the contract itself and the small box above that points out that contract law applies to that contract to give it life, make it enforceable, govern its terms, govern performance and breach factors and determine if remedies are owed for any occurring breach. The left to right arrow from the student to the institution stands for the tuition or other consideration flowing to the institution in return for provision of the products.
12. A couple of extra points should be made about 1D. At the top left is a Disintermediation box. This runs parallel to the sections of the work that address how the education sector is subject to forces of disruptive innovation which includes disintermediation forces that can allow the student or those that control the product factor inputs from 1A to connect outside the institution intermediation space to achieve in isolation some of the things the institution does. For example, students may hire a tutor because they don't find the institution's TAs very helpful. Some are already accessing open source content and finding third party assessment firms to assess the work and declare the learning achievement. Institutions are not going anywhere, but they may lose some of their monopoly power and influence. For now they are well branded and their products have the authority that students want.
13. At the far right of 1D are sources of income for the institution and the arrow flowing down indicates income flow to the institution. Tuition is included. These elements are central to

the debates over the cost of education. The expense box below the institution ties the outflow of funds to the existence of the product factor inputs from 1A. If costs to the student or the taxpayer are to go down then either the assembling of inputs and associated expenses must be modified or the income sources must be adapted. The kinds of disruptive innovation occurring and that are bound to occur are doing and will do both.

14. Diagram 1E captures the mentioned outcomes (Outcome 5) that fall outside the education system. A job is not an education outcome. It flows hopefully from the education system.
15. Diagram 1F is a time focused graphic to show how these outcomes and products allow the student to move from one point pre-student contract through the student contract period to a new state of knowledge and post contract period where they can enjoy new opportunities and work and business success. That success depends on a myriad of actions and decisions of other parties, economic cycles and personal decisions and actions.
16. Diagram 1F also illustrates some of the gateways or obstacles that stand in the road of the student moving toward the desires state of knowledge and the opportunities beyond. There must be a program and a position in the program. Admission standards must be reasonable (not inflated beyond what is needed for the learning objective). Funding must be available. The quality of the program must be sufficient (merchantable) to help the student achieve the learning objective. The assessment program must be sufficient to validate the learning achievement.
17. 1F shows that in the post contract period you again have elements or outcomes that the contract parties do not control. Contracts and regulations must not link these outcomes or elements to contracts or quality assurance efforts because, to repeat, they do not relate to contract product risk and because management and regulatory authorities should set objectives that are achievable and not impossible for them to achieve alone.
18. 1F also illustrates the point that diverse products at the left must be sufficient to prepare a person for the opportunities at the right.
19. At the bottom of 1F is a second rightward arrow that shows that non-traditional modes of learning can also now be used to take

the learner to the objective where learning can again be credibly evaluated and declared.

20. Finally, 1F has in the post contract space a left aiming arrow establishing that in today's world the process just keeps on going and we go back and start again. This changes the kind of learning outcomes that need to be set and the kind of assessment systems and credentials that must be offered.

32.3 Diagram 2 Explanatory Notes

1. The Diagram 2 group of graphics deals more with the public and government world, but ultimately it relates back again to the student and institution relationship which lies at the centre of everything. 2A starts with the Constitution in jurisdictions that have constitutional government. In federal states, national and provincial legislative bodies are given the power to make laws and those empowered bodies can and do delegate some of that power to subordinate officials and legally separate statutory agencies. National governments may have some related powers, but it is often the sub-national governments (States and Provinces) that have jurisdiction over education or property and civil rights (contracts and business).
2. Generally, these education regulating legislative bodies or delegates do not have the exclusive authority to provide education. Again, private education is not a delegated government power.
3. These governments take two primary steps in the education world. First, as illustrated in 2B, they may directly provide education as the legal entity that enters student contracts (rare) or legislatively pass laws, institution specific charters or laws that address groups of institutions (e.g. Universities Acts), to allow for the creation of new corporate entities that are mandated to provide education services. They also pass regular corporations laws that allow any person or group to incorporate and create new legal entities that can freely contract with consumers for the provision of education services. When it comes to students, student markets and contracts there is little difference between the private (non-government) entities created under education specific laws (e.g. Universities) and corporations that are

created under incorporation statutes. The same contract law applies.

4. Secondly, these constitutionally empowered governments may choose to regulate for quality assurance purposes the student and institution relationship and this is captured by 2C. The quality regulator is above the institution because most of the laws target the education service provider or institution. That is because they have to target an entity that can act or not act to protect consumers. The institution is regulated, however, because of what it does. If the entity was just a shell and did not offer products it would not have to be regulated because no consumer risk would exist. That is captured by the box above the contract box lying between the institution and student. The institution could be anyone of the institution types found in 2B because they all serve that common student market. They are united by that market and by the contract and contract law.
5. Diagram 2C illustrates the distinctions between contracts, law and business policy. Law and legal requirements flow from the constitution diagram 2A and legal duties are owed back to the government agency. The parties to the regulatory relationship are that government agency and the regulated institution. The up and down arrows stand for legal requirements that apply to and the duties owed by the regulated institution. Business policy comes from within the institution entity as owners or authorized managers dictate who can make business policy. The parties impacted are those directed to do something by the policy or that benefit from the policy. The policy is not law and not contractual (unless contract intent is clear or the operation of law dictates that result). The contract is a volitional instrument that the two parties freely enter into. They agree to abide by its terms for mutually beneficial reasons. Only they are bound and protected by it and only they can enforce it.
6. The bottom part of 2C deals with what triggers regulation. The bottom part of the contract box between the institution and student states that the product risk is sufficient to warrant a regulated standard. The arrow then drops to the box below which says the risk level gives rise to regulator jurisdiction and the legal standard that is appropriate to the risk. Prohibitions are set so one cannot engage in the prohibited action unless the standards

are met and the risk is mitigated. When that compliance with the standard occurs and the risk is mitigated then permission to engage in the otherwise prohibited action is given and often the law will say it must be given when that occurs. If the risk is mitigated there is no justification for the prohibition.

32.4 Diagrams

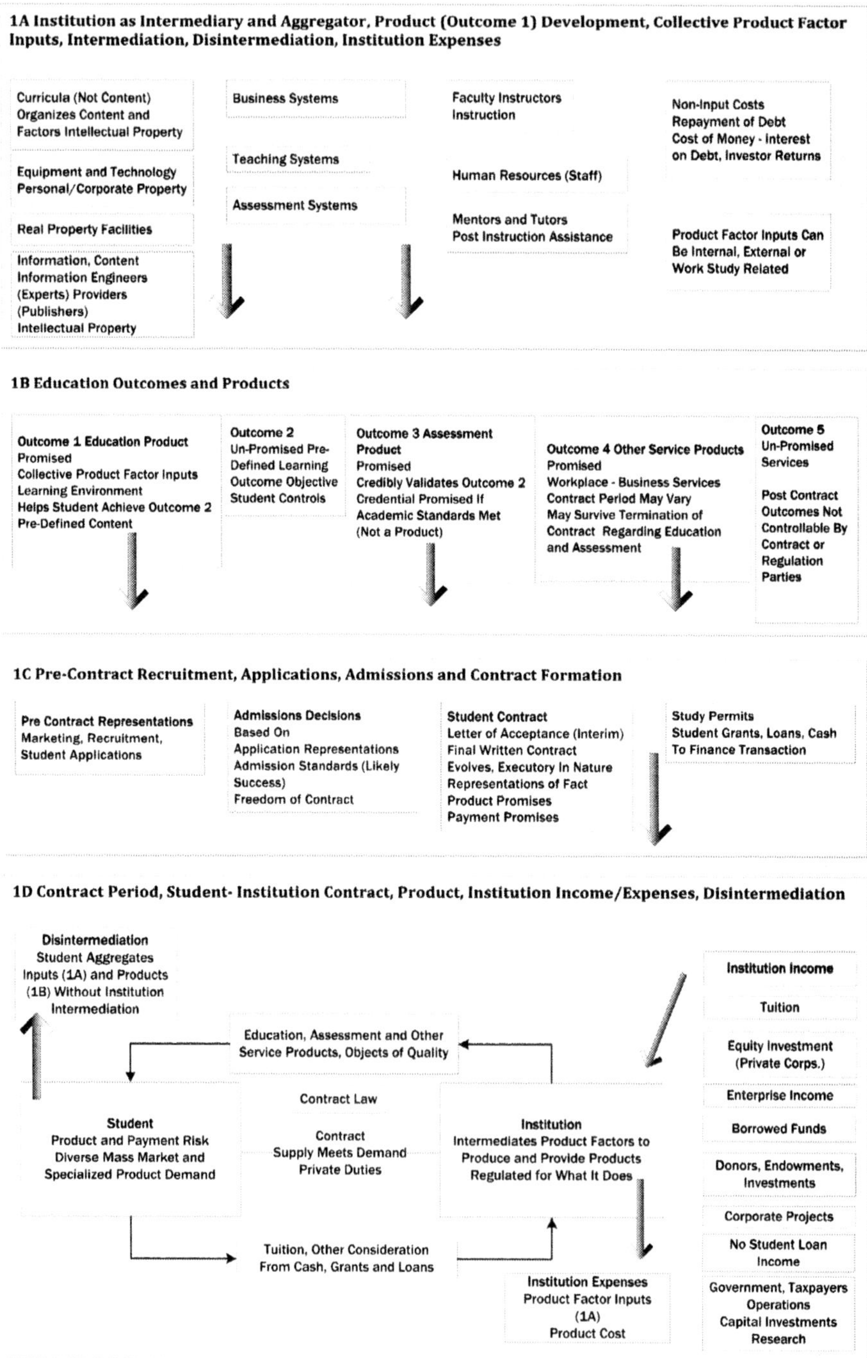

1E Post Contract (Un-Promised) Outcomes (Outcome 5), Un-Promised Services, Complex Cause and Effect

Workplace Success	Work Permit	Professional Organization Memberships
Business Success	Un-Promised Services	
Credential Evaluation	Credit Transfer	
Opportunities	Income, Compensation	

1F Gateways and Obstacles to Student Achievement of Desired Learning Objectives and State of Knowledge, Institution Model, Innovative Models

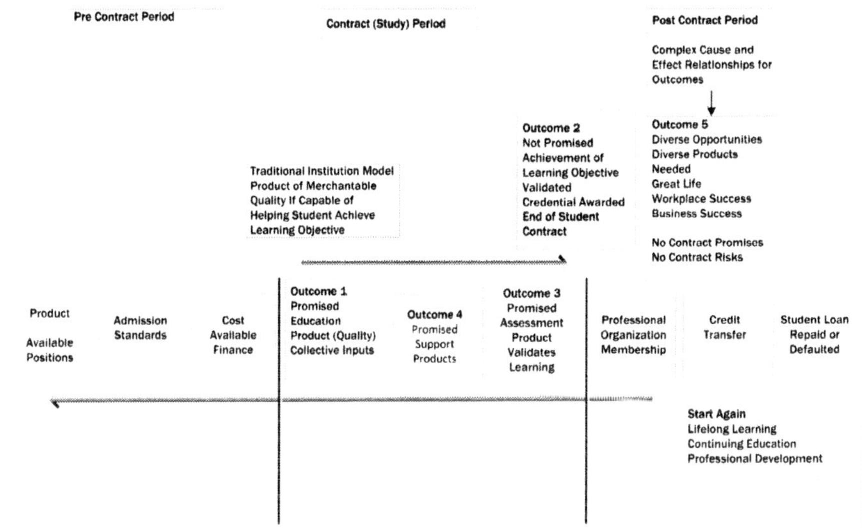

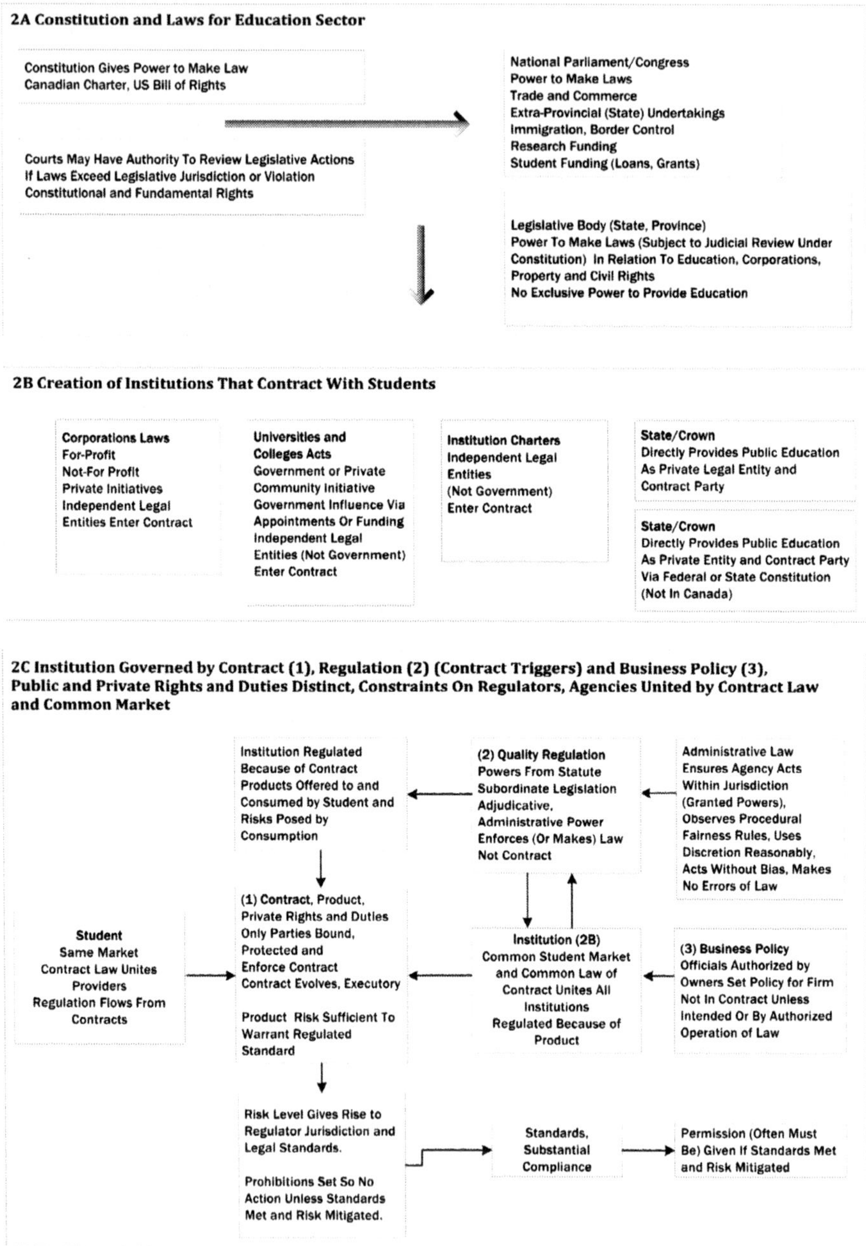
2A Constitution and Laws for Education Sector
Constitution Gives Power to Make Law
Canadian Charter, US Bill of Rights
Courts May Have Authority To Review Legislative Actions
If Laws Exceed Legislative Jurisdiction or Violation
Constitutional and Fundamental Rights
National Parliament/Congress
Power to Make Laws
Trade and Commerce
Extra-Provincial (State) Undertakings
Immigration, Border Control
Research Funding
Student Funding (Loans, Grants)
Legislative Body (State, Province)
Power To Make Laws (Subject to Judicial Review Under Constitution) In Relation To Education, Corporations, Property and Civil Rights
No Exclusive Power to Provide Education
2B Creation of Institutions That Contract With Students
Corporations Laws
For-Profit
Not-For Profit
Private Initiatives
Independent Legal Entities Enter Contract
Universities and Colleges Acts
Government or Private
Community Initiative
Government Influence Via Appointments Or Funding
Independent Legal Entities (Not Government)
Enter Contract
Institution Charters
Independent Legal Entities
(Not Government)
Enter Contract
State/Crown
Directly Provides Public Education
As Private Legal Entity and Contract Party
State/Crown
Directly Provides Public Education
As Private Entity and Contract Party
Via Federal or State Constitution
(Not In Canada)
2C Institution Governed by Contract (1), Regulation (2) (Contract Triggers) and Business Policy (3), Public and Private Rights and Duties Distinct, Constraints On Regulators, Agencies United by Contract Law and Common Market
Institution Regulated Because of Contract Products Offered to and Consumed by Student and Risks Posed by Consumption
(2) Quality Regulation
Powers From Statute
Subordinate Legislation
Adjudicative,
Administrative Power
Enforces (Or Makes) Law
Not Contract
Administrative Law
Ensures Agency Acts Within Jurisdiction (Granted Powers),
Observes Procedural Fairness Rules, Uses Discretion Reasonably,
Acts Without Bias, Makes No Errors of Law
Student
Same Market
Contract Law Unites Providers
Regulation Flows From Contracts
(1) Contract, Product,
Private Rights and Duties
Only Parties Bound,
Protected and Enforce Contract
Contract Evolves, Executory
Product Risk Sufficient To Warrant Regulated Standard
Institution (2B)
Common Student Market and Common Law of Contract Unites All Institutions
Regulated Because of Product
(3) Business Policy
Officials Authorized by Owners Set Policy for Firm
Not In Contract Unless Intended Or By Authorized Operation of Law
Risk Level Gives Rise to Regulator Jurisdiction and Legal Standards.
Prohibitions Set So No Action Unless Standards Met and Risk Mitigated.
Standards, Substantial Compliance
Permission (Often Must Be) Given If Standards Met and Risk Mitigated

(Endnotes)

1 Education International states on its website that it is the voice of teachers and other education employees across the globe. It is a global federation of about 400 unions in more than 170 countries and territories and represents 30 million teachers and education employees in education institutions from early childhood to university.

2 New World Dictionary, Second College Edition.

3 Rabindranath Tagore (1861-1941), O'Connell, K. M. (2003) Encyclopaedia of Informal Education.

4 Maharishi Mahesh Yogi, The Science of Being and Art of Living, Maharishi International University Press, 1966.

5 Sir Ken Robinson, Bring On the Learning Revolution, TED Conference, May 24, 2012 (follow-up from his famous 2006 lecture).

6 The Diplomacy of Knowledge, Globe and Mail, Feb. 17, 2012.

7 For example, Canadian Colleges Insert, Globe and Mail, Feb. 29, 2012. This point about the need for most workers to have substantial post-secondary training appears almost daily in the media and political forums.

8 This is a definition we have used for so long that its genesis is unclear. Similar words are expressed in trade negotiation materials. The source may have been Dorothy Riddle at Service Growth Consultants in Vancouver B.C.

9 In January of 2012, the Institute of International Education reported that over 43,000 American students are enrolled in academic degree programs outside of the US. News reports exist in Canada of students attending foreign law and medical schools and the numbers are significant.

10 For example: Students hold Day of Action across Canada—educationisaright.ca.

11 Black's Law Dictionary, Fifth Edition.

12 President Barrack Obama to both Houses of Congress Sept. 2011.

13 From parentcentral.ca, April 30—May 4, 2012.

14 Universities are becoming too business-like, conference told, Vancouver Sun October 19, 2010. BBC (Sean Coughlan) 2011, Universities to compete on places - Universities must show how tuition is spent and have to bid for places - Is the student customer always right? - Student complaints about universities rise by 33% - Students to get best-buy facts and consumer rights - What will market forces mean for universities?

15 Speaker at a conference sponsored by the Academica Group, Vancouver B.C. in 2011.

16 University Affairs Newsletter, April 2012, Judith Knelman.

17 For example, the Pennsylvania State Constitution addresses public education in Article III, Section 14 which states: The General Assembly shall provide for the maintenance and

support of a thorough and efficient system of public education to serve the needs of the Commonwealth. In Pennsylvania the State Constitution (the same is the case in many other states) gives plenary or absolute power to the legislative branch of government.

18 Is It Possible to Accurately Forecast Labour Market Need, Study Prepared by the Canadian Council of Learning for the BC Ministry of Advanced Education, January 10, 2007.

19 Possible Teacher Enrollment Caps in BC, Vancouver Sun, January 2011. Commissioned Report for BC Ministry of Advanced Education on Predicting Future Labor Needs, January 10, 2007, Canadian Council for Learning.

One in Five University Grads in Europe Overqualified for Their Jobs (Report), *Chronicle of Higher Education* February, 2012. Shortage of educated workers threatens oil-sands expansion: Financial Post Feb. 21, 2012. Toronto labour market short engineering, IT, and technical sales graduates: Feb. 2012 March 7, 2012. Engineering schools struggling to replace retiring personnel in profession: Toronto Star. Proportion of British graduates in low-skilled work increases: Times Higher Education, March 6, 2012. Note: Canadian media extensively reported that two thirds of new Ontario teachers did not find work in 2011.

20 From Free to Choose, Milton and rose Friedman, Harvest Books.

21 Ibid.

22 Canada Act 1982, Statutes of the United Kingdom, Schedule 2, Constitution Act 1982, Part 1: Canadian Charter of Rights and Freedoms.

23 Ibid, Section 7.

24 Two Concepts of Liberty: Oxford University Press 1969. From Four Essays on Liberty by Sir Isaiah Berlin.

25 Development as Freedom, Amartya Sen (1998 Nobel Prize, Economics), Anchor Books, Random House. 2000.

26 Ibid.

27 Ontario MPP Glen Murray tells Canadian Club that the private sector should invest more in post-secondary education - Toronto Start Published On Fri Mar 9 2012 - The uneasy ties between Canada's universities and wealthy business magnates, Theresa Tedesco March 9, 2012, March 12, 2012 - Aaron Lynett/National Post.

28 Many of these ideas were taken from The Law of Schools and Universities by Lazar and Noah Sarna, Lexis Nexis 2007 and from the article entitled In Loco Parentis to Consumerism: A Legal Analysis of the Contractual Relationship Between Institution and Student, K.B. Melear, NASPA Journal Vol. 40, no. 4, Summer 2003. Additional points were taken from an Academica Group (of London, Ontario) conference in Vancouver BC in 2011 where several university presidents, including Ross Paul (former President of the University of Windsor and Laurentian University), talked about how their institutions had changed.

29 Ibid.

30 Ibid.

31 Many of these points were drawn from the following books and presentations. 1. A. Bartlett Giamatti, former President of Yale and former Commissioner of Baseball. In Duderstadt, J.J. (2002). Higher Education in the Digital Age. Westport: Praeger, p. xi. 2. The university according to Cohen and March 1986. Cohen U.D. and March J.G. 1986. Leadership and Ambiguity: The American College President. 2nd Edition. Boston.

32 Supra, Ross Paul Address.

33 Supra, Sarna and Melear.

34 Economist, Print Edition, April 22nd 2010.

35 Gott v. Berea College (156 Ky. 376, 161 S.W. 204 [1913])(Court of Appeals of Kentucky).

36 William Kaplin, The Law of Higher Education: A Comprehensive Guide to Legal Implications of Administrative Decision Making, 2nd ed. (San Francisco: Jossey-Bass, 1985) at pages 3, 4, 107 and conclusion. Supra (Sarna) at p. 118.

37 From In Loco Parentis to Consumerism: A Legal Analysis of the Contractual Relationship Between Institution and Student, K.B. Melear, NASPA Journal Vol. 40, no. 4, Summer 2003.

38 Ibid. Also the chapter entitled "Contracts with Students" in Contemporary Issues in Higher Education Law (2nd edition), Richard Fossey, Kerry Brian Melear, and Joseph C. Beckham, eds. (2011)

39 Ibid. Citing Lawson & Daniels, 1974).

40 Dixon v. Alabama State Board of Education (1961). From Melear supra, (Lawson & Daniels, 1974; Zirkel & Reichner, 1986) (Fowler, 1984, p. 408; Grossi & Edwards, 1997).

41 Supra (Sarna), at pages 81 to 103 (103).

42 Ibid.

43 Cases exist in Canada and other jurisdictions, but key USA cases include Koblitz v. Western Reserve University (1901) and Anthony v. Syracuse University (1928). See also: Bickel and Lake (1999).

44 Chezik v. Delaware Law School (1987) and Van de Zilver v. Rutgers University (1997).

45 Blasser v. Royal Institution for the Advancement of Learning (1985) 24 D.L.R. (4th) 507, (Q.C.A.), para. 40. Cited in Sarna, The Law of Schools and Universities, Supra.

46 Davis v. Regis College 2d (Colo.App. 1991) at pages 1098, 1099, 1100 . Harris v. Blake , 798 F.2d 419 (10th Cir. 1986). Attaran v. University of B.C. [1998] B.C.J. No. 115 (B.C.S.C), Holmes J. at para. 39.

47 Supra (Melear) p. 193.

48 Noah Sarna Blog on Court Jurisdiction Over Academic Disputes Grounded in Contract or Tort.

49 Gauthier v. Saint-Germain (CanLII) published french, but discussed in Nazik Amdiss and University of Ottawa, Ltd. 2010 ONSC 4738 (CanLII).

50 Mulligan v. Laurentian University, 2007 CanLII 44947, Ontario Div. Ct.

51 Jaffer v. York University, 2010 ONCA 654 CanLII, Ont. C.A.

52 Supra, Jaffer v. York University and Gauthier c. Saint-Germain above.

53 United Kingdom Office of the Independent Adjudicator. Private Career Training Institutions Act (BC) s. 15a.1.

54 Are students always right? BBC 2011 - Student complaints up 33% BBC 2011 - Students to get best buy facts and consumer rights BBC 2011 - What will market focus mean for universities in the UK BBC 2011—Private Higher Education, A Global Revolution, Philip G. Altbach and Daniel C. Levy (State Uni. of NY at Albany).

Get Me a Job Or Give Me My Money Back, Macleans March 7, 2011. Law Grads Sue Alma Mater (Grads of New York Law School claim they were duped by marketing campaigns that reported fraudulent employment statistics intended to deceive prospective students - NBC August 2011). 20 more US law schools face suits over job-placement rates, Chronicle of Higher Education, March 14, 2012.

55 Essentials of Canadian Law, The Law of Contracts, John D. McCamus. Canadian Encyclopedic Digest, Westlaw, Carswell and Thompson Reuters.

56 Lakehead case. From Sarna, Supra.

57 Reid Hoffman, Founder of LinkedIn, Global Public Square with Fareed Zakaria, CNN, March 25, 2012.

58 The University of Alberta is an example. It announced that it was inviting suggestions that will push it into the 21st century. University of Alberta News, March 2012.

59 Examples include, Thornton v. Harvard University, 2 F. Supp.2d 89 (D.Mass. 1998), Hysaw v. Washburn University of Topeka, 690 F. Supp. 940, 946 (D.Kan. 1987), Reynolds v. Sterling College, Inc., 750 A.2d 1020 (Vt. 2000) (Supreme Court of Vermont).

60 This is again a definition that we have used for so long that its genesis is now unclear. You can find similar words in trade agreements.

61 Free Online Dictionary, West's Encyclopedia of American Law, Edition 2. Copyright 2008 The Gale Group, Inc. New World Dictionary, Second College Edition, Websters.

62 Close the Immigrant Success Gap, Michael Ignatieff and Maurizio Bevilacqua, National Post, 2008 - Flap Over Foreign Workers, BC Business, January 2007, p. 47, Mark Van Manen, Vancouver Sun. - Exploitation of Guest Workers Erodes Wage Levels and Standards, Jim Sinclair, Business in Vancouver (Date Unknown). - BC Should Consider Legislation to Speed the Way for Foreign Workers, Vancouver Sun Editorial, Date Unknown. Professional Bodies Need To Loosen Up, MP Jason Kenney, Conservative, Canadian Press, Date Unknown. - Canada Must Be More Aggressive About Keeping Skilled Immigrants (Internationally Educated Graduates), CanWest, October 27, 2007, Pauline Tam. - Government of Canada Announced Internationally Trained Workers Initiative, April 25, 2005, Canada Immigration Website.

63 Permanent beta: Why your career is a work in progress. By Reid Hoffman and Ben Casnocha , Special to CNN, May 9, 2012.

64 Frustrated by the fact that despite rising demand for Sheridan College's (government funded) degree programs Ontario graduate schools refuse to recognize those degrees, Sheridan president Jeff Zabudsky said the Ontario government should not build new undergrad universities and instead rely on existing colleges like Sheridan, Toronto Star, Feb. 8, 2012. This is also a growing issue in British Columbia, Canada.

65 Jobs Without People and People Without Jobs, Ontario's Labor Market Future, Dr. Rick Miner.

66 College publication article from George Burton, Canadore College's President, in May of 2012.

67 Immigrants to get Skills Tests Abroad, Postmedia News, March 29, 2012.

68 Example - National Association of Credential Evaluation Services (NACES) is active in the USA. Comparable Canadian groups are developing. There are also organizations like the Canadian Information Centre for International Credentials that provide information about credential evaluation, but not evaluation services.

69 Degree Authorization Act, SBC 2002, c 24, Consolidated Statutes of British Columbia.

70 Olar v. Laurentian University, 2008 ONCA 699 (CanLII) — 2008-10-10, Court of Appeal for Ontario.

71 Supra, Private Career Training Institutions Act (BC), s. 26 bylaws.

72 Ibid, s. 32.

73 Supra, MacDonald v. University of British Columbia.

74 Supra, Private Career Training Institutions Act, regulations and PCTIA Bylaws.

75 R. in Right of Canada v. Saskatchewan Wheat Pool, Supreme Court of Canada, 1983 Carswell Nat 92, [1983] 3 W.W.R. 97, [1983] 1 S.C.R. 205, (sub nom. Canada v. Saskatchewan Wheat Pool) 23 C.C.L.T. 121, 143 D.L.R. (3d) 9, 45 N.R. 425, J.E. 83-246. Holland 2008.doc; IBT Local 362 v. Midland.doc; Moldown v. SGEU 1995.doc; Hillyard v. Pittman 1991.doc; Kripps 1990.doc

76 Supra, Sarna, page 62

77 Two BC examples illustrate the points made, but many jurisdictions use common models. Private Career Training Institutions Act, SBC 2003, c 79. Degree Authorization Act, SBC 2002, c 24.

78 Ibid.

79 For example, Finstad v. Washburn University of Topeka, Supreme Court of Kansas.

80 Smart Regulation, Report on Actions and Plans: Fall 2005 Update. Treasury Board, Government of Canada.

81 Barrack Obama to Joint Houses of Congress Sept. 2011.

82 Roncarelli v. Duplessis, [1959] SCR 121, Supreme Court of Canada.

83 Research from the University of Illinois finds that the majority of undergrads seek out online content beyond what is provided by their professors. Students use materials, including online lectures, from Ivy League universities and reputable "brands" like the Mayo Clinic. The study also observes that students reject asking traditional authority figures like professors or librarians for help, and instead rely on their friends' recommendations. The Chronicle of Higher Education, April 25, 2012.

84 Don Tapscott and Anthony D. Williams, MacroWikinomics, Penguin Canada, Chapter 8, Rethinking the University: Collaborative Learning.

85 We don't claim to have invented this phrase, but its source is unclear. It was likely Malcolm Gladwell.

86 From broadcast interviews with authors Don Tapscott or Malcom Gladwell.

87 Supra, Ross Paul Address to Academic Conference 2011.

88 Ibid.

89 Ibid.

90 Ibid.

91 There are literally hundreds of books or articles on telecommuting or home based businesses. A few recent example are listed here. Freedom key to workplace of the future, Susanne Gargiulo for CNN November 19, 2011. - Job search firm calls for National Work from Home Day, Derek Abma, Postmedia News August 24, 2011. - Remote workers aren't going anywhere—literally. By Deborah L. Cohen, Reuters August 28, 2009. - Peter Thomson and Alison Maitland, co-authors of the book "Future Work: How businesses can adapt and thrive in the new world of work.

92 Expanding Graduate Programs and Renewing the Professoriate: What's the Connection? May 4th, 2012, Ian D. Clark, David Trick and Richard Van. This article appeared on the site of the Confederation of University Faculty Associations. This association fits the characterization noted. In their article, the authors favor limiting positions to projected workplace needs, but it is not known if they fully support OCUFA's views or the views of Education International in terms of opposing more open markets for quality assured providers and products.

93 The University of Manitoba's actuarial program is among the first programs to earn accreditation from the Canadian Institute of Actuaries (CIA). The accreditation will provide students with the option to apply to the CIA for exceptions from some of the early actuarial exams. This will make progress toward CIA Fellowship more predictable and will reduce the duplication of students' efforts between the professional exams and their university studies. This is one of many examples of how dispersed learning can be centrally validated by third parties.

94 A consistent point made in several annual surveys conducted by Macleans magazine in Canada.

95 Nearly every European Union country has committed to reducing their expenditures on universities, reports *Times Higher Education, Feb. 9, 2012.* The Commission on the Reform of Ontario's Public Services made several recommendations related to post-secondary education, February 2012.

96 Drummond Report (Ontario), Globe and Mail, Canada, February 16, 2012.

97 BC challenges PSE sector to cut spending by 1% (Provincial Budget 2012). The Ontario Ministry of Training, Colleges and Universities wants colleges and universities to realize 3% savings, Toronto Star Feb. 23, 2012. UK undergraduate course offerings cut by 27% over 6 years (BBC). Some universities are cutting enrollment, Macleans, Josh Dehaas, March 1st, 2012. University of Calgary to cut back on enrolment to help balance budget: *Calgary Herald.* University of Winnipeg department chairs raise concerns over austerity measures that threaten the integrity of the institution, Winnipeg Free Press March 20, 2012. Eleven Cambrian programs face suspension (cancellation), Sudbury Star March 21, 2012.

98 Many of these issues play out in the context of a debate over humanities and liberals arts education v. technical and business skills education. A few related articles are listed here. Can private universities survive in Canada? Brian Hutchinson, National Post, Dec.13, 2008. It's time for private universities (so humanities are taught) Todd Pettigrew, Macleans November 15th, 2010. The decline of the B.A. continues Macleans Nov. 2010. University Vocational or Academic Focus, "Is the university an educational institution or a vocational one?" Macleans, Rudayna Bahubeshi, September 22nd, 2011. Why liberal arts matter, Michael S. Roth, Special to CNN May 21, 2011. Washington State's public-private partnership fund and its targeted support for students in science, technology and all high demand fields shifts the purposes of college away from the civic and personal toward the economic and vocational, undermining the broader goals that have historically been part of American college education (Seattle Public Television, December 2011).

99 Muhammad. Yunus, Creating a World Without Poverty, Social Business and the Future of Capitalism, 2007.

100 Richard Susskind books, The Future of Law, The End of Lawyers.

101 The Guardian, April 24, 2012. Other examples: Backed by a $300-million investment by Microsoft, Barnes & Noble is transforming its college-textbook and digital divisions into a new subsidiary aimed at turning more students on to e-textbooks. Chronicle of Higher Education April 30, 2012. The British government recruited Wikipedia founder Jimmy Wales to advise it on how to make all publicly-funded academic research in Britain available online to anyone who wants to read or use it. Wales will advise on the common standards that will have to be agreed and adopted for open access to be a success, Times Higher Education, May 2, 2012.

102 Inside Higher Education, April 18, 2012.

103 New York Times, May 2, 2012.

104 May 11, 2012, Chronicle of Higher Education.

105 Chronicle of Higher Education, March 18, 2012.

106 Inside Higher Education, April 4, 2011.

107 Jerry Brown of Pricewaterhouse Coopers was referring to traditional TV media and content when he made this observation, but he could have been talking about education.

108 Supra, Tapscott, Macro Wikinomics, Chapter on Universities.

109 Cited in Trading It All Away: The WTO Services Negotiations and the Threat to Canada's Public Health and Educations Systems" March, 2000, Maude Barlow, Council of Canadians. The quote is used by Ms. Barlow to criticize trade initiatives that potentially cover education services. We use it to illustrate legal realities.

110 Here They Go Again, BCTF's Teacher Magazine, September 1999, Ellen Gould.

111 For example, Newsletter of Canadian Federation of Students January 2001, Vol. 7, No. 4.

112 Times of London Higher Education edition, January 13, 2012.

113 Simon Fraser University and Capilano College in Vancouver have both expressed interest in and at one point a least began to pursue US accreditation. Canadian examples of articles related to this issue of national and uniform standards are as follows: Canada not as smart as it thought it was. Universities losing competitive advantage (Fewer Canadian college students per capital than competitors). John Ivison, National Post October 17, 2009. National Post, October 21, 2009. National Post October 20, 2009. - Why Canada can't get world-class post-secondary education Erin Millar, May 6th, 2008, December 19, 2008 Macleans. - National Strategy, March 6, 2008 Macleans. - Capilano College president says Canada needs a federal postsecondary ministry, November 1, 2007. - Georgia Straight. Capilano College may pursue USA accreditation. - Judith Maxwell, president of Canadian Policy Research Networks.2007. - Organization for Economic Cooperation and Development annual report on education. Canada received more M's (data missing) than actual data and more than for any other country - The Canadian Council for Learning, December 2006 report titled Canadian Post-Secondary Education: A Positive Record,An Uncertain Future.

114 Bologna Process 1999. Twenty nine countries signed on initially and seventeen more joined later.

115 David Sovka, Academica Group News Services.

116 Ibid, David Sovka is a marketer at Comosun College in Victoria BC.

117 For example: BC Council for International Education and its Education Quality Assurance Program or the Canadian government's Imagine Canada Brand.

118 University of British Columbia News Release, August 2011, Macleans August 12, 2011.

119 Ibid.
120 Supra, MacDonald v. University of British Columbia.
121 Supra, N. Sarna, The Law of Schools and Universities, Melear In Loco Parentis (Cherry & Geary, 1992; Hirshberg, 1994). Stamatakos (1990).
122 Nishina v. Azuma Foods (Canada) Co., Ltd., 2010 BCSC 502 (CanLII), Supreme Court of British Columbia._
123 Supra, Saran, The Law of Schools and Universities, p. 10.
124 Supra, In Blasser, Rothman J.A. Sarna, p. 114.
125 Supra Sarna, his comments on judicial review in the education sector.
126 Mckinney v. University of Guelph [1990] 3 S.C.R. 229. Supra Sarna 115.
127 Supra, Sarna, p. 116.
128 Ibid.
129 Supra, Mckinney v. University of Guelph [1990] 3 S.C.R. 229.
130 Supra, Saran, p. 117.
131 Supra, Sarna, p. 120.
132 Supra, Sarna, p. 143 149, 159, 160.
133 Supra, Sarna, p. 113.
134 Principles of Administrative Law, 4th Edition, Jones, De Villars, Thomson-Carswell, Chapter 11, Errors of Law.
135 Ibid.
136 Mattel, Inc. v. 3894207 Canada Inc., 2006 SCC 22.
137 March 14, 2012, Lawsuits Over Job-Placement Rates Threaten More Law Schools, Chronicle for Higher Education.
138 In McKay v. CDI Career Development Institutes Ltd. [1999] B.C.J. No. 561 (BCSC)—the court refused to certify a request for a class action based on the alleged failure of the private training school to deliver the training advertised and to find jobs for its graduates. Nevertheless, the court admitted there were situations where a court might accept such a claim (Altine v. Institut Demers B.E. 2001 BE-641 (Que. CA) and other citations.
139 Free Online Dictionary, West's Encyclopedia of American Law, Edition 2. Copyright 2008 The Gale Group, Inc. New World Dictionary, Second College Edition, Websters.
140 International Workshop Agreement, Quality Management Systems, Guidelines for the Application of ISO 9001, 2000 in Education.
141 Supra PCTI Act. But common to many education regulation statutes.
142 Inside Higher Education, January 16, 2012.
143 Is It Possible to Accurately Forecast Labour Market Needs? Canadian Council on Learning, Prepared for BC Ministry of Advanced Education, January 2007.
144 Canada's Employment Quality Declines: Financial Post January 25, 2012.
145 Revamp Medical Schools, CMA Chief, National Post, Vancouver Sun, Canwest 2006. Adding Fuel to the Doctor Crisis, Five Million Canadians Without a Family Doctor, Macleans Jan. 14, 2008. Aspiring MDs Forced Overseas for Studies, 1500 Abroad, National Post (Date Unknown). Fraser Institute Study, Stop Recruiting Foreign Doctors to Resolve Shortages.
146 Higher Education Act of 1965 as amended, 20 U.S.C. 1070.
147 Career College Association d.b.a. Association of Private Sector Colleges and Universities v. US Department of Education.

148 Queen's University Considers Suspending its BFA program due to resource shortages (2012). Ontario is experiencing the worst teacher oversupply situation in Canada. York University's education faculty says fewer spaces may hinder a faculty's ability to support graduate programs or its ability to offer a B.Ed. Academica Group News Summary Nov. 9, 2011.

149 Voltaire's Bastards, The Dictatorship of Reason in the West, John Ralston Saul.

150 Roslyn Kunin and Associates, Vancouver, BC, Canada. Taxpayers' Costs to Support Higher Education: A Comparison of Public, Private Not-for-Profit and Private For-Profit Institutions, Robert Shapiro and Nam D. Pham, Sonecon Group, September 2010.

151 Chapter 2, Section 3 of the Student Aid BC Policy Manual refers to maintaining "acceptable" levels of risk. Institutions must (Section 5 Policy Manual) take measures to ensure that the incidence of loan defaults by its students is minimized. Section 5 says SABC will set specific rates, but these do not appear in written policy statements. Section 1 of Chapter 2 addresses issues of student success.

152 These are terms arising from Canadian and BC laws and policies. There is the federal Canada Student Financial Assistance Act SC 1994, c. 28 Consolidated Statutes of Canada and the Pan Canadian Designation Framework, but no BC legislation targeted at designations exists.

153 As of early May 2012, a petition is scheduled to be filed under the BC Judicial Review Procedure Act, [RSBC 1996] Chapter 241. The decisions subject to review involve a large number of private institutions that had designations not renewed because of reasons allegedly related to high default rates for student cohorts.

154 Career College Association as Association of Private Sector Colleges and Universities v. US Department of Education.

155 Canada Student Financial Assistance Act (CSFAA), SC 1994, c. 28 Consolidated Statutes of Canada, section 3(a). See Also, Order Designating the Appropriate Authority for a Province with Respect to the Act, SI/95-79.

156 United States District Court, District of Columbia, Career College Association, American Institute of Technology, and Microcomputer Technology Institute, Plaintiffs, v. The United States Department of Education and Lamar Alexander, Secretary of Education, Defendants. Civ. A. No. 92-1345-LFO.Aug. 31, 1992, 1992 WL 233837.

157 Fair Access to Regulated Professions and Compulsory Trades Act, Statutes of Ontario 2006, Chapter 31.

158 The study was done by Millenial Branding, a Generation Y consulting firm in 2012.

159 The list of home schooled and self-taught persons is endless. In addition to those listed there was Abraham Lincoln, Leonardo Da Vinci, Ben Franklin, Robbie Burns, Isaac Newton, William Faulkner, Thomas Huxley, Mark Twain. Modern day home schooled children have often been shown to have equal or superior academic results. This is not to criticize classroom focused teaching. It just illustrates that multiple models work.

160 The Ottawa Citizen, May 6, 2012.

161 Supra, Tapsott Macro-Wikinomics.

162 Taddy Blecher was named a Young Global Leader by the World Economic Forum and was a 2006 recipient of the Skoll Foundation's Social Entrepreneur Award.

163 Quebec and students: it's actually worse than you think, Macleans, May 11, 2012.

164 MacDonald v. University of British Columbia, 2003 BCSC 1103 (CanLII), 2003-07-11 Supreme Court of British Columbia. MacDonald et al. v. The University of British Columbia, 2004 BCSC 1299 (CanLII), 2004-10-08 Supreme Court of British Columbia. These courts presented reasons mainly focused on administrative law and judicial review as opposed to contract law, but contracts were acknowledged and contract law principles were addressed. These cases could be examples of where pleadings focused on contract law may (Emphasis Added) have led to different results. See sections on the Historical Anomaly of Judicial Review and Educational Institutions. This case is not likely a strong precedent for the principle that an institution can increase tuition any amount at any time just because a contract allows for simple increases. Individual case facts and contract terms will be important.

165 Creating a World Without Poverty, Social Business and the Future of Capitalism, Muhammad Yunus, Winner of the Nobel Peace Prize. Public Affairs and Perseus Books Group 2007. Yunus points out how government, corporate and NGO models all have unique strengths and weaknesses when it comes to addressing social issues.

166 John Watson Task Force on the Private Career Training Institutions Act, BC Canada, 2007.

167 Technologies of Freedom, Ithiel de Sola Poo, Belknap Press of Harvard University Press 1983. From book review by John Boon in the Saskatchewan Law Review March 1984.

168 Ibid.

169 Ibid.

170 This happened with Japanese and American cars decades ago. With respect to media see Macleans magazine July 6, 2009. The article analyzes the newspaper industry and quotes the book Disrupting Class: How Disruptive Innovation will change the Way the World Learns, Clayton Christen, Michael Horn, Curtis Johnson. See Also: Rethinking Education in an Age of Technology - Digital Revolution and Schooling in America, Allan Collins and Richard Halverson - Rethinking Education, Stephen Murgatroyd - Open Letter to Learners of this Planet, World Is Open/How web technology is revolutionizing education, Curtis Bonk, Professor at Indiana University USA. The Future of Law by Richard Susskind and Law In A Digital Age by M.E. Katsh.

CPSIA information can be obtained at www.ICGtesting.com
Printed in the USA
LVOW08s0333150114

369410LV00001BA/8/P

9 780988 016101